P9-BZF-487

Phil Ballard
Michael Moncur

Sams **Teach Yourself**

# Ajax, JavaScript and PHP

All
in **One**

**SAMS** 800 East 96th Street, Indianapolis, Indiana, 46240 USA

## Sams Teach Yourself Ajax, JavaScript, and PHP All in One

Copyright © 2009 by Sams Publishing

All rights reserved. No part of this book shall be reproduced, stored in a retrieval system, or transmitted by any means, electronic, mechanical, photocopying, recording, or otherwise, without written permission from the publisher. No patent liability is assumed with respect to the use of the information contained herein. Although every precaution has been taken in the preparation of this book, the publisher and author assume no responsibility for errors or omissions. Nor is any liability assumed for damages resulting from the use of the information contained herein.

ISBN-13: 978-0-672-32965-4
ISBN-10: 0-672-32965-4

Library of Congress Cataloging-in-Publication Data

Ballard, Phil.

 Sams teach yourself Ajax, JavaScript, and PHP all in one / Phil

Ballard, Michael Moncur.

 p. cm.

Includes index.

 ISBN 978-0-672-32965-4 (pbk. : CD-ROM)

1. Ajax (Web site development technology) 2. JavaScript (Computer program language)
3. PHP (Computer program language) 4. Web site development. I. Moncur, Michael G.
II. Title. III. Title: Teach yourself Ajax, JavaScript, and PHP all in one.

 TK5105.8885.A52B38 2008

 006.7'6–dc22

                            2008022476

Printed in the United States of America

Second Printing: October 2008

### Trademarks

All terms mentioned in this book that are known to be trademarks or service marks have been appropriately capitalized. Sams Publishing cannot attest to the accuracy of this information. Use of a term in this book should not be regarded as affecting the validity of any trademark or service mark.

### Warning and Disclaimer

Every effort has been made to make this book as complete and as accurate as possible, but no warranty or fitness is implied. The information provided is on an "as is" basis. The authors and the publisher shall have neither liability nor responsibility to any person or entity with respect to any loss or damages arising from the information contained in this book or from the use of the CD or programs accompanying it.

### Bulk Sales

Sams Publishing offers excellent discounts on this book when ordered in quantity for bulk purchases or special sales. For more information, please contact

**U.S. Corporate and Government Sales**
**1-800-382-3419**
**corpsales@pearsontechgroup.com**

For sales outside of the U.S., please contact

**International Sales**
**international@pearson.com**

**Editor-in-Chief**
*Mark Taub*

**Acquisitions Editor**
*Mark Taber*

**Managing Editor**
*Patrick Kanouse*

**Project Editor**
*Mandie Frank*

**Indexer**
*Ken Johnson*

**Proofreader**
*Paula Lowell*

**Publishing Coordinator**
*Vanessa Evans*

**Multimedia Developer**
*Dan Scherf*

**Designer**
*Gary Adair*

**Composition**
*TnT Design, Inc.*

The Safari® Enabled icon on the cover of your favorite technology book means the book is available through Safari Bookshelf. When you buy this book, you get free access to the online edition for 45 days. Safari Bookshelf is an electronic reference library that lets you easily search thousands of technical books, find code samples, download chapters, and access technical information whenever and wherever you need it.

To gain 45-day Safari Enabled access to this book:

▶ Go to http://www.informit.com/onlineedition

▶ Complete the brief registration form

▶ Enter the coupon code 37H1-TGKI-1KQV-LRIZ-VM1R

If you have difficulty registering on Safari Bookshelf or accessing the online edition, please email customer-service@safaribooksonline.com.

# Contents at a Glance

# Table of Contents

Introduction

Sams Teach Yourself Ajax, JavaScript, and PHP All in One

# About the Author

**Phil Ballard**, the author of *Sams Teach Yourself Ajax in 10 Minutes*, graduated in 1980 with an honors degree in electronics from the University of Leeds, England. Following an early career as a research scientist with a major multinational, he spent a few years in commercial and managerial roles within the high technology sector, later working full time as a software engineering consultant.

Operating as "The Mouse Whisperer" (http://www.mousewhisperer.co.uk), Ballard has spent recent years involved solely in website and intranet design and development for an international portfolio of clients.

**Michael Moncur** is a freelance webmaster and author. He runs a network of websites, including the Web's oldest site about famous quotations, online since 1994. He wrote *Sams Teach Yourself JavaScript in 24 Hours* and has also written several bestselling books about networking, certification programs, and databases. He lives with his wife in Salt Lake City, Utah.

# We Want to Hear from You!

As the reader of this book, *you* are our most important critic and commentator. We value your opinion and want to know what we're doing right, what we could do better, what areas you'd like to see us publish in, and any other words of wisdom you're willing to pass our way.

You can email or write me directly to let me know what you did or didn't like about this book—as well as what we can do to make our books stronger.

*Please note that I cannot help you with technical problems related to the topic of this book, and that due to the high volume of mail I receive, I might not be able to reply to every message.*

When you write, please be sure to include this book's title and author as well as your name and phone or email address. I will carefully review your comments and share them with the author and editors who worked on the book.

E-mail:     webdev@samspublishing.com

Mail:       Mark Taub
            Associate Publisher
            Sams Publishing
            800 East 96th Street
            Indianapolis, IN 46240 USA

# Reader Services

Visit our website and register this book at informit.com/register for convenient access to any updates, downloads, or errata that might be available for this book.

# Introduction

Over the last decade or so, the World Wide Web has grown in scope from being a relatively simple information repository to becoming the first stop for many people when seeking entertainment, education, news, or business resources.

Websites themselves need no longer be limited to a number of static pages containing text and perhaps simple images; the tools now available allow the development of highly interactive and engaging pages involving animations, visual effects, context-sensitive content, embedded productivity tools, and much more.

The list of technologies available for producing such pages is broad. However, those based on Open Source licenses have become, and remain, highly popular due to their typically low (often zero) entry cost, and to the huge resource of user-contributed scripts, tutorials, tools, and other resources for these tools and applications available via the Internet and elsewhere.

In this book, we give a detailed account of how to program fluid, interactive websites using server- and client-side coding techniques and tools, as well as how to combine these to produce a slick, desktop-application-like user experience using Ajax.

The programming languages used in this book include the ubiquitous JavaScript (for client-side programming) and the immensely popular open-source PHP language (for server-side scripting, and available with the majority of web-hosting packages). The nuts and bolts of Ajax programming are described in detail, as well as the use of several advanced open-source frameworks that contain ready-written code for quickly building state-of-the-art interactive sites.

> The CD that accompanies this book provides all the tools required on your journey through learning to program in PHP, JavaScript, and Ajax.

**On the CD**

## What Is Ajax?

Ajax stands for *Asynchronous JavaScript And XML*. Although strictly speaking Ajax is not itself a technology, it mixes well-known programming techniques in an uncommon way to enable web developers to build Internet applications with much more appealing user interfaces than those to which we have become accustomed.

When using popular desktop applications, we expect the results of our work to be made available immediately, without fuss, and without our having to wait for the whole screen to be redrawn by the program. While using a spreadsheet such as Excel, for instance, we expect the changes we make in one cell to propagate immediately through the neighboring cells while we continue to type, scroll the page, or use the mouse.

Unfortunately, this sort of interaction has seldom been available to users of web-based applications. Much more common is the experience of entering data into form fields, clicking on a button or a hyperlink and then sitting back while the page slowly reloads to exhibit the results of the request. In addition, we often find that the majority of the reloaded page consists of elements that are identical to those of the previous page and that have therefore been reloaded unnecessarily; background images, logos, and menus are frequent offenders.

Ajax promises us a solution to this problem. By working as an extra layer between the user's browser and the web server, Ajax handles server communications in the background, submitting server requests and processing the returned data. The results may then be integrated seamlessly into the page being viewed, without that page needing to be refreshed or a new one being loaded.

In Ajax applications, such server requests are not necessarily synchronized with user actions such as clicking on buttons or links. A well-written Ajax application may already have asked of the server, and received, the data required by the user—perhaps before the user even knew she wanted it. This is the meaning of the *asynchronous* part of the Ajax acronym.

The parts of an Ajax application that happen "under the hood" of the user's browser, such as sending server queries and dealing with the returned data, are written in *JavaScript*, and *XML* is an increasingly popular means of coding and transferring formatted information used by Ajax to efficiently transfer data between server and client.

We'll look at all these techniques, and how they can be made to work together, as we work through the chapters.

# Who This Book Is For

This volume is aimed primarily at web developers seeking to build better interfaces for the users of their web applications and programmers from desktop environments looking to transfer their applications to the Internet.

It also proves useful to web designers eager to learn how the latest techniques can offer new outlets for their creativity. Although the nature of PHP, JavaScript, and Ajax applications means that they require some programming, all the required technologies are explained from first principles within the book, so even those with little or no programming experience should be able to follow the lessons without a great deal of difficulty.

## How To Use This Book

All the technologies—including a refresher of WWW basics—are explained from first principles, so that even non-programmers or those unfamiliar with these languages should be able to follow the development of the concepts with little problem.

The book is divided into parts, each dedicated to a particular technology or discussion topic. Within each part, the chapters each specialize in a given aspect or subtopic. It should therefore be easy to follow the instructional flow of the book by a quick look through the table of contents.

However, if you are already a competent programmer in one or more of the technologies used—in PHP for instance, or in JavaScript—then feel free to speed-read or skip the sections that you don't need.

To try out many of the examples you'll need access to a web server that supports PHP, and a means to upload files into your web space (probably FTP). Most web hosts include PHP in their hosting packages, or can do so on request at minimal or no cost.

Alternatively, the CD that accompanies this book contains everything required to set up a web serving environment on your own computer. This package is called XAMPP, and it contains everything you need to develop fully functional, interactive websites like those described in this book, ready to be deployed to a web-based server at a later date if you so choose. Look out for the boxes marked "On the CD" as you work through the book.

## Conventions Used In This Book

This book contains special elements as described by the following:

These boxes highlight information that can make your programming more efficient and effective.

**By the Way**

These boxes provide additional information related to material you just read.

**Watch Out!**

These boxes focus your attention on problems or side effects that can occur in specific situations.

▼  **Try It Yourself**

The Try It Yourself section offers suggestions for creating your own scripts, experimenting further, or applying the techniques learned throughout the chapter. This will help you create practical applications based on what you've learned.

▲

**On the CD**

Sections like this remind you about relevant information or tools available on the CD that accompanies the book.

A special monospace font is used on programming-related terms and language.

# Setting Up Your Workspace

While you can write the code in this book using just a simple text editor, to run the examples you'll need a computer (with Windows, Mac, or Linux operating system) running a modern browser such as Internet Explorer or Firefox.

**Did you Know?**

You can download Microsoft Windows Explorer from http://www.microsoft.com/ and the latest version of Firefox from http://www.mozilla.com/.

You will also need to load files on to a web server—if you already have a web host that supports PHP, you can use your web space there. Alternatively, the accompanying CD has everything you need to set up your own web server for private use, either on your own PC or another on your network.

# What's on the CD

The accompanying CD contains everything you could need to get the best from this book. Included on the CD you'll find

- ▶ **XAMPP**, a complete open source compilation you can use to easily install the Apache web server, PHP language, and MySQL database manager on your computer. Versions are provided for Linux, Mac, and Windows environments.

- ▶ **jEdit**, a Java-based programmer's editor that's perfect for creating or modifying code. The CD includes files for Java, Mac, or Windows.

- ▶ A selection of **open source frameworks** for developing sophisticated web applications. Programming examples based on some of these frameworks are presented towards the end of the book.

# PART I

# Web Basics Refresher

# CHAPTER 1

# Workings of the Web

## What You'll Learn in This Chapter:

▶ A Short History of the Internet
▶ The World Wide Web
▶ Introducing HTTP
▶ The HTTP Request and Response
▶ HTML Forms

We have a lot of ground to cover in this book, so let's get to it. We'll begin by reviewing in this chapter what the World Wide Web is and where it came from. Afterward we'll take a look at some of the major components that make it work, especially the HTTP protocol used to request and deliver web pages.

## A Short History of the Internet

In the late 1950s, the U.S. government formed the Advanced Research Projects Agency (ARPA). This was largely a response to the Russian success in launching the *Sputnik* satellite and employed some of the country's top scientific intellects in research work with U.S. military applications.

During the 1960s, the agency created a decentralized computer network known as ARPAnet. This embryonic network initially linked four computers located at the University of California at Los Angeles, Stanford Research Institute, the University of California at Santa Barbara, and the University of Utah, with more nodes added in the early 1970s.

The network had initially been designed using the then-new technology of packet switching and was intended as a communication system that would remain functional even if some nodes should be destroyed by a nuclear attack.

Email was implemented in 1972, closely followed by the telnet protocol for logging on to remote computers and the File Transfer Protocol (FTP), enabling file transfer between computers.

This developing network was enhanced further in subsequent years with improvements to many facets of its protocols and tools. However, it was not until 1989 when Tim Berners-Lee and his colleagues at the European particle physics laboratory CERN (*Conseil Europeen pour le Recherche Nucleaire*) proposed the concept of linking documents with *hypertext* that the now familiar World Wide Web began to take shape. The year 1993 saw the introduction of Mosaic, the first graphical web browser and forerunner of the famous Netscape Navigator.

The use of hypertext pages and hyperlinks helped to define the page-based interface model that we still regard as the norm for web applications today.

# The World Wide Web

The World Wide Web operates using a client/server networking principle. When you enter the URL (the web address) of a web page into your browser and click on "Go," you ask the browser to make an *HTTP request* of the particular computer having that address. On receiving this request, that computer returns ("serves") the required page to you in a form that your browser can interpret and display. Figure 1.1 illustrates this relationship. In the case of the Internet, of course, the server and client computers may be located anywhere in the world.

**FIGURE 1.1**
How web servers and clients (browsers) interact.

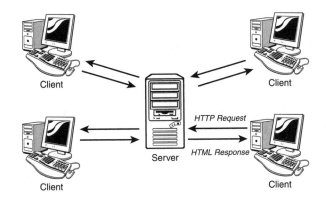

Later we'll discuss the nitty-gritty of HTTP requests in more detail. For now, suffice it to say that your HTTP request contains several pieces of information needed so that your page may be correctly identified and served to you, including the following:

- ▶ The domain at which the page is stored (for example, mydomain.com)

- ▶ The name of the page (This is the name of a file in the web server's file system— for example, mypage.html.)

- ▶ The names and values of any parameters that you want to send with your request

## What Is a Web Page?

Anyone with some experience using the World Wide Web will be familiar with the term *web page*. The traditional user interface for websites involves the visitor navigating among a series of connected *pages* each containing text, images, and so forth, much like the pages of a magazine.

Generally speaking, each web page is actually a separate file on the server. The collection of individual pages constituting a website is managed by a program called a *web server*.

## Web Servers

A web server is a program that interprets HTTP requests and delivers the appropriate web page in a form that your browser can understand. Many examples are available, most running under either UNIX/Linux operating systems or under some version of Microsoft Windows.

> The term *web server* is often used in popular speech to refer to both the web server program—such as Apache—and the computer on which it runs.

**Watch Out!**

Perhaps the best-known server application is the *Apache Web Server* from the Apache Software Foundation (http://www.apache.org), an open source project used to serve millions of websites around the world (see Figure 1.2).

Another example is Microsoft's IIS (Internet Information Services), often used on host computers running the Microsoft Windows operating system.

> Not all Windows-based web hosts use IIS. Various other web servers are available for Windows, including a version of the popular Apache Web Server.

**By the Way**

**FIGURE 1.2**
The Apache
Software
Foundation
home page at
http://www.
apache.org/
displayed in
Internet
Explorer.

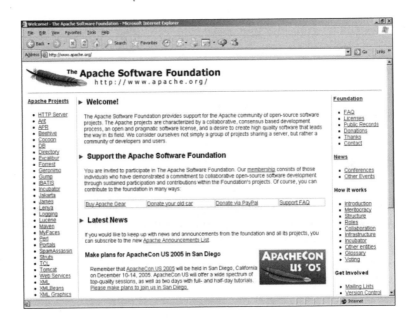

## Server-Side Programming

Server-side programs, scripts, or languages, refer to programs that run on the server computer. Many languages and tools are available for server-side programming, including PHP, Java, and ASP (the latter being available only on servers running the Microsoft Windows operating system). Sophisticated server setups often also include databases of information that can be addressed by server-side scripts.

**By the Way**

> Server-side programming in this book is carried out using the popular PHP scripting language, which is flexible, is easy to use, and can be run on nearly all servers. Ajax, however, can function equally well with any server-side scripting language.

The purposes of such scripts are many and various. In general, however, they all are designed to preprocess a web page before it is returned to you. By this we mean that some or all of the page content will have been modified to suit the context of your request—perhaps to display train times to a particular destination and on a specific date, or to show only those products from a catalog that match your stated hobbies and interests.

In this way server-side scripting allows web pages to be served with rich and varied content that would be beyond the scope of any design using only static pages—that is, pages with fixed content.

# Web Browsers

A *web browser* is a program on a web surfer's computer that is used to interpret and display web pages. The first graphical web browser, Mosaic, eventually developed into the famous range of browsers produced by Netscape.

---

By *graphical* web browser we mean one that can display not only the text elements of an HTML document but also images and colors. Typically, such browsers have a point-and-click interface using a mouse or similar pointing device.

There also exist text-based web browsers, the best known of which is Lynx (http://lynx.browser.org/), which display HTML pages on character-based displays such as terminals, terminal emulators, and operating systems with command-line interfaces such as DOS.

---

**By the Way**

The Netscape series of browsers, once the most successful available, were eventually joined by Microsoft's Internet Explorer offering, which subsequently went on to dominate the market.

Recent competitive efforts, though, have introduced a wide range of competing browser products including Opera, Safari, Konqueror, and especially Mozilla's Firefox, an open source web browser that has recently gained an enthusiastic following (see Figure 1.3).

Browsers are readily available for many computer operating systems, including the various versions of Microsoft Windows, UNIX/Linux, and Macintosh, as well as for other computing devices ranging from mobile telephones to PDAs (Personal Digital Assistants) and pocket computers.

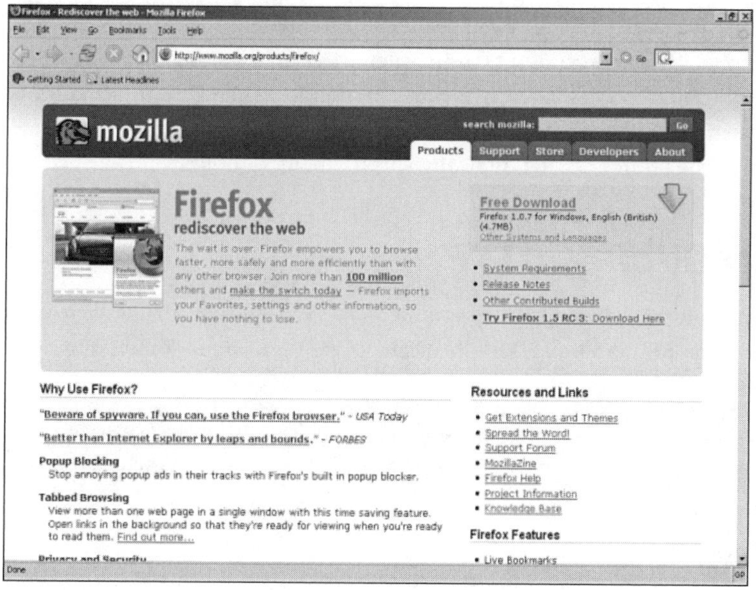

**FIGURE 1.3**
The Firefox browser from Mozilla.org browsing the Firefox Project home page.

## Client-Side Programming

We have already discussed how server scripts can improve your web experience by offering pages that contain rich and varied content created at the server and inserted into the page before it is sent to you.

Client-side programming, on the other hand, happens not at the server but right inside the user's browser *after* the page has been received. Such scripts allow you to carry out many tasks relating to the data in the received page, including performing calculations, changing display colors and styles, checking the validity of user input, and much more.

Nearly all browsers support some version or other of a client-side scripting language called JavaScript, which is an integral part of Ajax and is the language we'll be using in this book for client-side programming.

## DNS—The Domain Name Service

Every computer connected to the Internet has a unique numerical address (called an *IP address*) assigned to it. However, when you want to view a particular website in your browser, you don't generally want to type in a series of numbers—you want to use the domain name of the site in question. After all, it's much easier to remember www.somedomain.com than something like 198.105.232.4.

When you request a web page by its domain name, your Internet service provider submits that domain name to a DNS server, which tries to look up the database entry associated with the name and obtain the corresponding IP address. If it's successful, you are connected to the site; otherwise, you receive an error.

The many DNS servers around the Internet are connected together into a network that constantly updates itself as changes are made. When DNS information for a website changes, the revised address information is propagated throughout the DNS servers of the entire Internet, typically within about 24 hours.

# Introducing HTTP

Various protocols are used for communication over the World Wide Web, perhaps the most important being *HTTP*, the protocol that is also fundamental to Ajax applications.

When you request a web page by typing its address into your web browser, that request is sent using HTTP. The browser is an *HTTP client*, and the web page server is (unsurprisingly) an *HTTP server*.

In essence, HTTP defines a set of rules regarding how messages and other data should be formatted and exchanged between servers and browsers.

For a detailed account of HTTP, Sams Publishing offers the *HTTP Developer's Handbook* by Chris Shiflett.

**Did you Know?**

# The HTTP Request and Response

The HTTP protocol can be likened to a conversation based on a series of questions and answers, which we refer to respectively as *HTTP requests* and *HTTP responses*.

The contents of HTTP requests and responses are easy to read and understand, being near to plain English in their syntax.

This section examines the structure of these requests and responses, along with a few examples of the sorts of data they may contain.

## The HTTP Request

After opening a connection to the intended server, the HTTP client transmits a request in the following format:

- ▶ An opening line
- ▶ Optionally, a number of *header lines*
- ▶ A blank line
- ▶ Optionally, a message body

The opening line is generally split into three parts; the name of the *method*, the path to the required *server resource*, and the *HTTP version* being used. A typical opening line might read:

```
GET /sams/testpage.html HTTP/1.0
```

In this line we are telling the server that we are sending an HTTP request of type GET (explained more fully in the next section), we are sending this using HTTP version 1.0, and the server resource we require (including its local path) is

```
/sams/testpage.html.
```

In this example the server resource we seek is on our own server, so we have quoted a relative path. It could of course be on another server elsewhere, in which case the server resource would include the full URL.

**By the Way**

Header lines are used to send information about the request, or about the data being sent in the message body. One parameter and value pair is sent per line, the parameter and value being separated by a colon. Here's an example:

```
User-Agent: [name of program sending request]
```

For instance, Internet Explorer v5.5 offers something like the following:

```
User-agent: Mozilla/4.0 (compatible; MSIE 5.5; Windows NT 5.0)
```

A further example of a common request header is the `Accept:` header, which states what sort(s) of information will be found acceptable as a response from the server:

```
Accept: text/plain, text/html
```

By issuing the header in the preceding example, the request is informing the server that the sending application can accept either plain text or HTML responses (that is, it is not equipped to deal with, say, an audio or video file) .

**By the Way**

HTTP request methods include POST, GET, PUT, DELETE, and HEAD. By far the most interesting for the purposes of this book are the GET and POST requests. The PUT, DELETE, and HEAD requests are not covered here.

## The HTTP Response

In answer to such a request, the server typically issues an HTTP response, the first line of which is often referred to as the *status line*. In that line the server echoes the HTTP version and gives a response status code (which is a three-digit integer) and a short message known as a *reason phrase*. Here's an example HTTP response:

```
HTTP/1.0 200 OK
```

The response status code and reason phrase are essentially intended as machine- and human-readable versions of the same message, though the reason phrase may actually vary a little from server to server. Table 1.1 lists some examples of common status codes and reason phrases. The first digit of the status code usually gives some clue about the nature of the message:

▶ 1**—Information

▶ 2**—Success

▶ 3**—Redirected

▶ 4**—Client error

▶ 5**—Server error

**TABLE 1.1** Some Commonly Encountered HTTP Response Status Codes

| Status Code | Explanation |
|---|---|
| 200 - OK | The request succeeded. |
| 204 - No Content | The document contains no data. |
| 301 - Moved Permanently | The resource has permanently moved to a different URI. |
| 401 - Not Authorized | The request needs user authentication. |
| 403 - Forbidden | The server has refused to fulfill the request. |
| 404 - Not Found | The requested resource does not exist on the server. |
| 408 - Request Timeout | The client failed to send a request in the time allowed by the server. |
| 500 - Server Error | Due to a malfunctioning script, server configuration error or similar. |

A detailed list of status codes is maintained by the World Wide Web Consortium, W3C, and is available at http://www.w3.org/Protocols/rfc2616/ rfc2616-sec10.html.

*Did you Know?*

The response may also contain header lines each containing a header and value pair similar to those of the HTTP request but generally containing information about the server and/or the resource being returned:

```
Server: Apache/1.3.22
Last-Modified: Fri, 24 Dec 1999 13:33:59 GMT
```

# HTML Forms

Web pages often contain fields where you can enter information. Examples include select boxes, check boxes, and fields where you can type information. Table 1.2 lists some popular HTML form tags.

**TABLE 1.2** Some Common HTML Form Tags

| Tag | Description |
|---|---|
| <form>...</form> | Container for the entire form |
| <input /> | Data entry element; includes text, password, check box and radio button fields, and submit and reset buttons |
| <select>...</select> | Drop-down select box |
| <option>...</option> | Selectable option within select box |
| <textarea>...</textarea> | Text entry field with multiple rows |

After you have completed the form you are usually invited to submit it, using an appropriately labeled button or other page element.

At this point, the HTML form constructs and sends an HTTP request from the user-entered data. The form can use either the GET or POST request type, as specified in the method attribute of the <form> tag.

## GET and POST Requests

Occasionally you may hear it said that the difference between GET and POST requests is that GET requests are just for GETting (that is, retrieving) data, whereas POST requests can have many uses, such as uploading data, sending mail, and so on.

Although there may be some merit in this rule of thumb, it's instructive to consider the differences between these two HTTP requests in terms of how they are constructed.

A GET request encodes the message it sends into a *query string*, which is appended to the URL of the server resource. A POST request, on the other hand, sends its message in the *message body* of the request. What actually happens at this point is that the entered data is encoded and sent, via an HTTP request, to the URL declared in the action attribute of the form, where the submitted data will be processed in some way.

Whether the HTTP request is of type GET or POST and the URL to which the form is sent are both determined in the HTML markup of the form. Let's look at the HTML code of a typical form:

```
<form action="http://www.sometargetdomain.com/somepage.htm"
➥    method="post">
Your Surname: <input type="text" size="50" name="surname" />
<br />
<input type="submit" value="Send" />
</form>
```

This snippet of code, when embedded in a web page, produces the simple form shown in Figure 1.4.

Let's take a look at the code, line by line. First, we begin the form by using the <form> tag, and in this example we give the tag two attributes. The action attribute determines the URL to which the submitted form will be sent. This may be to another page on the same server and described by a relative path, or to a remote domain, as in the code behind the form in Figure 1.4.

Next we find the attribute method, which determines whether we want the data to be submitted with a GET or a POST request.

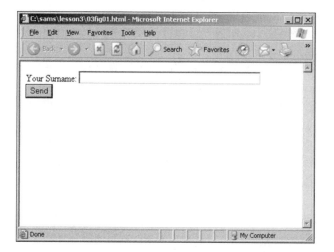

**FIGURE 1.4**
A simple HTML form.

Now suppose that we completed the form by entering the value *Ballard* into the surname field. On submitting the form by clicking the Send button, we are taken to http://www.sometargetdomain.com/somepage.htm, where the submitted data will be processed—perhaps adding the surname to a database, for example.

The variable surname (the name attribute given to the Your Surname input field) and its value (the data we entered in that field) will also have been sent to this destination page, encoded into the body of the POST request and invisible to users.

Now suppose that the first line of the form code reads as follows:

```
<form action="http://www.sometargetdomain.com/somepage.htm"
➥    method="get">
```

On using the form, we would still be taken to the same destination, and the same variable and its value would also be transmitted. This time, however, the form would construct and send a GET request containing the data from the form. Looking at the address bar of the browser, after successfully submitting the form, we would find that it now contains:

```
http://www.example.com/page.htm?surname=Ballard
```

Here we can see how the parameter and its value have been appended to the URL. If the form had contained further input fields, the values entered in those fields would also have been appended to the URL as *parameter=value* pairs, with each pair separated by an & character. Here's an example in which we assume that the form has a further text input field called firstname:

```
http://www.example.com/page.htm?surname=Ballard&firstname=Phil
```

Some characters, such as spaces and various punctuation marks, are not allowed to be transmitted in their original form. The HTML form encodes these characters into a form that can be transmitted correctly. An equivalent process decodes these values at the receiving page before processing them, thus making the encoding/decoding operation essentially invisible to the user. We can, however, see what this encoding looks like by making a GET request and examining the URL constructed in doing so.

Suppose that instead of the surname field in our form we have a fullname field that asks for the full name of the user and encodes that information into a GET request. Then, after submitting the form, we might see the following URL in the browser:

`http://www.example.com/page.htm?fullname=Phil+Ballard`

Here the space in the name has been replaced by the + character; the decoding process at the receiving end removes this character and replaces the space.

In many cases, you may use either the POST or GET method for your form submissions and achieve essentially identical results. The difference becomes important, however, when you learn how to construct server calls in Ajax applications.

The XMLHTTPRequest object at the heart of all Ajax applications uses HTTP to make requests of the server and receive responses. The content of these HTTP requests are essentially identical to those generated when an HTML form is submitted.

## Summary

This chapter reviewed the history and architecture of the World Wide Web, and covered some basics of server requests and responses using the HTTP protocol.

In particular, we discussed how GET and POST requests are constructed, and how they are used in HTML forms. Additionally, we saw some examples of responses to these requests that we might receive from the server.

# CHAPTER 2

# Writing and Styling Pages in HTML and CSS

## What You'll Learn in This Chapter:

- ▶ Introducing HTML
- ▶ Elements of an HTML Page
- ▶ A More Advanced HTML Page
- ▶ Some Useful HTML Tags
- ▶ Adding Your Own Style
- ▶ Defining the Rules
- ▶ Add a Little `class`
- ▶ Applying Styles
- ▶ Formatting Text with Styles
- ▶ Adding Lines

In this chapter we introduce HTML, the markup language behind virtually every page of the World Wide Web. A sound knowledge of HTML provides an excellent foundation for the Ajax applications discussed in later chapters.

# Introducing HTML

It wouldn't be appropriate to try to give an exhaustive account of HTML (Hypertext Markup Language)—or, indeed, any of the other component technologies of Ajax—within this book. Instead we'll review the fundamental principles and give some code examples to illustrate them, paying particular attention to the subjects that will become relevant when we start to develop Ajax applications.

## What Is HTML?

The World Wide Web is constructed from many millions of individual pages, and those pages are, in general, written in Hypertext Markup Language, better known as HTML.

That name gives away a lot of information about the nature of HTML. We use it to mark up our text documents so that web browsers know how to display them and to define hypertext links within them to provide navigation within or between them.

Anyone who (like me) can remember the old pre-WYSIWYG word processing programs will already be familiar with text markup. Most of these old applications required that special characters be placed at the beginning and end of sections of text that you wanted to be displayed as (for instance) bold, italic, or underlined text.

## What Tools Are Needed to Write HTML?

Because the elements used in HTML markup employ only ordinary keyboard characters, all you really need is a good text editor to construct HTML pages. Many are available, and most operating systems have at least one such program already installed. If you're using some version of Windows, for example, the built-in Notepad application works just fine.

Although Notepad is a perfectly serviceable text editor, many so-called *programmers' editors* are available offering useful additional functions such as line numbering and syntax highlighting. Many of these are under open source licences and can be downloaded and used at no cost. It is well worth considering using such an editor, especially for larger or more complex programming tasks.

The use of word processing software can cause problems due to unwanted markup and other symbols that such programs often embed in the output code. If you choose to use a word processor, make sure that it is capable of saving files as plain ASCII text.

The CD accompanying this book contains the popular and capable jEdit programmer's editor.

## Our First HTML Document

Let's jump right in and create a simple HTML document. Open your chosen editor and enter the text shown in Listing 2.1. The HTML markup elements (often referred to as *tags*) are the character strings enclosed by < and >.

**LISTING 2.1**   `testpage.html`

```
<!DOCTYPE HTML PUBLIC "-//W3C//DTD HTML 4.01 Transitional//EN"
➥"http://www.w3.org/TR/html4/loose.dtd">
<html>
<head>
<title>A Simple HTML Document</title>
```

**LISTING 2.1**    Continued

```
</head>
<body>
<h1>My HTML Page</h1>
Welcome to my first page written in HTML.<br />
This is simply a text document with HTML markup to show some
words in <b>bold</b> and some other words in <i>italics</i>.
<br />
</body>
</html>
```

Now save the document somewhere on your computer, giving it the name
`testpage.html`.

If you now load that page into your favorite browser, such as Internet Explorer or
Firefox, you should see something like the window displayed in Figure 2.1.

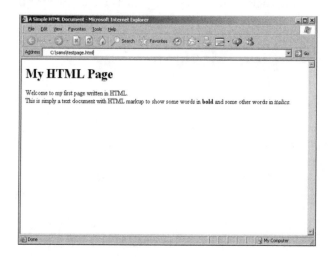

**FIGURE 2.1**
Our test document displayed in Internet Explorer.

# Elements of an HTML Page

Let's look at Listing 2.1 in a little more detail.

The first element on the page is known as the `DOCTYPE` element. Its purpose is to
notify the browser of the "flavor" of HTML used in the document. The `DOCTYPE` element used throughout this book refers to *HTML 4.0 Transitional,* a fairly forgiving
version of the HTML specification that allows the use of some earlier markup styles
and structures in addition to the latest HTML 4.0 specifications.

The `DOCTYPE` element must always occur right at the beginning of the HTML document.

Next, note that the remainder of the document is enclosed by the elements <html> at the start of the page and </html> at the end. These tags notify the browser that what lies between should be interpreted and displayed as an HTML document.

**Watch**
*Out!*

> Although many modern browsers correctly display HTML without these tags, it is bad practice to omit them. Even if the page is shown correctly on your own PC, you have no idea what operating system and browser a visitor may be using—he or she may not be so lucky.

The document within these outer tags is split into two further sections. The first is enclosed in <head> and </head> tags, and the second is contained between <body> and </body>. Essentially, the document's head section is used to store information about the document that is not to be displayed in the browser window, whereas the body of the document contains text to be interpreted and displayed to the user via the browser window.

## The <head> of the Document

From Listing 2.1 we can see that the head section of our simple HTML document contains only one line—the words A Simple HTML Document enclosed in <title> and </title> tags.

Remember that the head section contains information that is not to be displayed in the browser window. This is not, then, the title displayed at the top of our page text, as you can confirm by looking again at Figure 2.1. Neither does the document title refer to the filename of the document, which in this case is testpage.html.

In fact, the document title fulfils a number of functions, among them:

▶ Search engines often use the page title (among other factors) to help them decide what a page is about.

▶ When you bookmark a page, it is generally saved by default as the document title.

▶ Most browsers, when minimized, display the title of the current document on their icon or taskbar button.

It's important, therefore, to choose a meaningful and descriptive title for each page that you create.

Many other element types are used in the head section of a document, including link, meta, and script elements. Although we don't give an account of them here, they are described throughout the book as they occur.

# The Document <body>

Referring again to Listing 2.1, we can clearly see that the content of the document's body section is made up of the text we want to display on the page, plus some tags that help us to define how that text should look.

To define that certain words should appear in bold type, for example, we enclose those words in <b> and </b> tags. Similarly, to convert certain words into an italic typeface, we can use the <i> and </i> tags.

The heading, My HTML Page, is enclosed between <h1> and </h1> tags. These indicate that we intend the enclosed text to be a heading. HTML allows for six levels of headings, from h1 (the most prominent) to h6. You can use any of the intermediate values h2, h3, h4, and h5 to display pages having various levels of subtitles, for instance corresponding to chapter, section, and paragraph headings. Anything displayed within header tags is displayed on a line by itself.

All the tags discussed so far have been *containers*—that is, they consist of opening and closing tags between which you place the text that you want these tags to act upon. Some elements, however, are not containers but can be used alone. Listing 2.1 shows one such element: the <br /> tag, which signifies a line break. Another example is <hr /> (a horizontal line).

---

If you want to write in the body section of the HTML page but *don't* want it to be interpreted by the browser and therefore displayed on the screen, you may do so by writing it as a *comment*. HTML comments start with the character string <!-- and end with the string --> as in this example:

```
<!-- this is just a comment and won't be displayed in the browser -->
```

*Did you Know?*

---

# Adding Attributes to HTML Elements

Occasionally there is a need to specify exactly how a markup tag should behave. In such cases you can add (usually within the opening tag) parameter and value pairs, known as *attributes*, to change the behavior of the element:

```
<body bgcolor="#cccccc">
… page content goes here …
</body>
```

In this example, the behavior of the <body> tag has been modified by adjusting its BGCOLOR (background color) property to a light gray. Figure 2.2 shows the effect this has if applied to our file testpage.html:

**FIGURE 2.2**
Our test page
with the body
color changed
to gray.

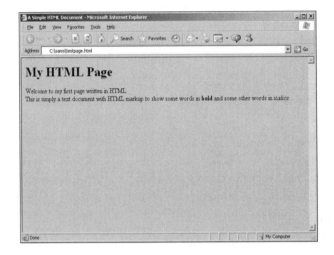

**Did you Know?** Color values in HTML are coded using a hexadecimal system. Each color value is made up of three component values, corresponding to red, green, and blue. Each of the color values can range from hex 00 to hex ff (zero to 255 in decimal notation). The three hex numbers are concatenated into a string prefixed with a hash character (#). The color value #000000 therefore corresponds to black, and #ffffff to pure white.

## Images

Images can be inserted in our page by means of the <img /> tag. In this case we specify the source file of the image as a parameter by using the src attribute. Other aspects of the image display that we can alter this way include the borders, width, and height of the image:

```
<img src="myimagefile.jpg" border="2" width="250" height="175" />
```

Border width, image width, and image height are in numbers of *pixels* (the "dots" formed by individual picture elements on the screen).

**Did you Know?** A further useful attribute for images is alt, which is an abbreviation of *alternative text*. This specifies a short description of the image that will be offered to users whose browsers cannot, or are configured not to, display images. Alternative text can also be important in making your website accessible to those with visual impairment and other disabilities:

```
<img src="myimagefile.jpg" alt="Description of Image" />
```

## Tables

Often you want to display information in tabular format, and HTML has a set of elements designed specifically for this purpose:

```
<table>
<tr><th>Column Header 1</th><th>Column Header 2</th></tr>
<tr><td>Data Cell 1</td><td>Data Cell 2</td></tr>
<tr><td>Data Cell 3</td><td>Data Cell 4</td></tr>
</table>
```

The `<table>` and `</table>` tags contain a nested hierarchy of other tags, including `<tr>` and `</tr>`, which define individual table rows; `<th>` and `</th>`, which indicate cells in the table's header; and `<td>` and `</td>`, which contain individual cells of table data.

Look ahead to Figure 2.3 to see an example of how a table looks when displayed in a browser window.

## Hyperlinks

Hypertext links (*hyperlinks*) are fundamental to the operation of HTML. By clicking on a hyperlink, you can navigate to a new location, be that to another point on the current page or to some point on a different page on another website entirely.

Links are contained within an `<a>`, or anchor tag, a container tag that encloses the content that will become the link. The destination of the link is passed to this tag as a parameter `href`:

```
Here is <a href="newpage.html">my hyperlink</a>
```

Clicking on the words `my hyperlink` in the preceding example results in the browser requesting the page newpage.html.

---

A hyperlink can contain images as well as, or instead of, text. Look at this example:

```
<a href="newpage.html"><img src="picfile.gif" /></a>
```

Here, a user can click on the image `picfile.gif` to navigate to `newpage.html`.

*Did you Know?*

---

# A More Advanced HTML Page

Let's revisit our `testpage.html` and add some extra elements. Listing 2.2 shows `seville.html`, developed from our original HTML page but with different content in the `<body>` section of the document. Figure 2.3 shows how the page looks when displayed, this time in Mozilla Firefox.

Now we have applied a background tint to the body area of the document. The content of the body area has been centered on the page, and that content now includes an image (which we've given a two-pixel-wide border), a heading and a subheading, a simple table, and some text.

**LISTING 2.2**   seville.html

```
<!DOCTYPE HTML PUBLIC "-//W3C//DTD HTML 4.01
➥Transitional//EN" "http://www.w3.org/TR/html4/loose.dtd">
<html>
<head>
<title>A Simple HTML Document</title>
</head>
<body bgcolor="#cccccc">
<center>
<img src="cathedral.jpg" border="2" alt="Cathedral" />
<h1>Guide to Seville</h1>
<h3>A brief guide to the attractions</h3>
<table border="2">
<tr>
  <th bgcolor="#aaaaaa">Attraction</th>
  <th bgcolor="#aaaaaa">Description</th>
</tr>
<tr>
  <td>Cathedral</td>
  <td>Dating back to the 15th century</td>
</tr>
<tr>
  <td>Alcazar</td>
  <td>The medieval Islamic palace</td>
</tr>
</table>
<p>Enjoy your stay in beautiful Seville.</p>
</center>
</body>
</html>
```

Let's take a closer look at some of the code.

First, we used the BGCOLOR property of the <body> tag to provide the overall background tint for the page:

```
<body bgcolor="#cccccc">
```

Everything in the body area is contained between the <center> tag (immediately after the body tag) and its partner </center>, immediately before the closing body tag. This ensures that all of our content is centered on the page.

The main heading is enclosed in <h1> … </h1> tags as previously, but is now followed by a subheading using <h3> … </h3> tags to provide a slightly smaller font size.

By using the border property in our opening `<table>` tag, we set a border width of two pixels for the table:

```
<table border="2">
```

Meanwhile we darkened the background of the table's header cells slightly by using the BGCOLOR property of the `<th>` elements:

```
<th bgcolor="#aaaaaa">Vegetables</th>
```

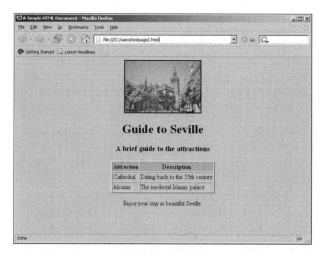

**FIGURE 2.3**
testpage2.html
shown in Mozilla
Firefox.

# Some Useful HTML Tags

Table 2.1 lists some of the more popular HTML tags.

**TABLE 2.1** Some Common HTML Markup Elements

**Document Tags**

| | |
|---|---|
| `<html>..</html>` | The entire document |
| `<head>..</head>` | Document head |
| `<body>..</body>` | Document body |
| `<title>..</title>` | Document title |

**Style Tags**

| | |
|---|---|
| `<a>..</a>` | Hyperlink |
| `<b>..</b>` | Bold text |
| `<em>..</em>` | Emphasized text |
| `<font>..</font>` | Changed font |
| `<i>..</i>` | Italic text |

**TABLE 2.1**    Continued

**Style Tags**

| | |
|---|---|
| `<small>..</small>` | Small text |
| `<table>..</table>` | Table |
| `<tr>..</tr>` | Table row |
| `<th>..</th>` | Cell in table header |
| `<td>..</td>` | Cell in table body |
| `<ul>..</ul>` | Bulleted list |
| `<ol>..</ol>` | Ordered (numbered) list |
| `<li>..</li>` | List item in bulleted or ordered list |

***Did you Know?***

The World Wide Web Consortium is responsible for administering the definitions of HTML, HTTP, XML, and many other web technologies. Its website is at http://www.w3.org/.

# Adding Your Own Style

As you've already learned, HTML was written as a markup language for defining the structure of a document (paragraphs, headings, tables, and so on). Although it was never intended to become a desktop publishing tool, it does include some basic formatting attributes, such as font-size, align and the aforementioned bgcolor. In 1996, the W3C first recommended the idea of Cascading Style Sheets (CSS) to format HTML documents. The recommendation, which was updated in mid-1998, enables web developers to separate the structure and format of their documents.

The CSS recommendation describes the following three types of style sheets:

▶ **Embedded**   The style properties are included (within the `<style>` tags) at the top of the HTML document. A style assigned to a particular tag applies to all those tags in this type of document. In this book, you'll see embedded style sheets most often.

▶ **Inline**   The style properties are included throughout the HTML page. Each HTML tag receives its own style attributes as they occur in the page.

▶ **Linked**   The style properties are stored in a separate file. That file can be linked to any HTML document using a `<link>` tag placed within the `<head>` tags.

In the following sections, you'll learn how to construct these style sheets and how to apply them to your documents.

Even without all the formatting benefits that style sheets provide, web developers can rejoice in knowing that using style sheets will no doubt be the biggest timesaver they've ever encountered. Because you can apply style sheets to as many HTML documents as you like, making changes takes a matter of minutes rather than days.

Before the advent of style sheets, if you wanted to change the appearance of a particular tag in your website, you would have to open each document, find the tag you wanted to change, make the change, save the document, and continue on to the next document. With style sheets, you can change the tag in a single style sheet document and have the changes take effect immediately in all the pages linked to it.

*Did you Know?*

# Defining the Rules

Style sheet rules are made up of selectors (the HTML tags that receive the style) and declarations (the style sheet properties and their values). In the following example, the selector is the body tag and the declaration is made up of the style property (background) and its value (black). This example sets the background color for the entire document to black.

```
body {background:black}
```

You can see that, in a style sheet, the HTML tag is not surrounded by brackets as it would be in the HTML document, and the declaration is surrounded by curly braces. Declarations can contain more than one property. The following example also sets the text color for this page to white. Notice that the two properties are separated by a semicolon.

```
body {background:black; color:white}
```

If you want to apply the same rules to several HTML tags, you could group those rules together, as in the following example:

```
body, td, h1 {
            background:black;
            color:white
            }
```

# Add a Little class

As the old saying goes, rules are made to be broken. What if you don't want every single h1 heading in your document to be white on a black background? Maybe you want every other h1 heading to be yellow on a white background. Let me introduce you to the class attribute. You can apply this attribute to almost every HTML tag, and it's almost like creating your own tags.

Figure 2.4 shows a fairly standard HTML page that uses an aqua table at the top of the page to hold the navigation links, and places other tabular content in yellow tables throughout the document. You can see the HTML document for that page in Figure 2.5.

**FIGURE 2.4**
An HTML page that formats two tables differently.

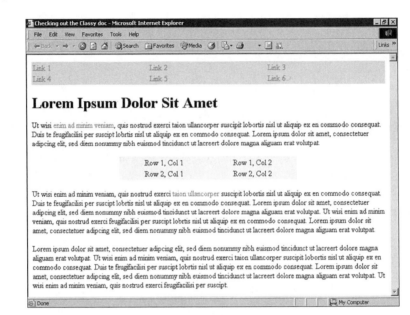

**FIGURE 2.5**
The HTML document for the page in Figure 2.4. Notice the class attribute in each `<table>` tag.

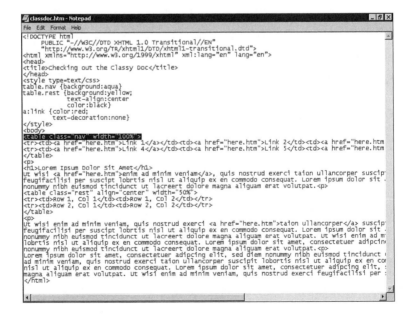

Take a closer look at the style properties in Figure 2.5. This document defines two table styles within the <style> tags. The HTML tag name `table` is followed by a period (.) and the class names (`nav` and `rest`).

```
table.nav {background:aqua}
table.rest {background:yellow;
            text-align:center;
            color:black}
```

When the table is referenced in the body of the document, you must apply the `class` attribute to tell the browser which style properties should be applied. The HTML markup for each table in this example appears in the following HTML code. You can see that the `class` name appears within quotations just like the other HTML attributes (and as with the `width` attribute shown here).

```
<table class="nav" width="100%">
<table class="rest" width=50%>
```

# Applying Styles

Before moving on, we'll quickly cover how to apply style properties to your documents. Remember, you have three methods to add style sheets: embedded, linked, and inline. We'll discuss each one in turn.

## Embedded Styles

All the styles are defined at the top of the HTML document within the <head> tags because they contain information about the entire document. The styles defined here apply only to the one document in which they appear. If you plan to use these same styles in another document, you need to add them there as well.

```
<head>
<style type="text/css">
table.nav {background:aqua}
table.rest {background:yellow;
            text-align:center;
            color:black}
a:link {color:red;
        text-decoration:none}
</style>
</head>
```

The <style> tag almost always includes the `type="text/css"` attribute, so you should get used to adding it.

## Linked Styles

Linked style sheets hold all the style properties in a separate file. You then link the file into each HTML document where you want those style properties to appear.

```
<head>
<link rel="stylesheet" href="mystyles.css" type="text/css">
</head>
```

With this method, I've created a separate file called mystyles.css (for cascading style sheet) that contains all my style properties. You can see that the same type="text/css" attribute shows up here. Following are the entire contents of the mystyles.css file. These are the same styles that showed up in the preceding embedded styles example, but now they appear in a separate text file.

```
table.nav {background:aqua}
table.rest {background:yellow;
           text-align:center;
           color:black}
a:link {color:red;
        text-decoration:none}
```

## Inline Styles

With inline styles, the style properties are added to the HTML tag as the tag is entered. This means that if I want the same style to appear on all the <h1> tags in my document, I would have to type those styles in all the <h1> tags. Look at the following example. I am still using the same style properties, as in the previous examples, but now you can see how the two tables would be created using inline styles.

```
<table style="background:aqua" width="100%">

<table style="background:yellow; text-align:center;
              color:black" width="100%">
```

Using inline styles, the <style> tag becomes the style attribute. Multiple style properties are still separated by semicolons, but the entire group of properties for each tag is grouped within each HTML tag. This type of style sheet is fine for documents in which you need to apply styles to only one or two elements, but you wouldn't want to do all that work when you have a lot of styles to add.

## Cascading Precedence

Web browsers give precedence to the style that appears closest to the tag. So, inline styles (which appear as attributes within the tag itself) are most important. Embedded styles (which appear at the top of the HTML file) are applied next, and linked styles (which appear in another file altogether) are applied last.

Imagine that you have created an embedded style for the <h1> tag, but want to change that style for one occurrence of the <h1> tag in that document. You would create an inline style for that new <h1> tag. The browsers recognize that fact and change the style for that tag to reflect the inline style.

Style sheet precedence is supposed to place more importance on embedded styles than on linked style sheets. In actual practice, however, you'll find that both Internet Explorer and Netscape treat linked sheets as more important than embedded sheets (but they do treat inline styles as more important than either of the other two). You'll find that you have better luck if you use either linked or embedded styles, but not both.

# Formatting Text with Styles

Text is the most important element of any Web page. Without text, there is nothing on the page to help people decide whether it's worth coming back.

Text on an HTML page is structured by the <body>, <p>, <td>, <tr>, <th>, <h1> <h6>, and <li> tags (among others). You can add your own style preferences to each of these tags using the style properties shown in Table 2.2.

In the following example, we've added some embedded style elements that set the font, font size, and font color for the body text of a basic HTML page. In Figure 2.6, you can see how those styles change the appearance of the document in the browser.

```
<!DOCTYPE html
    PUBLIC "-//W3C//DTD XHTML 1.0 Transitional//EN"
    "http://www.w3.org/TR/xhtml1/DTD/xhtml1-transitional.dtd">
<html xmlns="http://www.w3.org/1999/xhtml"
    xml:lang="en" lang="en">
<head>
<title>My First Web Page</title>
<style type="text/css">
body {font-family:"Arial";
    font-size:"12pt";
    color:red}
</style>
</head>
<body>
<p>This is my <b><i>first</i></b> Web page.</p>
</body>
</html>
```

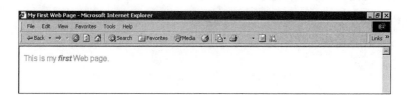

**FIGURE 2.6**
The browser applies the style attributes to the text in the <body> tags.

Table 2.2 lists the many style properties that you can use to format your text.

**TABLE 2.2** Style Properties for Text

| Property | Description of Use and Values |
|---|---|
| background | Sets the background color for the text. |
| color | Sets the text color for the text. |
| font-family | Sets the font for the text. |
| font-size | Can be a point size, a percentage of the size of another tag, or xx-small to xx-large. |
| font-style | normal (which is assumed) or italic. |
| font-weight | extra-light to extra-bold. |
| text-align | left, right, center, or justify (full). |
| text-indent | Can be a fixed length or a percentage. |
| text-decoration | underline, overline, strikethrough, and none. |

Microsoft maintains a brief tutorial for style sheets on its typography site (http://www.microsoft.com/typography/default.mspx). The tutorial teaches Web page authors how style sheets can enhance their documents. The <style> tag for one of those examples is shown in the following code. This is impressive because of the many different styles and classes defined in this document. You can see that you are only limited by your own imagination. You can see the page this style code created in Figure 2.7.

```
<style type="text/css">
body {background: coral}
.copy {color: Black;
    font-size: 11px;
    line-height: 14px;
    font-family: Verdana, Arial, Helvetica, sans-serif}
a:link {text-decoration: none;
    font-size: 20px;
    color: black;
    font-family: Impact, Arial Black, Arial,
                 Helvetica, sans-serif}
.star {color: white;
    font-size: 350px;
    font-family: Arial, Arial, helvetica, sans-serif}
.subhead {color: black;
    font-size: 28px;
    margin-top: 12px;
    margin-left: 20px;
    line-height: 32px;
    font-family: Impact, Arial Black, Arial,
                 Helvetica, sans-serif}
.what {color: black;
    font-size: 22px;
    margin-left: 20px;
    font-weight: bold;
    font-style: italic;
    font-family: Times New Roman, times, serif}
.quott {color: black;
```

```
    font-size: 120px;
    line-height: 120px;
    margin-top: -24px;
    margin-left: -4px;
    font-family: Arial Black, Arial, helvetica, sans-serif}
.quotb {color: black;
    font-size: 120px;
    line-height: 120px;
    margin-right: -1px;
    margin-top: -33px;
    font-family: Arial Black, Arial, helvetica, sans-serif}
.quote {color: red;
    font-size: 24px;
    line-height: 28px;
    margin-top: -153px;
    font-family: Impact, Arial Black, Arial,
                 Helvetica, sans-serif}
.footer {color: cornsilk;
    background: red;
    font-size: 22px;
    margin-left: 20px;
    margin-top: 16px;
    font-family: Impact, Arial Black, Arial,
                 Helvetica, sans-serif}
.headline {color: black;
    font-size: 80px;
    line-height: 90px;
    margin-left: 20px;
    font-family: Impact, Arial Black, Arial,
                 Helvetica, sans-serif}
.mast {color: cornsilk;
    font-size: 90px;
    font-style: italic;
    font-family: Impact, Arial Black, Arial,
                 Helvetica, sans-serif}
</style>
```

**FIGURE 2.7**
The preceding style code produced this page, found at http://www.microsoft.com/typography/css/gallery/slide3.htm.

None of the most popular web browsers react the same way to all the style sheet properties. Your best bet is to remember to test everything before you publish it. Webmaster Stop maintains a table of style sheet properties mapped to the most popular browsers. Check out this table (http://www.webmasterstop.com/118.html) to find out whether the style sheet properties you plan to use are supported by specific browsers.

## Link Styles

You have probably seen those bright blue underlined hyperlinks on the Web. Style sheets have the following selectors to help you change the look of them:

- `a:link`   Sets the styles for unvisited links.

- `a:visited`   Sets the styles for visited links.

- `a:active`   Sets the styles for the link while it is linking.

- `a:hover`   Sets the style for the link while your mouse is hovering.

Table 2.3 shows some of the style properties you can assign to your links.

**TABLE 2.3**   Style Properties for the Anchor Styles

| Property | Description of Use and Values |
|---|---|
| background-color | Sets the background color for the link. |
| color | Sets the text color for the link. |
| font-family | Sets the font for the text of the link. |
| text-decoration | underline, overline, strikethrough, and none. |

One of the most popular style sheet effects on the Web right now is to remove the underlining on hyperlinks. To do this on your pages, just add the `text-decoration:none` declaration to the a styles, as shown in the following example:

```
a:link {color:yellow;
        text-decoration:none}
```

If you like the look of the underlined hyperlink, you're in luck. You don't have to specify anything at all. Underlining is assumed for all a styles.

## Color Styles

As you can see in Table 2.4, you can apply color to your HTML tags in two different ways: with `color` or with `background`.

**TABLE 2.4**   Style Properties for Color

| Property | Description of Use and Values |
| --- | --- |
| color | Sets the color of the text. |
| background | Sets the background of the page or text. |

Don't forget to test your pages before you publish them. Not all colors work together. If you've specified a black background color and a black text color, you have a problem because no one will be able to see your text.

Watch
Out!

# Adding Lines

A horizontal line, or horizontal rule as it is named in HTML, is one of the easiest tags to use. You can insert the <hr /> tag anywhere in your document to insert a horizontal line that extends across the space available. Take a look at the following sample HTML. It shows three <hr> tags: two used as a section break between text and the other used inside a table cell. Figure 2.8 shows how they appear in the browser.

```
<!DOCTYPE html
     PUBLIC "-//W3C//DTD XHTML 1.0 Transitional//EN"
     "http://www.w3.org/TR/xhtml1/DTD/xhtml1-transitional.dtd">
<html xmlns="http://www.w3.org/1999/xhtml"
     xml:lang="en" lang="en">
<head>
<title>Horizontal Lines</title>
<style type="text/css">
td {text-align=center}
</style>
</head>
<body>
<p>This is a horizontal line.</p>
<hr />
<p>This is another horizontal line.</p>
<hr />

<table width="50%" rules=cols>
  <tr>
   <td>This is also a<hr />horizontal line.</td>
   <td>There is <br />no line on this<br />side
       of the table.</td>
  </tr>
</table>
</body>
</html>
```

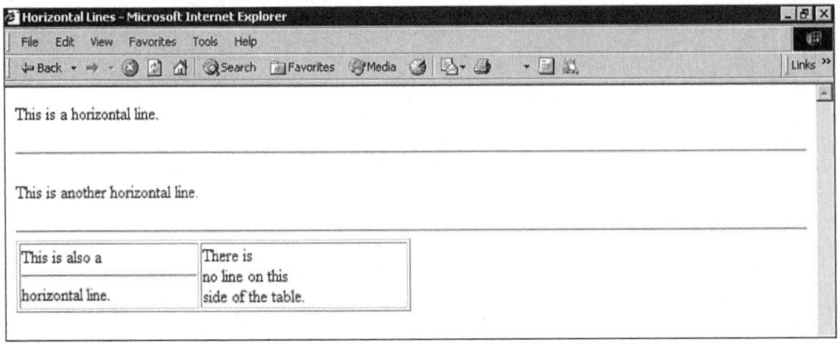

**FIGURE 2.8**
The <hr /> tag inserts a horizontal line that stretches across the available horizontal space.

## Margin Styles

Style sheets give you another important advantage: You can specify the margins of almost any HTML element. The margins can be defined in pt, in, cm, or px sizes.

```
body {margin-left: 100px;
     margin-right: 100px;
     margin-top: 50px}
```

You can set the margin-left, margin-right, and margin-top properties individually or combine them into one property called margin that applies the sizes to the top, right, and left margins.

```
body {margin: 100px 100px 50px}
```

## Summary

This chapter discussed the basics of web page layout using Hypertext Markup Language, including the structure of HTML documents, examples of HTML page elements, and page styling using both element attributes and cascading style sheets.

# CHAPTER 3

# Anatomy of an Ajax Application

## What You'll Learn in This Chapter:

▶ The Need for Ajax
▶ Introducing Ajax
▶ The Constituent Parts of Ajax
▶ Putting It All Together

In this chapter you will learn about the individual building blocks of Ajax and how they fit together to form the architecture of an Ajax application. Subsequent chapters will examine these components in more detail, finally assembling them into a working Ajax application.

## The Need for Ajax

In the following parts of the book, we shall discuss each of the core components in detail.

Before discussing the individual components, though, let's look in more detail at what we want from our Ajax application.

### Traditional Versus Ajax Client-Server Interactions

Chapter 1 discussed the traditional page-based model of a website user interface. When you interact with such a website, individual pages containing text, images, data entry forms, and so forth are presented one at a time. Each page must be dealt with individually before navigating to the next.

For instance, you may complete the data entry fields of a form, editing and re-editing your entries as much as you want, knowing that the data will not be sent to the server until the form is finally submitted.

Figure 3.1 illustrates this interaction.

**FIGURE 3.1**
Traditional
client–server
interactions.

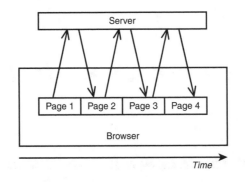

After you submit a form or follow a navigation link, you then must wait while the browser screen refreshes to display the new or revised page that has been delivered by the server.

As your experience as an Internet user grows, using this interface becomes almost second nature. You learn certain rules of thumb that help to keep you out of trouble, such as "don't click the Submit button a second time," and "don't click the Back button after submitting a form."

Unfortunately, interfaces built using this model have a few drawbacks. First, there is a significant delay while each new or revised page is loaded. This interrupts what we, as users, perceive as the "flow" of the application.

Furthermore, a *whole* page must be loaded on each occasion, even when most of its content is identical to that of the previous page. Items common to many pages on a website, such as header, footer, and navigation sections, can amount to a significant proportion of the data contained in the page.

Figure 3.2 illustrates a website displaying pages before and after the submission of a form, showing how much identical content has been reloaded and how relatively little of the display has actually changed.

This unnecessary download of data wastes bandwidth and further exacerbates the delay in loading each new page.

**By the Way**

> *Bandwidth* refers to the capacity of a communications channel to carry information. On the Internet, bandwidth is usually measured in bps (bits per second) or in higher multiples such as Mbps (million bits per second).

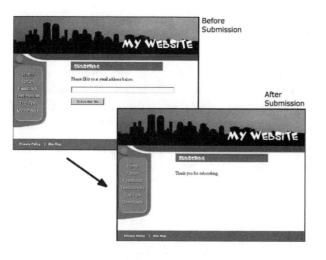

Before
Submission

After
Submission

**FIGURE 3.2**
Many page
items are
reloaded unnec-
essarily.

# The Rich User Experience

The combined effect of the issues just described is to offer a much inferior user experience compared to that provided by the vast majority of desktop applications.

On the desktop, you expect the display contents of a program to remain visible and the interface elements to respond to commands while the computing processes occur quietly in the background. As I write this chapter using a word processor, for example, I can save the document to disk, scroll or page up and down, and alter font faces and sizes without having to wait on each occasion for the entire display to be refreshed.

Ajax allows you to add to your web application interfaces some of this functionality more commonly seen in desktop applications and often referred to as a *rich user experience*.

# Introducing Ajax

To improve the user's experience, you need to add some extra capabilities to the traditional page-based interface design. You want your user's page to be interactive, responding to the user's actions with revised content, and be updated without any interruptions for page loads or screen refreshes.

To achieve this, Ajax builds an extra layer of processing between the web page and the server.

This layer, often referred to as an *Ajax Engine* or *Ajax Framework*, intercepts requests from the user and in the background handles server communications quietly, unobtrusively, and *asynchronously*. By this we mean that server requests and responses no longer need to coincide with particular user actions but may happen at any time convenient to the user and to the correct operation of the application. The browser does not freeze and await the completion by the server of the last request but instead lets the user carry on scrolling, clicking, and typing in the current page.

The updating of page elements to reflect the revised information received from the server is also looked after by Ajax, happening dynamically while the page continues to be used.

Figure 3.3 represents how these interactions take place.

**FIGURE 3.3**
Ajax client–server interaction.

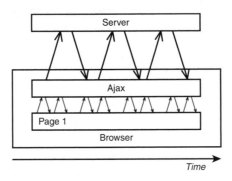

## A Real Ajax Application—Google Suggest

To see an example of an Ajax application in action, let's have a look at *Google Suggest*. This application extends the familiar Google search engine interface to offer the user suggestions for suitable search terms, based on what he has so far typed.

With each key pressed by the user, the application's Ajax layer queries Google's server for suitably similar search phrases and presents the returned data in a drop-down box. Along with each suggested phrase is listed the number of results that would be expected for a search conducted using that phrase. At any point the user has the option to select one of these suggestions instead of continuing to type and have Google process the selected search.

Because the server is queried with every keypress, this drop-down list updates dynamically as the user types—with no waiting for page refreshes or similar interruptions.

Figure 3.4 shows the program in action. You can try it for yourself by following the links from Google's home page at http://www.google.com/webhp?complete=1&hl=en.

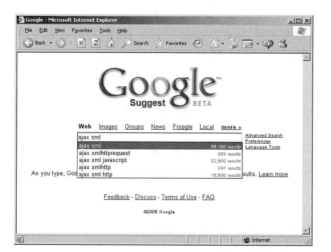

**FIGURE 3.4**
An example of an Ajax application—Google Suggest.

Next let's identify the individual components of such an Ajax application and see how they work together.

> Google has presented other Ajax-enabled applications that you can try, including the *gmail* web mail service and the *Google Maps* street mapping program. See the Google website at http://www.google.com/ for details.

*By the Way*

# The Constituent Parts of Ajax

Now let's examine the components of an Ajax application one at a time.

## The XMLHTTPRequest **Object**

When you click on a hyperlink or submit an HTML form, you send an HTTP request to the server, which responds by serving to you a new or revised page. For your web application to work asynchronously, however, you must have a means to send HTTP requests to the server *without* an associated request to display a new page.

You can do so by means of the XMLHTTPRequest *object*. This JavaScript object is capable of making a connection to the server and issuing an HTTP request without the necessity of an associated page load.

In following chapters you will learn what objects are, see how an instance of this object can be created, and see how its properties and methods can be used by JavaScript routines included in the web page to establish asynchronous communications with the server.

> As a security measure, the XMLHTTPRequest object can generally only make calls to URLs within the same domain as the calling page and cannot directly call a remote server.

Chapter 5, "Working with the Document Object Model" will introduce the concept of objects in general, and this subject will be expanded in Chapter 7 "Using Functions and Objects."

Chapter 10, "The Heart of Ajax"—the XMLHTTPPRequest Object, discusses how to create an instance of the XMLHTTPRequest object and reviews the object's properties and methods.

## Talking with the Server

In the traditional style of web page, when you issue a server request via a hyperlink or a form submission, the server accepts that request, carries out any required server-side processing, and subsequently serves to you a new page with content appropriate to the action you have undertaken.

While this processing takes place, the user interface is effectively frozen. You are made quite aware of this, when the server has completed its task, by the appearance in the browser of the new or revised page.

With asynchronous server requests, however, such communications occur in the background, and the completion of such a request does not necessarily coincide with a screen refresh or a new page being loaded. You must therefore make other arrangements to find out what progress the server has made in dealing with the request.

The XMLHTTPRequest object possesses a convenient property to report on the progress of the server request. You can examine this property using JavaScript routines to determine the point at which the server has completed its task and the results are available for use.

Your Ajax armory must therefore include a routine to monitor the status of a request and to act accordingly. We'll look at this in more detail in Chapter 11, "Talking with the Server."

## What Happens at the Server?

So far as the server-side script is concerned, the communication from the XMLHTTPRequest object is just another HTTP request. Ajax applications care little about what languages or operating environments exist at the server; provided that the client-side Ajax layer receives a timely and correctly formatted HTTP response from the server, everything will work just fine.

It is possible to build simple Ajax applications with no server-side scripting at all, simply by having the XMLHTTPRequest object call a static server resource such as an XML or text file.

Ajax applications may make calls to various other server-side resources such as web services. Later in the book we'll look at some examples of calling web services using protocols such as SOAP and REST.

> In this book we'll be using the popular PHP scripting language for our server-side routines, but if you are more comfortable with ASP, JSP, or some other server-side language, go right ahead and use it in your Ajax applications.

*By the Way*

## Dealing with the Server Response

Once notified that an asynchronous request has been successfully completed, you may then utilize the information returned by the server.

Ajax allows for this information to be returned in a number of formats, including ASCII text and XML data.

Depending on the nature of the application, you may then translate, display, or otherwise process this information within the current page.

We'll look into these issues in Chapter 12, "Using the Returned Data."

## Other Housekeeping Tasks

An Ajax application will be required to carry out a number of other duties, too. Examples include detecting error conditions and handling them appropriately, and keeping the user informed about the status of submitted Ajax requests.

You will see various examples in later chapters.

# Putting It All Together

Suppose that you want to design a new Ajax application, or update a legacy web application to include Ajax techniques. How do you go about it?

First you need to decide what page events and user actions will be responsible for causing the sending of an asynchronous HTTP request. You may decide, for example, that the action of moving the mouse cursor over an image will result in a request being sent to the server to retrieve further information about the subject of the picture, or that the clicking of a button will generate a server request for information with which to populate the fields on a form.

JavaScript can be used to execute instructions on occurrences such as these, by employing event handlers. The details of how will be covered in detail in the following chapters. In your Ajax applications, such methods will be responsible for initiating asynchronous HTTP requests via XMLHTTPRequest.

Having made the request, you need to write routines to monitor the progress of that request until you hear from the server that the request has been successfully completed.

Finally, after receiving notification that the server has completed its task, you need a routine to retrieve the information returned from the server and apply it in the application. You may, for example, want to use the newly returned data to change the contents of the page's body text, populate the fields of a form, or pop open an information window.

Figure 3.5 shows the flow diagram of all this.

**FIGURE 3.5**
How the components of an Ajax application work together.

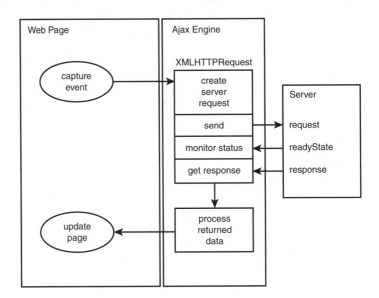

In Chapter 13, "Our First Ajax Application," you'll use what you have learned to construct a complete Ajax application.

## Ajax Frameworks

While it is essential for a complete understanding of Ajax to understand what role each of the individual components plays, it is thankfully not necessary to rewrite all of your code for each new application. Your Ajax code can be stored as a reusable library of common Ajax routines, ready to be reused wherever they may be needed. There are also many commercial and open-source frameworks that you can use in your projects to do the "heavy lifting."

We shall look at both of these techniques later in the book, where we develop our own JavaScript library for Ajax, and also consider several of the more popular open-source libraries.

# Summary

This chapter discussed the shortcomings of the traditional web interface, identifying specific problems we want to overcome. We also introduced the various building blocks of an Ajax application and discussed how they work together.

In the following chapters we shall look at these components in more detail, eventually using them to build a complete Ajax application.

That concludes Part I of the book, "Web Basics Refresher." In Part II we shall begin to explore client-side programming using JavaScript.

# PART II

# Introducing Web Scripting with JavaScript

# CHAPTER 4

# Creating Simple Scripts in JavaScript

As has already been discussed earlier in the book, JavaScript is a client-side scripting language for web pages. You can include JavaScript commands directly in the HTML document, and the script will be executed when the page is viewed in a browser.

During this chapter, you will create a simple script, edit it, and test it using a web browser. Along the way you'll learn the basic tasks involved in creating and using scripts.

## Tools for Scripting

Unlike many programming languages, you won't need any special software to create JavaScript scripts. In fact, you probably already have everything you need.

## Text Editors

The first tool you'll need to work with JavaScript is a *text editor*. JavaScript scripts are stored in simple text files, usually as part of HTML documents. Any editor that can store ASCII text files will work. Our discussion of programmers' editors in Chapter 2, "Writing and Styling Pages in HTML and CSS" is equally relevant to our work here in JavaScript (and, in fact, to the coding we carry out in PHP, later in the book).

> The CD that accompanies the book contains versions of the jEdit programmer's editor for use on Java, Macintosh, and Windows platforms. This editor will work just fine for coding your JavaScript programs.

## Browsers

You'll need two other things to work with JavaScript: a web browser and a computer to run it on. I recommend that you use the latest version of Mozilla Firefox or Microsoft Internet Explorer. See the Mozilla (http://www.mozilla.com) or Microsoft (http://www.microsoft.com) website to download a copy.

At a minimum, you should have Firefox 1.0, Netscape 7.0, or Internet Explorer 6.0 or later. You can choose whichever browser you like for your web browsing, but for developing JavaScript you should have more than one browser—at a minimum, Firefox and Internet Explorer. This will allow you to test your scripts in the common browsers users will employ on your site.

**By the Way**

> If you plan on making your scripts available over the Internet, you'll also need a web server, or access to one. However, you can use most of the JavaScript examples in this book directly from your computer's hard disk.

# Displaying Time with JavaScript

One common and easy use for JavaScript is to display dates and times. Because JavaScript runs on the browser, the times it displays will be in the user's current time zone. However, you can also use JavaScript to calculate "universal" (UTC) time.

**By the Way**

> UTC stands for Universal Time (Coordinated), and is the atomic time standard based on the old GMT (Greenwich Mean Time) standard. This is the time at the Prime Meridian, which runs through Greenwich, London, England.

As a basic introduction to JavaScript, you will now create a simple script that displays the current time and the UTC time within a web page, starting with the next section.

# Beginning the Script

Your script, like most JavaScript programs, begins with the HTML `<script>` tag. You use the `<script>` and `</script>` tags to enclose a script within the HTML document.

> Remember to include only valid JavaScript statements between the starting and ending `<script>` tags. If the browser finds anything but valid JavaScript statements within the `<script>` tags, it will display a JavaScript error message.

**Watch Out!**

To begin creating the script, open your favorite text editor and type the beginning and ending `<script>` tags as shown.

```
<script LANGUAGE="JavaScript" type="text/javascript"> </script>
```

Because this script does not use any of the new features of JavaScript 1.1 or later, you won't need to specify a version number in the `<script>` tag. This script should work with all browsers going back to Netscape 2.0 or Internet Explorer 3.0.

# Adding JavaScript Statements

Your script now needs to determine the local and UTC times, and then display them to the browser. Fortunately, all of the hard parts, such as converting between date formats, are built in to the JavaScript interpreter.

## Storing Data in Variables

To begin the script, you will use a *variable* to store the current date. You will learn more about variables in Chapter 6, "Using Variables, Strings, and Arrays." A variable is a container that can hold a value—a number, some text, or in this case, a date.

To start writing the script, add the following line after the first `<script>` tag. Be sure to use the same combination of capital and lowercase letters in your version because JavaScript commands and variable names are case sensitive.

```
now = new Date();
```

This statement creates a variable called now and stores the current date and time in it. This statement and the others you will use in this script use JavaScript's built-in Date object, which enables you to conveniently handle dates and times. You'll learn more about working with dates in Chapter 9, "Using Built-In Functions and Libraries."

> Notice the semicolon at the end of the previous statement. This tells the browser that it has reached the end of a statement. Semicolons are optional, but using them helps you avoid some common errors. We'll use them throughout this book for clarity.

## Calculating the Results

Internally, JavaScript stores dates as the number of milliseconds since January 1, 1970. Fortunately, JavaScript includes a number of functions to convert dates and times in various ways, so you don't have to figure out how to convert milliseconds to day, date, and time.

To continue your script, add the following two statements before the final </script> tag:

```
localtime = now.toString();
utctime = now.toGMTString();
```

These statements create two new variables: localtime, containing the current time and date in a nice readable format, and utctime, containing the UTC equivalent.

> The localtime and utctime variables store a piece of text, such as January 1, 2001 12:00 PM. In programming parlance, a piece of text is called a *string*. You will learn more about strings in Chapter 6.

## Creating Output

You now have two variables—localtime and utctime—which contain the results we want from our script. Of course, these variables don't do us much good unless we can see them. JavaScript includes a number of ways to display information, and one of the simplest is the document.write statement.

The document.write statement displays a text string, a number, or anything else you throw at it. Because your JavaScript program will be used within a web page, the output will be displayed as part of the page. To display the result, add these statements before the final </script> tag:

```
document.write("<b>Local time:</b> " + localtime + "<br>");
document.write("<b>UTC time:</b> " + utctime);
```

These statements tell the browser to add some text to the web page containing your script. The output will include some brief strings introducing the results, and the contents of the localtime and utctime variables.

Notice the HTML tags, such as <b>, within the quotation marks—because JavaScript's output appears within a web page, it needs to be formatted using HTML. The <br> tag in the first line ensures that the two times will be displayed on separate lines.

---

Notice the plus signs (+) used between the text and variables in the previous statements. In this case, it tells the browser to combine the values into one string of text. If you use the plus sign between two numbers, they are added together.

***By the Way***

---

# Adding the Script to a Web Page

You should now have a complete script that calculates a result and displays it. Your listing should match Listing 4.1.

**LISTING 4.1** The Complete Date and Time Script

```
<script language="JavaScript" type="text/javascript">
now = new Date();
localtime = now.toString();
utctime = now.toGMTString();
document.write("<b>Local time:</b> " + localtime + "<BR>");
document.write("<b>UTC time:</b> " + utctime);
</script>
```

To use your script, you'll need to add it to an HTML document. In its most basic form, the HTML document should include opening and closing <html> tags, <head> tags, and <body> tags.

If you add these tags to the document containing your script along with a descriptive heading, you should end up with something like Listing 4.2.

**LISTING 4.2** The Date and Time Script in an HTML Document

```
<html>
<head><title>Displaying Times and Dates</title></head>
<body>
<h1>Current Date and Time</h1>
<p>
<script language="JavaScript" type="text/javascript">
now = new Date();
localtime = now.toString();
utctime = now.toGMTString();
document.write("<b>Local time:</b> " + localtime + "<BR>");
document.write("<b>UTC time:</b> " + utctime);
```

**LISTING 4.2    Continued**

```
</script>
</p>
</body>
</html>
```

Now that you have a complete HTML document, save it with the `.htm` or `.html` extension.

**By the Way**

> Notepad and other Windows text editors might try to be helpful and add the `.txt` extension to your script. Be sure your saved file has the correct extension.

# Testing the Script

To test your script, you simply need to load the HTML document you created in a web browser. Start Netscape or Internet Explorer and select Open from the File menu. Click the Choose File or Browse button, and then find your HTML file. After you've selected it, click the Open button to view the page.

If you typed the script correctly, your browser should display the result of the script, as shown in Figure 4.1. (Of course, your result won't be the same as mine, but it should be the same as the setting of your computer's clock.)

A note about Internet Explorer 6.0 and above: Depending on your security settings, the script might not execute, and a yellow highlighted bar on the top of the browser might display a security warning. In this case, click the yellow bar and select Allow Blocked Content to allow your script to run. (This happens because the default security settings allow JavaScript in online documents, but not in local files.)

**FIGURE 4.1**
Firefox displays the results of the Date and Time script.

## Modifying the Script

Although the current script does indeed display the current date and time, its display isn't nearly as attractive as the clock on your wall or desk. To remedy that, you can use some additional JavaScript features and a bit of HTML to display a large clock.

To display a large clock, we need the hours, minutes, and seconds in separate variables. Once again, JavaScript has built-in functions to do most of the work:

```
hours = now.getHours();
mins = now.getMinutes();
secs = now.getSeconds();
```

These statements load the hours, mins, and secs variables with the components of the time using JavaScript's built-in date functions.

After the hours, minutes, and seconds are in separate variables, you can create document.write statements to display them:

```
document.write("<h1>");
document.write(hours + ":" + mins + ":" + secs);
document.write("</h1>");
```

The first statement displays an HTML <h1> header tag to display the clock in a large typeface. The second statement displays the hours, mins, and secs variables, separated by colons, and the third adds the closing </font> tag.

You can add the preceding statements to the original date and time script to add the large clock display. Listing 4.3 shows the complete modified version of the script.

**LISTING 4.3**   **The Date and Time Script with Large Clock Display**

```
<html>
<head><title>Displaying Times and Dates</title></head>
<body>
<h1>Current Date and Time</h1>
<p>
<script language="JavaScript">
now = new Date();
localtime = now.toString();
utctime = now.toGMTString();
document.write("<b>Local time:</b> " + localtime + "<BR>");
document.write("<b>UTC time:</b> " + utctime);
hours = now.getHours();
mins = now.getMinutes();
secs = now.getSeconds();
document.write("<h1>");
document.write(hours + ":" + mins + ":" + secs);
document.write("</h1>");
</script>
</p>
</body>
</html>
```

Now that you have modified the script, save the HTML file and open the modified file in your browser. If you left the browser running, you can simply use the Reload button to load the new version of the script. Try it and verify that the same time is displayed in both the upper portion of the window and the new large clock. Figure 4.2 shows the results.

**Current Date and Time**

Local time: Mon Dec 5 23:42:55 MST 2005
UTC time: Tue, 6 Dec 2005 06:42:55 UTC

23:42:55

**By the Way**

> The time formatting produced by this script isn't perfect: Hours after noon are in 24-hour time, and there are no leading zeroes, so 12:04 is displayed as 12:4. See Chapter 9 for solutions to these issues.

## Dealing with JavaScript Errors

As you develop more complex JavaScript applications, you're going to run into errors from time to time. JavaScript errors are usually caused by mistyped JavaScript statements.

To see an example of a JavaScript error message, modify the statement you added in the previous section. We'll use a common error: omitting one of the parentheses. Change the last `document.write` statement in Listing 4.3 to read

```
document.write("</h1>";
```

Save your HTML document again and load the document into the browser. Depending on the browser version you're using, one of two things will happen: Either an error message will be displayed, or the script will simply fail to execute.

If an error message is displayed, you're halfway to fixing the problem by adding the missing parenthesis. If no error was displayed, you should configure your browser to display error messages so that you can diagnose future problems:

▶ In Netscape or Firefox, type **javascript:** into the browser's Location field to display the JavaScript Console. In Firefox, you can also select Tools, JavaScript Console from the menu. The console is shown in Figure 4.3, displaying the error message you created in this example.

▶ In Internet Explorer, select Tools, Internet Options. On the Advanced page, uncheck the Disable Script Debugging box and check the Display a Notification About Every Script Error box. (If this is disabled, a yellow icon in the status bar will still notify you of errors.)

Notice the field at the bottom of the JavaScript Console. This enables you to type a JavaScript statement, which will be executed immediately. This is a handy way to test JavaScript's features.

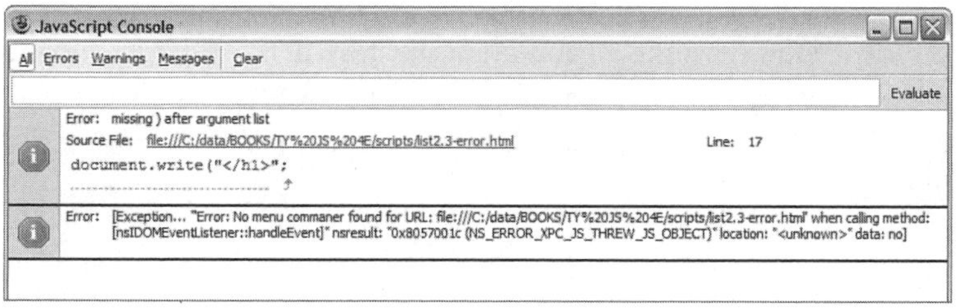

**By the Way**

**FIGURE 4.3**
Firefox's JavaScript Console displays an error message.

The error we get in this case is `missing )` `after argument list` (Firefox) or `Expected ')'` (Internet Explorer), which turns out to be exactly the problem. Be warned, however, that error messages aren't always this enlightening.

While Internet Explorer displays error dialog boxes for each error, Firefox's JavaScript Console displays a single list of errors and allows you to test commands. For this reason, you might find it useful to install Firefox for debugging and testing JavaScript, even if Internet Explorer is your primary browser.

## Statements

Statements are the basic units of a JavaScript program. A statement is a section of code that performs a single action. For example, consider the following three statements, each of which return part of the current time:

```
hours = now.getHours();
mins = now.getMinutes();
secs = now.getSeconds();
```

Although a statement is typically a single line of JavaScript, this is not a rule—it's possible to break a statement across multiple lines, or to include more than one statement in a single line.

A semicolon marks the end of a statement. You can also omit the semicolon if you start a new line after the statement. If you combine statements into a single line, you must use semicolons to separate them.

## Combining Tasks with Functions

In the basic scripts you've examined so far, you've seen some JavaScript statements that have a section in parentheses, like this:

```
document.write("Testing.");
```

This is an example of a *function*. Functions provide a simple way to handle a task, such as adding output to a web page. JavaScript includes a wide variety of built-in functions, which you will learn about throughout this book. A statement that uses a function, as in the preceding example, is referred to as a *function call*.

Functions take parameters (the expression inside the parentheses) to tell them what to do. Additionally, a function can return a value to a waiting variable. For example, the following function call prompts the user for a response and stores it in the text variable:

```
text = prompt("Enter some text.")
```

You can also create your own functions. This is useful for two main reasons: First, you can separate logical portions of your script to make it easier to understand. Second, and more importantly, you can use the function several times or with different data to avoid repeating script statements.

> You will learn how to define, call, and return values from your own functions in Chapter 7, "Using Functions and Objects."

## Variables

Variables are containers that can store a number, a string of text, or another value. For example, the following statement creates a variable called fred and assigns it the value 27:

```
var fred = 27;
```

JavaScript variables can contain numbers, text strings, and other values. You'll learn more about them in Chapter 6, "Using Variables, Strings, and Arrays."

## Conditionals

Although event handlers notify your script when something happens, you might want to check certain conditions yourself. For example, did the user enter a valid email address?

JavaScript supports *conditional statements*, which enable you to answer questions like this. A typical conditional uses the `if` statement, as in this example:

```
if (count==1) alert("The countdown has reached 1.");
```

This compares the variable `count` with the constant 1, and displays an alert message to the user if they are the same. You will use conditional statements like this in most of your scripts.

---

You'll learn more about conditionals in Chapter 8, "Controlling Flow with Conditions and Loops."

*By the Way*

---

## Loops

Another useful feature of JavaScript—and most other programming languages—is the capability to create *loops*, or groups of statements that repeat a certain number of times. For example, these statements display the same alert 10 times, greatly annoying the user:

```
for (i=1; i<=10; i++) {
   Alert("Yes, it's yet another alert!");
}
```

The `for` statement is one of several statements JavaScript uses for loops. This is the sort of thing computers are supposed to be good at: performing repetitive tasks. You will use loops in many of your scripts, in much more useful ways than this example.

---

Loops are covered in detail in Chapter 8.

*By the Way*

---

## Event Handlers

As already mentioned, not all scripts are located within `<script>` tags. You can also use scripts as *event handlers*. Although this might sound like a complex programming term, it actually means exactly what it says: Event handlers are scripts that handle events.

In real life, an event is something that happens to you. For example, the things you write on your calendar are events: "Dentist appointment" or "Fred's birthday." You also encounter unscheduled events in your life: for example, a traffic ticket, an IRS audit, or an unexpected visit from relatives.

Whether events are scheduled or unscheduled, you probably have normal ways of handling them. Your event handlers might include things such as *When Fred's birthday arrives, send him a present* or *When relatives visit unexpectedly, turn out the lights and pretend nobody is home.*

Event handlers in JavaScript are similar: They tell the browser what to do when a certain event occurs. The events JavaScript deals with aren't as exciting as the ones you deal with—they include such events as *When the mouse button clicks* and *When this page is finished loading.* Nevertheless, they're a very useful part of JavaScript.

Many JavaScript events (such as mouse clicks) are caused by the user. Rather than doing things in a set order, your script can respond to the user's actions. Other events don't involve the user directly—for example, an event is triggered when an HTML document finishes loading.

Each event handler is associated with a particular browser object, and you can specify the event handler in the tag that defines the object. For example, images and text links have an event, onMouseOver, that happens when the mouse pointer moves over the object. Here is a typical HTML image tag with an event handler:

```
<img src="button.gif" onMouseOver="highlight();">
```

You specify the event handler as an attribute to the HTML tag and include the JavaScript statement to handle the event within the quotation marks. This is an ideal use for functions because function names are short and to the point and can refer to a whole series of statements.

See the Try It Yourself section at the end of this chapter for a complete example of an event handler within an HTML document.

## Which Script Runs First?

You can actually have several scripts within a web document: one or more sets of <script> tags, external JavaScript files, and any number of event handlers. With all of these scripts, you might wonder how the browser knows which to execute first. Fortunately, this is done in a logical fashion:

▶ Sets of <script> tags within the <head> section of an HTML document are handled first, whether they include embedded code or refer to a JavaScript file. Because these scripts cannot create output in the web page, it's a good place to define functions for use later.

▶ Sets of <script> tags within the <body> section of the HTML document are executed after those in the <head> section, while the web page loads and displays. If there is more than one script in the body, they are executed in order.

▶ Event handlers are executed when their events happen. For example, the onLoad event handler is executed when the body of a web page loads. Because the <head> section is loaded before any events, you can define functions there and use them in event handlers.

# JavaScript Syntax Rules

JavaScript is a simple language, but you do need to be careful to use its *syntax*—the rules that define how you use the language—correctly. The rest of this book covers many aspects of JavaScript syntax, but there are a few basic rules you should understand to avoid errors.

## Case Sensitivity

Almost everything in JavaScript is *case sensitive*: you cannot use lowercase and capital letters interchangeably. Here are a few general rules:

▶ JavaScript keywords, such as for and if, are always lowercase.

▶ Built-in objects such as Math and Date are capitalized.

▶ DOM object names are usually lowercase, but their methods are often a combination of capitals and lowercase. Usually capitals are used for all but the first word, as in toLowerCase and getElementById.

When in doubt, follow the exact case used in this book or another JavaScript reference. If you use the wrong case, the browser will usually display an error message.

## Variable, Object, and Function Names

When you define your own variables, objects, or functions, you can choose their names. Names can include uppercase letters, lowercase letters, numbers, and the underscore (_) character. Names must begin with a letter or underscore.

You can choose whether to use capitals or lowercase in your variable names, but remember that JavaScript is case sensitive: score, Score, and SCORE would be considered three different variables. Be sure to use the same name each time you refer to a variable.

## Reserved Words

One more rule for variable names—they must not be *reserved words*. These include the words that make up the JavaScript language, such as `if` and `for`, DOM object names such as `window` and `document`, and built-in object names such as `Math` and `Date`.

## Spacing

Blank space (known as *whitespace* by programmers) is ignored by JavaScript. You can include spaces and tabs within a line, or blank lines, without causing an error. Blank space often makes the script more readable.

# Using Comments

JavaScript *comments* enable you to include documentation within your script. This will be useful if someone else tries to understand the script, or even if you try to understand it after a long break. To include comments in a JavaScript program, begin a line with two slashes, as in this example:

```
//this is a comment.
```

You can also begin a comment with two slashes in the middle of a line, which is useful for documenting a script. In this case, everything on the line after the slashes is treated as a comment and ignored by the browser. For example,

```
a = a + 1; // add one to the value of a
```

JavaScript also supports C-style comments, which begin with `/*` and end with `*/`. These comments can extend across more than one line, as the following example demonstrates:

```
/*This script includes a variety
of features, including this comment. */
```

Because JavaScript statements within a comment are ignored, C-style comments are often used for *commenting out* sections of code. If you have some lines of JavaScript that you want to temporarily take out of the picture while you debug a script, you can add `/*` at the beginning of the section and `*/` at the end.

**By the Way**

> Because these comments are part of JavaScript syntax, they are only valid inside `<script>` tags or within an external JavaScript file.

# Best Practices for JavaScript

You should now be familiar with the basic rules for writing valid JavaScript. Along with following the rules, it's also a good idea to follow *best practices*. The following practices may not be required, but you'll save yourself and others some headaches if you follow them.

- ▶ **Use comments liberally**—These make your code easier for others to understand, and also easier for you to understand when you edit them later. They are also useful for marking the major divisions of a script.

- ▶ **Use a semicolon at the end of each statement, and only use one statement per line**—This will make your scripts easier to debug.

- ▶ **Use separate JavaScript files whenever possible**—This separates JavaScript from HTML and makes debugging easier, and also encourages you to write modular scripts that can be reused.

- ▶ **Avoid being browser-specific**—As you learn more about JavaScript, you'll learn some features that only work in one browser. Avoid them unless absolutely necessary, and always test your code in more than one browser.

- ▶ **Keep JavaScript optional**—Don't use JavaScript to perform an essential function on your site—for example, the primary navigation links. Whenever possible, users without JavaScript should be able to use your site, although it may not be quite as attractive or convenient. This strategy is known as *progressive enhancement*.

## Try It Yourself ▼

### Using an Event Handler

To conclude this chapter, here's a simple example of an event handler. This will demonstrate how you set up an event, which you'll use throughout this book, and how JavaScript works without <script> tags. Listing 4.6 shows an HTML document that includes a simple event handler.

**LISTING 4.6** An HTML Document with a Simple Event Handler

```
<html>
<head>
<title>Event Handler Example</title>
</head>
<body>
<h1>Event Handler Example</h1>
<p>
```

▼

**LISTING 4.6**    Continued

```
<a href="http://www.jsworkshop.com/"
onClick="alert('Aha! An Event!');">Click this link</a>
to test an event handler.
</p>
</body>
</html>
```

The event handler is defined with the following onClick attribute within the <a> tag that defines a link:

```
onClick="alert('Aha! An Event!');"
```

This event handler uses the built-in alert() function to display a message when you click on the link. In more complex scripts, you will usually define your own function to act as an event handler. Figure 4.4 shows this example in action.

**FIGURE 4.4**
The browser displays an alert when you click the link.

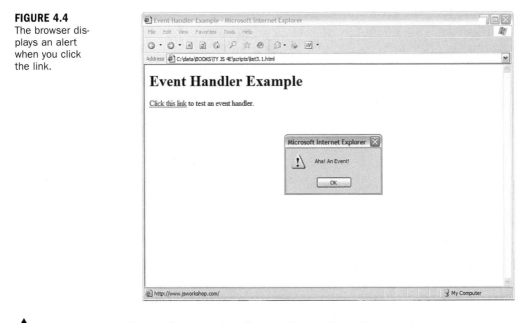

You'll use other event handlers similar to this in the next chapter.

# Summary

During this chapter, you wrote a simple JavaScript program and tested it using a browser. You learned about the tools you need to work with JavaScript—basically, an editor and a browser. You also learned how to modify and test scripts, and what happens when a JavaScript program runs into an error, and you learned how to use scripts in separate JavaScript files.

In the process of writing this script, you have used some of JavaScript's basic features: variables, the `document.write` statement, and functions for working with dates and times.

You've also been introduced to several components of JavaScript programming and syntax: functions, objects, event handlers, conditions, and loops. You learned how to use JavaScript comments to make your script easier to read, and looked at a simple example of an event handler.

In the next chapter, you'll look at the Document Object Model (DOM) and learn how you can use the objects within the DOM to work with web pages and interact with users.

# CHAPTER 5

# Working with the Document Object Model (DOM)

---

## What You'll Learn in This Chapter:

▶ Understanding Objects
▶ Understanding the Document Object Model (DOM)
▶ Working with Web Documents
▶ Accessing Browser History
▶ Working with the `location` Object

In this chapter, you'll be introduced to one of the most important tools you'll use with JavaScript: the Document Object Model (DOM), which lets your scripts manipulate web pages, windows, and documents.

Without the DOM, JavaScript would be just another scripting language—with the DOM, it becomes a powerful tool for making pages dynamic. This chapter will first discuss objects, then introduce the idea of the DOM and some of the objects you'll use most often.

## Understanding Objects

JavaScript supports *objects*. Like variables, objects can store data—but they can store two or more pieces of data at once.

The items of data stored in an object are called the *properties* of the object. For example, you could use objects to store information about people such as in an address book. The properties of each person object might include a name, an address, and a telephone number.

JavaScript uses periods to separate object names and property names. For example, for a person object called Bob, the properties might include Bob.address and Bob.phone.

Objects can also include *methods*. These are functions that work with the object's data. For example, our person object for the address book might include a `display()` method to display the person's information. In JavaScript terminology, the statement `Bob.display()` would display Bob's details.

**By the Way**

The `document.write` function we discussed in the previous chapter is actually the `write` method of the `document` object. You will learn more about this object later in this chapter.

Don't worry if this sounds confusing—you'll be exploring objects in much more detail later in this book. For now, you just need to know the basics. JavaScript supports three kinds of objects:

▶ *Built-in objects* are built in to the JavaScript language. You've already encountered one of these, `Date`. Other built-in objects include `Array` and `String`, which you'll explore in Chapter 6, "Using Variables, Strings, and Arrays" and `Math`, which is explained in Chapter 9, "Using Built-In Functions and Libraries."

▶ *DOM (Document Object Model) objects* represent various components of the browser and the current HTML document. For example, the `alert()` function you used earlier in this chapter is actually a method of the `window` object. You'll explore these in more detail in the course of this chapter.

▶ *Custom objects* are objects you create yourself. You'll learn to use custom objects in Chapter 7 "Using Functions and Objects."

# Understanding the Document Object Model (DOM)

One advantage that JavaScript has over basic HTML is that scripts can manipulate the web document and its contents. Your script can load a new page into the browser, work with parts of the browser window and document, open new windows, and even modify text within the page dynamically.

To work with the browser and documents, JavaScript uses a hierarchy of parent and child objects called the Document Object Model (DOM). These objects are organized into a tree-like structure, and represent all of the content and components of a web document.

**By the Way**

> The DOM is not part of the JavaScript language—rather, it's an API (application pro-gramming interface) built in to the browser. While the DOM is most often used with JavaScript, it can also be used by other languages, such as VBScript and Java.

The objects in the DOM have *properties*—variables that describe the web page or doc-ument, and *methods*—functions that enable you to work with parts of the web page.

When you refer to an object, you use the parent object name followed by the child object name or names, separated by periods. For example, JavaScript stores objects to represent images in a document as children of the document object. The following refers to the image9 object, a child of the document object, which is a child of the window object:

```
window.document.image9
```

The window object is the parent object for all of the objects we will be looking at in this chapter. Figure 5.1 shows this section of the DOM object hierarchy and a variety of its objects.

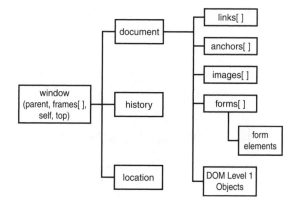

**FIGURE 5.1**
The DOM object hierarchy.

**By the Way**

> This diagram only includes the basic browser objects that will be covered in this chapter. These are actually a part of the DOM, but a full discussion of all DOM objects is beyond the scope of this book.

## History of the DOM

Starting with the introduction of JavaScript 1.0 in Netscape 2.0, browsers have included objects that represent parts of a web document and other browser features. However, there was never a true standard. While both Netscape and Microsoft

Internet Explorer included many of the same objects, there was no guarantee that the same objects would work the same way in both browsers, let alone in less common browsers.

The bad news is that there are still differences between the browsers—but here's the good news. Since the release of Netscape 3.0 and Internet Explorer 4.0, all of the basic objects (those covered in this chapter) are supported in much the same way in both browsers. With more recent browser releases, a much more advanced DOM is supported.

## DOM Levels

The W3C (World Wide Web Consortium) developed the DOM level 1 recommendation. This is a standard that defines not only basic objects, but an entire set of objects that encompass all parts of an HTML document. A level 2 DOM standard has also been released, and level 3 is under development.

Netscape 4 and Internet Explorer 4 supported their own DOMs that allowed more control over documents, but weren't standardized. Fortunately, starting with Internet Explorer 5 and Netscape 6, both support the W3C DOM, so you can support both browsers with simple, standards-compliant code. All of today's current browsers support the W3C DOM.

The basic object hierarchy described in this chapter is informally referred to as DOM level 0, and the objects are included in the DOM level 1 standard.

# Working with Web Documents

The document object represents a web document, or page. Web documents are displayed within browser windows, so it shouldn't surprise you to learn that the document object is a child of the window object.

Because the window object always represents the current window (the one containing the script), you can use window.document to refer to the current document. You can also simply refer to document, which automatically refers to the current window.

**By the Way**

> You've already used the document.write method to display text within a web document. The examples in earlier chapters only used a single window and document, so it was unnecessary to use window.document.write—but this longer syntax would have worked equally well.

If multiple windows or frames are in use, there might be several window objects, each with its own document object. To use one of these document objects, you use the name of the window and the name of the document.

In the following sections, you will look at some of the properties and methods of the document object that will be useful in your scripting.

# Getting Information About the Document

Several properties of the document object include information about the current document in general:

▶ document.URL specifies the document's URL. This is a simple text field. You can't change this property. If you need to send the user to a different location, use the window.location object, described later in this chapter.

▶ document.title lists the title of the current page, defined by the HTML <title> tag.

▶ document.referrer is the URL of the page the user was viewing prior to the current page—usually, the page with a link to the current page.

▶ document.lastModified is the date the document was last modified. This date is sent from the server along with the page.

▶ document.bgColor and document.fgColor are the background and foreground (text) colors for the document, corresponding to the BGCOLOR and TEXT attributes of the <body> tag.

▶ document.linkColor, document.alinkColor, and document.vlinkColor are the colors for links within the document. These correspond to the LINK, ALINK, and VLINK attributes of the <body> tag.

▶ document.cookie enables you to read or set a cookie for the document.

As an example of a document property, Listing 5.1 shows a short HTML document that displays its last modified date using JavaScript.

**LISTING 5.1**   Displaying the Last Modified Date

```
<html><head><title>Test Document</title></head>
<body>
<p>This page was last modified on:
<script language="JavaScript" type="text/javascript">
document.write(document.lastModified);
</script>
</p>
</body>
</html>
```

This can tell the user when the page was last changed. If you use JavaScript, you don't have to remember to update the date each time you modify the page. (You could also use the script to always print the current date instead of the last modified date, but that would be cheating.)

**By the Way**

> You might find that the `document.lastModified` property doesn't work on your web pages, or returns the wrong value. The date is received from the web server, and some servers do not maintain modification dates correctly.

## Writing Text in a Document

The simplest document object methods are also the ones you will use most often. In fact, you've used one of them already. The `document.write` method prints text as part of the HTML page in a document window. This statement is used whenever you need to include output in a web page.

An alternative statement, `document.writeln`, also prints text, but it also includes a newline (\n) character at the end. This is handy when you want your text to be the last thing on the line.

**Watch Out!**

> Bear in mind that the newline character is displayed as a space by the browser, except inside a <pre> container. You will need to use the <br> tag if you want an actual line break.

You can use these methods only within the body of the web page, so they will be executed when the page loads. You can't use these methods to add to a page that has already loaded without reloading it. You can write new content for a document, however, as the next section explains.

The document.write method can be used within a <script> tag in the body of an HTML document. You can also use it in a function, provided you include a call to the function within the body of the document.

## Using Links and Anchors

Another child of the document object is the link object. Actually, there can be multiple link objects in a document. Each one includes information about a link to another location or an anchor.

> Anchors are named places in an HTML document that can be jumped to directly. You define them with a tag like this: <a name="part2">. You can then link to them: <a href="#part2">.

**Did you Know?**

You can access `link` objects with the `links` array. Each member of the array is one of the `link` objects in the current page. A property of the array, `document.links.length`, indicates the number of links in the page.

Each `link` object (or member of the `links` array) has a list of properties defining the URL. The `href` property contains the entire URL, and other properties define portions of it. These are the same properties as the `location` object, defined later in this chapter.

You can refer to a property by indicating the link number and property name. For example, the following statement assigns the entire URL of the first link to the variable `link1`:

```
link1 = links[0].href;
```

The anchor objects are also children of the `document` object. Each anchor object represents an anchor in the current document—a particular location that can be jumped to directly.

Like links, you can access anchors with an array: `anchors`. Each element of this array is an anchor object. The `document.anchors.length` property gives you the number of elements in the `anchors` array.

# Accessing Browser History

The `history` object is another child (property) of the `window` object. This object holds information about the URLs that have been visited before and after the current one, and it includes methods to go to previous or next locations.

The `history` object has one property you can access:

- ▶ `history.length` keeps track of the length of the history list—in other words, the number of different locations that the user has visited.

> The `history` object has `current`, `previous`, and `next` properties that store URLs of documents in the history list. However, for security and privacy reasons, these objects are not normally accessible in today's browsers.

**By the Way**

The `history` object has three methods you can use to move through the history list:

▶ `history.go()` opens a URL from the history list. To use this method, specify a positive or negative number in parentheses. For example, `history.go(-2)` is equivalent to clicking the Back button twice.

▶ `history.back()` loads the previous URL in the history list—equivalent to clicking the Back button.

▶ `history.forward()` loads the next URL in the history list, if available. This is equivalent to clicking the Forward button.

You'll use these methods in the Try It Yourself section at the end of this chapter.

# Working with the `location` Object

A third child of the `window` object is the `location` object. This object stores information about the current URL stored in the window. For example, the following statement loads a URL into the current window:

```
window.location.href="http://www.starlingtech.com";
```

The `href` property used in this statement contains the entire URL of the window's current location. You can also access portions of the URL with various properties of the `location` object. To explain these properties, consider the following URL:

```
http://www.jsworkshop.com:80/test.cgi?lines=1#anchor
```

The following properties represent parts of the URL:

▶ `location.protocol` is the protocol part of the URL (`http:` in the example).

▶ `location.hostname` is the host name of the URL (`www.jsworkshop.com` in the example).

▶ `location.port` is the port number of the URL (`80` in the example).

▶ `location.pathname` is the filename part of the URL (`test.cgi` in the example).

▶ `location.search` is the query portion of the URL, if any (`lines=1` in the example). Queries are used mostly by CGI scripts.

▶ `location.hash` is the anchor name used in the URL, if any (`#anchor` in the example).

The `link` object, introduced earlier this chapter, also includes this list of properties for accessing portions of the URL.

**By the Way**

> Although the `location.href` property usually contains the same URL as the `document.URL` property described earlier in this chapter, you can't change the `document.URL` property. Always use `location.href` to load a new page.

The `location` object has two methods:

▶ `location.reload()` reloads the current document. This is the same as the Reload button on the browser's toolbar. If you optionally include the `true` parameter, it will ignore the browser's cache and force a reload whether the document has changed or not.

▶ `location.replace()` replaces the current location with a new one. This is similar to setting the `location` object's properties yourself. The difference is that the `replace` method does not affect the browser's history. In other words, the Back button can't be used to go to the previous location. This is useful for splash screens or temporary pages that it would be useless to return to.

## Try It Yourself ▼

### Creating Back and Forward Buttons

You can use the `back` and `forward` methods of the `history` object to add your own Back and Forward buttons to a web document. The browser already has Back and Forward buttons, of course, but it's occasionally useful to include your own links that serve the same purpose.

You will now create a script that displays Back and Forward buttons and use these methods to navigate the browser. Here's the code that will create the Back button:

```
<input type="button"
   onClick="history.back();" value="<-- Back">
```

The `<input>` tag defines a button labeled Back. The `onClick` event handler uses the `history.back()` method to go to the previous page in history. The code for the Forward button is similar:

```
<input type="button"
   onClick="history.forward();" value="Forward -->">
```

▼

With these out of the way, you just need to build the rest of the HTML document. Listing 5.2 shows the complete HTML document, and Figure 5.2 shows a browser's display of the document. After you load this document into a browser, visit other URLs and make sure the Back and Forward buttons work.

**LISTING 5.2    A Web Page That Uses JavaScript to Include Back and Forward Buttons**

```
<html>
<head><title>Back and Forward Buttons</title>
</head>
<body>
<h1>Back and Forward Buttons</h1>
<p>This page allows you to go back or forward to pages in the history list.
These should be equivalent to the back and forward arrow buttons in the
browser's toolbar.</p>
<p>
<input type="button"
    onClick="history.back();" value="<-- Back">
<input type="button"
    onClick="history.forward();" value="Forward -->">
</p>
</body>
</html>
```

**FIGURE 5.2**
The Back and Forward buttons in Internet Explorer.

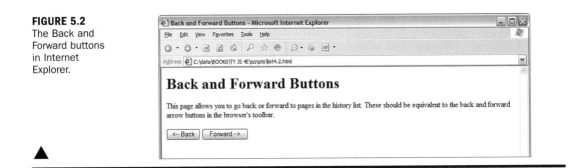

## Summary

In this chapter, you've learned about the Document Object Model (DOM), JavaScript's hierarchy of web page objects. You've learned how you can use the document object to work with documents, and used the history and location objects to control the current URL displayed in the browser.

You should now have a basic understanding of the DOM and some of its objects—you'll learn about more of the objects throughout this book.

# CHAPTER 6

# Using Variables, Strings, and Arrays

## What You'll Learn in This Chapter:

▶ Using Variables
▶ Understanding Expressions and Operators
▶ Data Types in JavaScript
▶ Converting Between Data Types
▶ Using `String` Objects
▶ Working with Substrings
▶ Using Numeric Arrays
▶ Using String Arrays
▶ Sorting a Numeric Array

Now that you have learned some of the fundamentals of JavaScript and the DOM, it's time to dig into more details of the JavaScript language.

In this chapter, you'll learn three tools for storing data in JavaScript: variables, which store numbers or text; strings, which are special variables for working with text; and arrays, which are multiple variables you can refer to by number.

## Using Variables

Unless you skipped the last few chapters of this book, you've already used a few variables. You probably can also figure out how to use a few more without any help. Nevertheless, there are some aspects of variables you haven't learned yet. We will now look at some of the details.

## Choosing Variable Names

Variables are named containers that can store data (for example, a number, a text string, or an object). As you learned earlier in this book, each variable has a name. There are specific rules you must follow when choosing a variable name:

▶ Variable names can include letters of the alphabet, both upper- and lower-case. They can also include the digits 0–9 and the underscore (_) character.

▶ Variable names cannot include spaces or any other punctuation characters.

▶ The first character of the variable name must be either a letter or an underscore.

▶ Variable names are case sensitive—totalnum, Totalnum, and TotalNum are separate variable names.

▶ There is no official limit on the length of variable names, but they must fit within one line.

Using these rules, the following are examples of valid variable names:

```
total_number_of_fish
LastInvoiceNumber
temp1
a
_var39
```

**By the Way**

You can choose to use either friendly, easy-to-read names or completely cryptic ones. Do yourself a favor: Use longer, friendly names whenever possible. Although you might remember the difference between a, b, x, and x1 right now, you might not after a good night's sleep.

## Using Local and Global Variables

Some computer languages require you to declare a variable before you use it. JavaScript includes the var keyword, which can be used to declare a variable. You can omit var in many cases; the variable is still declared the first time you assign a value to it.

To understand where to declare a variable, you will need to understand the concept of *scope*. A variable's scope is the area of the script in which that variable can be used. There are two types of variables:

▶ *Global variables* have the entire script (and other scripts in the same HTML document) as their scope. They can be used anywhere, even within functions.

▶ *Local variables* have a single function as their scope. They can be used only within the function they are created in.

To create a global variable, you declare it in the main script, outside any functions. You can use the var keyword to declare the variable, as in this example:

```
var students = 25;
```

This statement declares a variable called students and assigns it a value of 25. If this statement is used outside functions, it creates a global variable. The var keyword is optional in this case, so this statement is equivalent to the previous one:

```
students = 25;
```

Before you get in the habit of omitting the var keyword, be sure you understand exactly when it's required. It's actually a good idea to always use the var keyword—you'll avoid errors and make your script easier to read, and it won't usually cause any trouble.

> For the most part, the variables you've used in earlier chapters of this book have been global.

**By the Way**

A local variable belongs to a particular function. Any variable you declare with the var keyword in a function is a local variable. Additionally, the variables in the function's parameter list are always local variables.

To create a local variable within a function, you must use the var keyword. This forces JavaScript to create a local variable, even if there is a global variable with the same name.

You should now understand the difference between local and global variables. If you're still a bit confused, don't worry—if you use the var keyword every time, you'll usually end up with the right type of variable.

## Assigning Values to Variables

You can use the equal sign to assign a value to a variable. For example, this statement assigns the value 40 to the variable lines:

```
lines = 40;
```

You can use any expression to the right of the equal sign, including other variables. You have used this syntax earlier to add one to a variable:

```
lines = lines + 1;
```

Because incrementing or decrementing variables is quite common, JavaScript includes two types of shorthand for this syntax. The first is the += operator, which enables you to create the following shorter version of the preceding example:

```
lines += 1;
```

Similarly, you can subtract a number from a variable using the -= operator:

```
lines -= 1;
```

If you still think that's too much to type, JavaScript also includes the increment and decrement operators, ++ and --. This statement adds one to the value of lines:

```
lines++;
```

Similarly, this statement subtracts one from the value of lines:

```
lines--;
```

You can alternately use the ++ or -- operators before a variable name, as in ++lines. However, these are not identical. The difference is when the increment or decrement happens:

▶ If the operator is after the variable name, the increment or decrement happens *after* the current expression is evaluated.

▶ If the operator is before the variable name, the increment or decrement happens *before* the current expression is evaluated.

This difference is only an issue when you use the variable in an expression and increment or decrement it in the same statement. As an example, suppose you have assigned the lines variable the value 40. The following two statements have different effects:

```
alert(lines++);
alert(++lines);
```

The first statement displays an alert with the value 40, and then increments lines to 41. The second statement first increments lines to 41, then displays an alert with the value 41.

**By the Way**

These operators are strictly for your convenience. If it makes more sense to you to stick to lines = lines + 1, do it—your script won't suffer.

# Understanding Expressions and Operators

An *expression* is a combination of variables and values that the JavaScript inter-preter can evaluate to a single value. The characters that are used to combine these values, such as + and /, are called *operators*.

Along with variables and constant values, you can also use calls to functions that return results within an expression.

***Did you Know?***

## Using JavaScript Operators

You've already used some operators, such as the + sign (addition) and the incre-ment and decrement operators. Table 6.1 lists some of the most important operators you can use in JavaScript expressions.

**TABLE 6.1** Common JavaScript Operators

| Operator | Description | Example |
|---|---|---|
| + | Concatenate (combine) strings | message="this is" + " a test"; |
| + | Add | result = 5 + 7; |
| - | Subtract | score = score - 1; |
| * | Multiply | total = quantity * price; |
| / | Divide | average = sum / 4; |
| % | Modulo (remainder) | remainder = sum % 4; |
| ++ | Increment | tries++; |
| -- | Decrement | total--; |

Along with these, there are also many other operators used in conditional statements—you'll learn about these in Chapter 8, "Controlling Flow with Conditions and Loops."

## Operator Precedence

When you use more than one operator in an expression, JavaScript uses rules of *operator precedence* to decide how to calculate the value. Table 6.1 lists the operators from lowest to highest precedence, and operators with highest precedence are evalu-ated first. For example, consider this statement:

```
result = 4 + 5 * 3;
```

If you try to calculate this result, there are two ways to do it. You could multiply 5 * 3 first and then add 4 (result: 19) or add 4 + 5 first and then multiply by 3 (result: 27). JavaScript solves this dilemma by following the precedence rules: Because multiplication has a higher precedence than addition, it first multiplies 5 * 3 and then adds 4, producing a result of 19.

> If you're familiar with any other programming languages, you'll find that the operators and precedence in JavaScript work, for the most part, the same way as those in C, C++, and Java.

Sometimes operator precedence doesn't produce the result you want. For example, consider this statement:

```
result = a + b + c + d / 4;
```

This is an attempt to average four numbers by adding them all together and then dividing by four. However, because JavaScript gives division a higher precedence than addition, it will divide the d variable by 4 before adding the other numbers, producing an incorrect result.

You can control precedence by using parentheses. Here's the working statement to calculate an average:

```
result = (a + b + c + d) / 4;
```

The parentheses ensure that the four variables are added first, and then the sum is divided by four.

> If you're unsure about operator precedence, you can use parentheses to make sure things work the way you expect and to make your script more readable.

# Data Types in JavaScript

In some computer languages, you have to specify the type of data a variable will store: for example, a number or a string. In JavaScript, you don't need to specify a data type in most cases. However, you should know the types of data JavaScript can deal with.

These are the basic JavaScript data types:

▶ *Numbers*, such as 3, 25, or 1.4142138. JavaScript supports both integers and floating-point numbers.

▶ *Boolean*, or logical values. These can have one of two values: `true` or `false`. These are useful for indicating whether a certain condition is true.

> You'll learn more about Boolean values, and about using conditions in JavaScript, in Chapter 8.

▶ *Strings*, such as `"I am a jelly doughnut"`. These consist of one or more characters of text. (Strictly speaking, these are `String` objects, which you'll learn about later in this chapter.)

▶ *The null value*, represented by the keyword `null`. This is the value of an undefined variable. For example, the statement `document.write(fig)` will result in this value (and an error message) if the variable `fig` has not been previously used or defined.

Although JavaScript keeps track of the data type currently stored in each variable, it doesn't restrict you from changing types midstream. For example, suppose you declared a variable by assigning it a value:

```
total = 31;
```

This statement declares a variable called `total` and assigns it the value of 31. This is a numeric variable. Now suppose you changed the value of `total`:

```
total = "albatross";
```

This assigns a string value to `total`, replacing the numeric value. JavaScript will not display an error when this statement executes; it's perfectly valid, although it's probably not a very useful total.

> Although this feature of JavaScript is convenient and powerful, it can also make it easy to make a mistake. For example, if the `total` variable was later used in a mathematical calculation, the result would be invalid—but JavaScript does not warn you that you've made this mistake.

# Converting Between Data Types

JavaScript handles conversions between data types for you whenever it can. For example, you've already used statements like this:

```
document.write("The total is " + total);
```

This statement prints out a message such as `"The total is 40"`. Because the `document.write` function works with strings, the JavaScript interpreter automatically converts any nonstrings in the expression (in this case, the value of `total`) to strings before performing the function.

This works equally well with floating-point and Boolean values. However, there are some situations where it won't work. For example, the following statement will work fine if the value of `total` is 40:

```
average = total / 3;
```

However, the `total` variable could also contain a string; in this case, the preceding statement would result in an error.

In some situations, you might end up with a string containing a number, and need to convert it to a regular numeric variable. JavaScript includes two functions for this purpose:

- ▶ **parseInt()**—Converts a string to an integer number.

- ▶ **parseFloat()**—Converts a string to a floating-point number.

Both of these functions will read a number from the beginning of the string and return a numeric version. For example, these statements convert the string `"30 angry polar bears"` to a number:

```
stringvar = "30 angry polar bears";
numvar = parseInt(stringvar);
```

After these statements execute, the `numvar` variable contains the number 30. The nonnumeric portion of the string is ignored.

**By the Way**

> These functions look for a number of the appropriate type at the beginning of the string. If a valid number is not found, the function will return the special value NaN, meaning *not a number*.

# Using String **Objects**

You've already used several strings during the first few chapters of this book. Strings store a group of text characters, and are named similarly to other variables. As a simple example, this statement assigns the string This is a test to a string variable called test:

```
test = "This is a test";
```

## Creating a String **Object**

JavaScript stores strings as String objects. You usually don't need to worry about this, but it will explain some of the techniques for working with strings, which use methods (built-in functions) of the String object.

There are two ways to create a new String object. The first is the one you've already used, whereas the second uses object-oriented syntax. The following two statements create the same string:

```
test = "This is a test";
test = new String("This is a test");
```

The second statement uses the new keyword, which you use to create objects. This tells the browser to create a new String object containing the text This is a test, and assigns it to the variable test.

> Although you can create a string using object-oriented syntax, the standard JavaScript syntax is simpler, and there is no difference in the strings created by these two methods.

**By the Way**

## Assigning a Value

You can assign a value to a string in the same way as any other variable. Both of the examples in the previous section assigned an initial value to the string. You can also assign a value after the string has already been created. For example, the following statement replaces the contents of the test variable with a new string:

```
test = "This is only a test.";
```

You can also use the concatenation operator (+) to combine the values of two strings. Listing 6.1 shows a simple example of assigning and combining the values of strings.

**LISTING 6.1    Assigning Values to Strings and Combining Them**

```
<html>
<head>
<title>String Test</title>
</head>
<body>
<h1>String Test</h1>
<script language="JavaScript" type="text/javascript">;
test1 = "This is a test. ";
test2 = "This is only a test.";
both = test1 + test2;
alert(both);
</script>
</body>
</html>
```

This script assigns values to two string variables, test1 and test2, and then displays an alert with their combined value. If you load this HTML document in a browser, your output should resemble Figure 6.1.

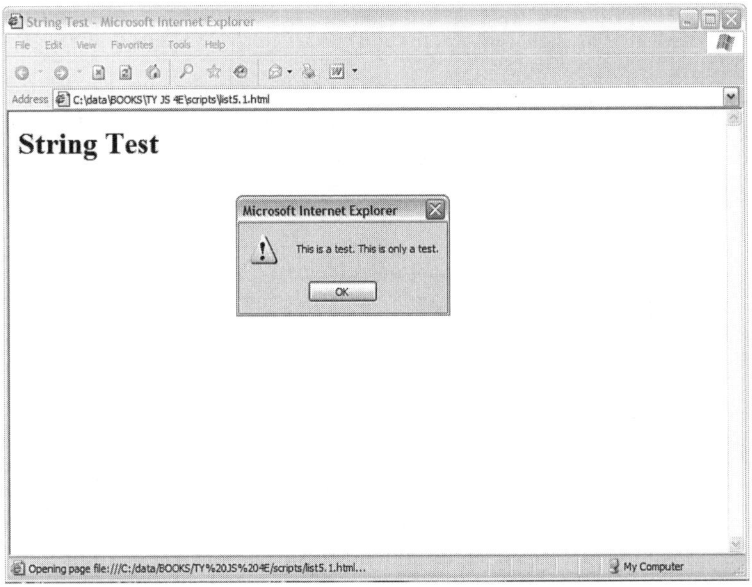

**FIGURE 6.1**
The output of
the string exam-
ple script.

In addition to using the + operator to concatenate two strings, you can use the += operator to add text to a string. For example, this statement adds a period to the current contents of the string sentence:

```
sentence += ".";
```

> The plus sign (+) is also used to add numbers in JavaScript. The browser knows whether to use addition or concatenation based on the types of data you use with the plus sign. If you use it between a number and a string, the number is converted to a string and concatenated.

By the Way

## Calculating the String's Length

From time to time, you might find it useful to know how many characters a string variable contains. You can do this with the `length` property of `String` objects, which you can use with any string. To use this property, type the string's name followed by `.length`.

For example, `test.length` refers to the length of the `test` string. Here is an example of this property:

```
test = "This is a test.";
document.write(test.length);
```

The first statement assigns the string `This is a test` to the `test` variable. The second statement displays the length of the string—in this case, 15 characters. The `length` property is a read-only property, so you cannot assign a value to it to change a string's length.

> Remember that although `test` refers to a string variable, the value of `test.length` is a number and can be used in any numeric expression.

By the Way

## Converting the String's Case

Two methods of the `String` object enable you to convert the contents of a string to all uppercase or all lowercase:

- ▶ **toUpperCase()**—Converts all characters in the string to uppercase.

- ▶ **toLowerCase()**—Converts all characters in the string to lowercase.

For example, the following statement displays the value of the `test` string variable in lowercase:

```
document.write(test.toLowerCase());
```

Assuming that this variable contained the text This Is A Test, the result would be the following string:

```
this is a test
```

Note that the statement doesn't change the value of the text variable. These methods return the upper- or lowercase version of the string, but they don't change the string itself. If you want to change the string's value, you can use a statement like this:

```
test = test.toLowerCase();
```

> Note that the syntax for these methods is similar to the length property introduced earlier. The difference is that methods always use parentheses, whereas properties don't. The toUpperCase and toLowerCase methods do not take any parameters, but you still need to use the parentheses.

# Working with Substrings

So far, you've worked with entire strings. JavaScript also enables you to work with *substrings*, or portions of a string. You can use the substring method to retrieve a portion of a string, or the charAt method to get a single character. These are explained in the following sections.

## Using Part of a String

The substring method returns a string consisting of a portion of the original string between two index values, which you must specify in parentheses. For example, the following statement displays the fourth through sixth characters of the text string:

```
document.write(text.substring(3,6));
```

At this point, you're probably wondering where the 3 and the 6 come from. There are three things you need to understand about the index parameters:

▶ Indexing starts with 0 for the first character of the string, so the fourth character is actually index 3.

▶ The second index is noninclusive. A second index of 6 includes up to index 5 (the sixth character).

▶ You can specify the two indexes in either order. The smaller one will be assumed to be the first index. In the previous example, (6,3) would have produced the same result. Of course, there is rarely a reason to use the reverse order.

As another example, suppose you defined a string called `alpha` to hold the alphabet:

```
alpha = "ABCDEFGHIJKLMNOPQRSTUVWXYZ";
```

The following are examples of the `substring()` method using this string:

▶ `alpha.substring(0,4)` returns ABCD.

▶ `alpha.substring(10,12)` returns KL.

▶ `alpha.substring(12,10)` also returns KL. Because it's smaller, 10 is used as the first index.

▶ `alpha.substring(6,7)` returns G.

▶ `alpha.substring(24,26)` returns YZ.

▶ `alpha.substring(0,26)` returns the entire alphabet.

▶ `alpha.substring(6,6)` returns the `null` value, an empty string. This is true whenever the two index values are the same.

## Getting a Single Character

The `charAt` method is a simple way to grab a single character from a string. You specify the character's index, or position, in parentheses. The indexes begin at 0 for the first character. Here are a few examples using the `alpha` string:

▶ `alpha.charAt(0)` returns A.

▶ `alpha.charAt(12)` returns M.

▶ `alpha.charAt(25)` returns Z.

▶ `alpha.charAt(27)` returns an empty string because there is no character at that position.

## Finding a Substring

Another use for substrings is to find a string within another string. One way to do this is with the `indexOf` method. To use this method, add `indexOf` to the string you want to search, and specify the string to search for in the parentheses. This example searches for "this" in the `test` string:

```
loc = test.indexOf("this");
```

> As with most JavaScript methods and property names, `indexOf` is case sensitive. Make sure you type it exactly as shown here when you use it in scripts.

The value returned in the `loc` variable is an index into the string, similar to the first index in the `substring` method. The first character of the string is index `0`.

You can specify an optional second parameter to indicate the index value to begin the search. For example, this statement searches for the word `fish` in the `temp` string, starting with the 20th character:

```
location = temp.indexOf("fish",19);
```

**By the Way**

> One use for the second parameter is to search for multiple occurrences of a string. After finding the first occurrence, you search starting with that location for the second one, and so on.

A second method, `lastIndexOf()`, works the same way, but finds the *last* occurrence of the string. It searches the string backwards, starting with the last character. For example, this statement finds the last occurrence of `Fred` in the `names` string:

```
location = names.lastIndexOf("Fred");
```

As with `indexOf()`, you can specify a location to search from as the second parameter. In this case, the string will be searched backward starting at that location.

# Using Numeric Arrays

An array is a numbered group of data items that you can treat as a single unit. For example, you might use an array called `scores` to store several scores for a game. Arrays can contain strings, numbers, objects, or other types of data. Each item in an array is called an *element* of the array.

## Creating a Numeric Array

Unlike most other types of JavaScript variables, you typically need to declare an array before you use it. The following example creates an array with four elements:

```
scores = new Array(4);
```

To assign a value to the array, you use an *index* in brackets. Indexes begin with 0, so the elements of the array in this example would be numbered 0 to 3. These statements assign values to the four elements of the array:

```
scores[0] = 39;
scores[1] = 40;
scores[2] = 100;
scores[3] = 49;
```

You can also declare an array and specify values for elements at the same time. This statement creates the same scores array in a single line:

```
scores = new Array(39,40,100,49);
```

In JavaScript 1.2 and later, you can also use a shorthand syntax to declare an array and specify its contents. The following statement is an alternative way to create the scores array:

```
scores = [39,40,100,49];
```

Remember to use parentheses when declaring an array with the new keyword, as in a=new Array(3,4,5), and use brackets when declaring an array without new, as in a=[3,4,5]. Otherwise, you'll run into JavaScript errors.

**Did you Know?**

## Understanding Array Length

Like strings, arrays have a length property. This tells you the number of elements in the array. If you specified the length when creating the array, this value becomes the length property's value. For example, these statements would print the number 30:

```
scores = new Array(30);
document.write(scores.length);
```

You can declare an array without a specific length, and change the length later by assigning values to elements or changing the `length` property. For example, these statements create a new array and assign values to two of its elements:

```
test = new Array();
test[0]=21;
test[5]=22;
```

In this example, because the largest index number assigned so far is 5, the array has a `length` property of 6—remember, elements are numbered starting at 0.

## Accessing Array Elements

You can read the contents of an array using the same notation you used when assigning values. For example, the following statements would display the values of the first three elements of the `scores` array:

```
scoredisp = "Scores: " + scores[0] + "," + scores[1] + "," + scores[2];
document.write(scoredisp);
```

Looking at this example, you might imagine it would be inconvenient to display all the elements of a large array. This is an ideal job for loops, which enable you to perform the same statements several times with different values. You'll learn all about loops in Chapter 8.

# Using String Arrays

So far, you've used arrays of numbers. JavaScript also allows you to use *string arrays*, or arrays of strings. This is a powerful feature that enables you to work with a large number of strings at the same time.

## Creating a String Array

You declare a string array in the same way as a numeric array—in fact, JavaScript does not make a distinction between them:

```
names = new Array(30);
```

You can then assign string values to the array elements:

```
names[0] = "Henry J. Tillman";
names[1] = "Sherlock Holmes";
```

As with numeric arrays, you can also specify a string array's contents when you create it. Either of the following statements would create the same string array as the preceding example:

```
names = new Array("Henry J. Tillman", "Sherlock Holmes");
names = ["Henry J. Tillman", "Sherlock Holmes"];
```

You can use string array elements anywhere you would use a string. You can even use the string methods introduced earlier. For example, the following statement prints the first five characters of the first element of the names array, resulting in Henry:

```
document.write(names[0].substring(0,5));
```

# Splitting a String

JavaScript includes a string method called split, which splits a string into its component parts. To use this method, specify the string to split and a character to divide the parts:

```
test = "John Q. Public";
parts = test.split(" ");
```

In this example, the test string contains the name John Q. Public. The split method in the second statement splits the name string at each space, resulting in three strings. These are stored in a string array called parts. After the example statements execute, the elements of parts contain the following:

▶  parts[0] = "John"

▶  parts[1] = "Q."

▶  parts[2] = "Public"

JavaScript also includes an array method, join, which performs the opposite function. This statement reassembles the parts array into a string:

```
fullname = parts.join(" ");
```

The value in the parentheses specifies a character to separate the parts of the array. In this case, a space is used, resulting in the final string John Q. Public. If you do not specify a character, commas are used.

## Sorting a String Array

JavaScript also includes a sort method for arrays, which returns an alphabetically sorted version of the array. For example, the following statements initialize an array of four names and sort it:

```
names[0] = "Public, John Q.";
names[1] = "Tillman, Henry J.";
names[2] = "Bush, George W.";
names[3] = "Mouse, Mickey";
sortednames = names.sort();
```

The last statement sorts the names array and stores the result in a new array, sortednames.

# Sorting a Numeric Array

Because the sort method sorts alphabetically, it won't work with a numeric array—at least not the way you'd expect. If an array contains the numbers 4, 10, 30, and 200, for example, it would sort them as 10, 200, 30, 4—not even close. Fortunately, there's a solution: You can specify a function in the sort method's parameters, and that function will be used to compare the numbers. The following code sorts a numeric array correctly:

```
function numcompare(a,b) {
    return a-b;
}
nums = new Array(30, 10, 200, 4);
sortednums = nums.sort(numcompare);
```

This example defines a simple function, numcompare, which subtracts the two numbers. After you specify this function in the sort method, the array is sorted in the correct numeric order: 4, 10, 30, 200.

**By the Way**

JavaScript expects the comparison function to return a negative number if a belongs before b, 0 if they are the same, or a positive number if a belongs after b. This is why a-b is all you need for the function to sort numerically.

## Try It Yourself                                                          ▼

## Sorting and Displaying Names

To gain more experience working with JavaScript's string and array features, you can create a script that enables the user to enter a list of names, and displays the list in sorted form.

Because this will be a larger script, you will create separate HTML and JavaScript files, as described in Chapter 4, "Creating Simple Scripts in JavaScript." First, the sort.html file will contain the HTML structure and form fields for the script to work with. Listing 6.2 shows the HTML document.

**LISTING 6.2**   The HTML Document for the Sorting Example

```html
<html>
<head>
<title>Array Sorting Example</title>
<script type="text/javascript" language="javascript" src="sort.js">
</script>
</head>
<body>
<h1>Sorting String Arrays</h1>
<p>Enter two or more names in the field below,
and the sorted list of names will appear in the
text area.</p>
<form name="theform">
Name:
<input type="text" name="newname" size="20">
<input type="button" name="addname" value="Add"
onclick="SortNames();">
<br>
<h2>Sorted Names</h2>
<textarea cols="60" rows="10" name="sorted">
The sorted names will appear here.
</textarea>
</form>
</body>
</html>
```

Because the script will be in a separate document, the <script> tag in the header of this document uses the src attribute to include a JavaScript file called sort.js. You will create this file next.

This document defines a form named theform, a text field named newname, an addname button, and a textarea named sorted. Your script will use these form fields as its user interface. Listing 6.2 shows the HTML document, and Listing 6.3 shows the JavaScript source file that it incorporates.

▼

▼

**LISTING 6.3    The JavaScript File for the Sorting Example**

```
// initialize the counter and the array
var numnames=0;
var names = new Array();
function SortNames() {
   // Get the name from the text field
   thename=document.theform.newname.value;
   // Add the name to the array
   names[numnames]=thename;
   // Increment the counter
   numnames++;
   // Sort the array
   names.sort();
   document.theform.sorted.value=names.join("\n");
}
```

The script begins by defining two variables with the var keyword: numnames will be a counter that increments as each name is added, and the names array will store the names.

When you type a name into the text field and click the button, the onclick event handler calls the SortNames function. This function stores the text field value in a variable, thename, and then adds the name to the names array using numnames as the index. It then increments numnames to prepare for the next name.

The final section of the script sorts the names and displays them. First, the sort() method is used to sort the names array. Next, the join() method is used to combine the names, separating them with line breaks, and display them in the textarea.

To test the script, save it as sort.js, and then load the sort.html file you created previously into a browser. You can then add some names and test the script. Figure 6.2 shows the result after sorting several names.

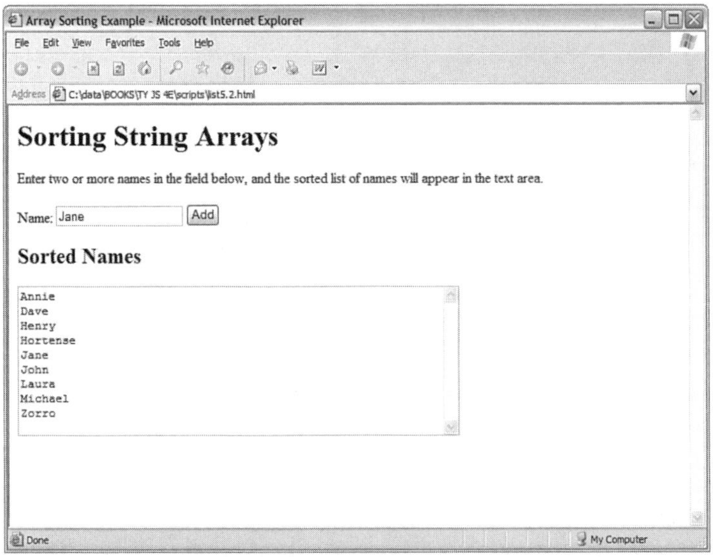

**FIGURE 6.2**
The output of the name-sorting example.

# Summary

During this chapter, you've focused on variables and how JavaScript handles them. You've learned how to name variables, how to declare them, and the differences between local and global variables. You also explored the data types supported by JavaScript and how to convert between them.

You also learned about JavaScript's more complex variables, strings and arrays, and looked at the features that enable you to perform operations on them, such as converting strings to uppercase or sorting arrays.

In the next chapter, you'll continue your JavaScript education by learning more about two additional key features: functions and objects.

# CHAPTER 7

# Using Functions and Objects

---

## *What You'll Learn in This Chapter:*

▶ Using Functions
▶ Introducing Objects
▶ Using Objects to Simplify Scripting
▶ Extending Built-in Objects

In this chapter, you'll learn about two more key JavaScript concepts that you'll use throughout the rest of this book. First, you'll learn the details of using functions, which enable you to group any number of statements into a block. This is useful for repeating sections of code, and you can also create functions that accept parameters and return values for later use.

Whereas functions enable you to group sections of code, objects enable you to group data—you can use them to combine related data items and functions for working with the data.

## Using Functions

The scripts you've seen so far are simple lists of instructions. The browser begins with the first statement after the `<script>` tag and follows each instruction in order until it reaches the closing `</script>` tag (or encounters an error).

Although this is a straightforward approach for short scripts, it can be confusing to read a longer script written in this fashion. To make it easier for you to organize your scripts, JavaScript supports functions, which you learned about in Chapter 4, "Creating Simple Scripts in JavaScript." In this section, you will learn how to define and use functions.

## Defining a Function

Functions are groups of JavaScript statements that can be treated as a single unit. To use a function, you must first define it. Here is a simple example of a function definition:

```
function Greet() {
    alert("Greetings.");
}
```

This defines a function that displays an alert message to the user. This begins with the `function` keyword. The function's name is `Greet`. Notice the parentheses after the function's name. As you'll learn next, the space between them is not always empty.

The first and last lines of the function definition include braces ({ and }). You use these to enclose all of the statements in the function. The browser uses the braces to determine where the function begins and ends.

Between the braces, this particular function contains a single line. This uses the built-in `alert` function, which displays an alert message. The message will contain the text "Greetings."

Function names are case sensitive. If you define a function such as `Greet` with a capital letter, be sure you use the identical name when you call the function.

Now, about those parentheses. The current `Greet` function always does the same thing: Each time you use it, it displays the same message. Although this avoids a bit of typing, it doesn't really provide much of an advantage.

To make your function more flexible, you can add *parameters*, also known as *arguments*. These are variables that are received by the function each time it is called. For example, you can add a parameter called `who` that tells the function the name of the person to greet. Here is the modified `Greet` function:

```
function Greet(who) {
    alert("Greetings, " + who);
}
```

Of course, to use this function, you should include it in an HTML document. Traditionally, the best place for a function definition is within the <head> section of the document. Because the statements in the <head> section are executed first, this ensures that the function is defined before it is used.

Listing 7.1 shows the `Greet` function embedded in the header section of an HTML document.

**LISTING 7.1**   The Greet Function in an HTML Document

```
<html>
<head>
<title>Functions</title>
<script language="JavaScript" type="text/javascript">
function Greet(who) {
    alert("Greetings, " + who);
}
</script>
</head>
<body>
This is the body of the page.
</body>
</html>
```

# Calling the Function

You have now defined a function and placed it in an HTML document. However, if you load Listing 7.1 into a browser, you'll notice that it does absolutely nothing. This is because the function is defined—ready to be used—but we haven't used it yet.

Making use of a function is referred to as *calling* the function. To call a function, use the function's name as a statement in a script. You will need to include the parentheses and the values for the function's parameters. For example, here's a statement that calls the Greet function:

```
Greet("Fred");
```

This tells the JavaScript interpreter to transfer control to the first statement in the Greet function. It also passes the parameter "Fred" to the function. This value will be assigned to the who variable inside the function.

> Functions can have more than one parameter. To define a function with multiple parameters, list a variable name for each parameter, separated by commas. To call the function, specify values for each parameter separated by commas.

**By the Way**

Listing 7.2 shows a complete HTML document that includes the function definition and a second script in the body of the page that actually calls the function. To demonstrate the usefulness of functions, we'll call it twice to greet two different people.

**LISTING 7.2**   The Complete Function Example

```
<html>
<head>
<title>Functions</title>
<script language="JavaScript" type="text/javascript">
function Greet(who) {
```

**LISTING 7.2** Continued

```
    alert("Greetings, " + who);
}
</script>
</head>
<body>
<h1>Function Example</h1>
<p>Prepare to be greeted twice.</p>
<script language="JavaScript" type="text/javascript">
Greet("Fred");
Greet("Ethel");
</script>
</body>
</html>>
```

This listing includes a second set of <script> tags in the body of the page. The second script includes two function calls to the Greet function, each with a different name.

Now that you have a script that actually does something, try loading it into a browser. You should see something like Figure 7.1, which shows the Greeting script running in Firefox.

**FIGURE 7.1**
The output of the Greeting example.

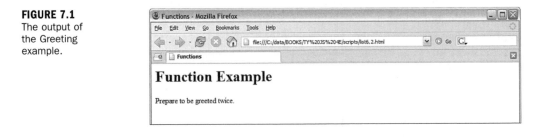

**By the Way**

> Notice that the second alert message isn't displayed until you click the OK button on the first alert. This is because JavaScript processing is halted while alerts are displayed.

## Returning a Value

The function you just created displays a message to the user, but functions can also return a value to the script that called them. This allows you to use functions to calculate values. As an example, you can create a function that averages four numbers.

Your function should begin with the function keyword, the function's name, and the parameters it accepts. We will use the variable names a, b, c, and d for the four numbers to average. Here is the first line of the function:

```
function Average(a,b,c,d) {
```

> I've also included the opening brace ({) on the first line of the function. This is a common style, but you can also place the brace on the next line, or on a line by itself.

**By the** Way

Next, the function needs to calculate the average of the four parameters. You can calculate this by adding them, and then dividing by the number of parameters (in this case, 4). Thus, here is the next line of the function:

```
result = (a + b + c + d) / 4;
```

This statement creates a variable called `result` and calculates the result by adding the four numbers, and then dividing by 4. (The parentheses are necessary to tell JavaScript to perform the addition before the division.)

To send this result back to the script that called the function, you use the `return` keyword. Here is the last part of the function:

```
return result;
}
```

Listing 7.3 shows the complete `Average` function in an HTML document. This HTML document also includes a small script in the `<body>` section that calls the `Average` function and displays the result.

**LISTING 7.3**   The Average **Function in an HTML Document**

```
<html>_
<head>
<title>Function Example</title>
<script language="JavaScript" type="text/javascript">
function Average(a,b,c,d) {
result = (a + b + c + d) / 4;
return result;
}
</script>
</head>
<body>
<p>The following is the result of the function call.</p>
<script LANGUAGE="JavaScript" type="text/javascript">
score = Average(3,4,5,6);
document.write("The average is: " + score);
</script>_
</body>
</html>
```

You can use a variable with the function call, as shown in this listing. This statement averages the numbers 3, 4, 5, and 6 and stores the result in a variable called `score`:

```
score = Average(3,4,5,6);
```

> You can also use the function call directly in an expression. For example, you could use the alert statement to display the result of the function alert(Average(1,2,3,4)) .

# Introducing Objects

In the previous chapter, you learned how to use variables to represent different kinds of data in JavaScript. JavaScript also supports *objects*, a more complex kind of variable that can store multiple data items and functions.

Although a variable can have only one value at a time, an object can contain multiple values, as well as functions for working with the values. This allows you to group related data items and the functions that deal with them into a single object.

In this chapter, you'll learn how to define and use your own objects. You've already worked with some of them, including

▶ **DOM objects**—Allow your scripts to interact with web pages. You learned about these in Chapter 5, "Working with the Document Object Model (DOM)."

▶ **Built-in objects**—Include strings and arrays, which you learned about in Chapter 6, "Using Variables, Strings, and Arrays."

The syntax for working with all three types of objects—DOM objects, built-in objects, and custom objects—is the same, so even if you don't end up creating your own objects, you should have a good understanding of JavaScript's object terminology and syntax.

## Creating Objects

When you created an array in the previous chapter, you used the following JavaScript statement:

```
scores = new Array(4);
```

The new keyword tells the JavaScript interpreter to use a function—in this case, the built-in Array function—to create an object. You'll create a function for a custom object later in this chapter.

## Object Properties and Values

Each object has one or more *properties*—essentially, variables that will be stored within the object. For example, in Chapter 5, you learned that the location.href property gives you the URL of the current document. The `href` property is one of the properties of the `location` object in the DOM.

You've also used the `length` property of `String` objects, as in the following example from the previous chapter:

```
test = "This is a test.";
document.write(test.length);
```

Like variables, each object property has a *value*. To read a property's value, you simply include the object name and property name, separated by a period, in any expression, as in `test.length` previously. You can change a property's value using the = operator, just like a variable. The following example sends the browser to a new URL by changing the `location.href` property:

```
location.href="http://www.jsworkshop.com/";
```

---

An object can also be a property of another object. This is referred to as a *child object*.

**By the Way**

---

## Understanding Methods

Along with properties, each object can have one or more *methods*. These are functions that work with the object's data. For example, the following JavaScript statement reloads the current document, as you learned in Chapter 5:

```
location.reload();
```

When you use `reload()`, you're using a method of the `location` object. Like normal functions, methods can accept arguments in parentheses, and can return values.

# Using Objects to Simplify Scripting

Although JavaScript's variables and arrays are versatile ways to store data, sometimes you need a more complicated structure. For example, suppose you are creating a script to work with a business card database that contains names, addresses, and phone numbers for a variety of people.

If you were using regular variables, you would need several separate variables for each person in the database: a name variable, an address variable, and so on. This would be very confusing.

Arrays would improve things slightly. You could have a names array, an addresses array, and a phone number array. Each person in the database would have an entry in each array. This would be more convenient, but still not perfect.

With objects, you can make the variables that store the database as logical as business cards. Each person is represented by a Card object, which has properties for name, address, and phone number. You can even add methods to the object to display or work with the information.

In the following sections, you'll use JavaScript to actually create the Card object and its properties and methods. Later in this chapter, you'll use the Card object in a script to display information for several members of the database.

## Defining an Object

The first step in creating an object is to name it and its properties. We've already decided to call the object a Card object. Each object will have the following properties:

- name
- address
- workphone
- homephone

The first step in using this object in a JavaScript program is to create a function to make new Card objects. This function is called the *constructor* for an object. Here is the constructor function for the Card object:

```
function Card(name,address,work,home) {
    this.name = name;
    this.address = address;
    this.workphone = work;
    this.homephone = home;
}
```

The constructor is a simple function that accepts parameters to initialize a new object and assigns them to the corresponding properties. This function accepts several parameters from the statement that calls the function, and then assigns them as properties of an object. Because the function is called Card, the object is the Card object.

Notice the this keyword. You'll use it anytime you create an object definition. Use this to refer to the current object—the one that is being created by the function.

## Defining an Object Method

Next, you will create a method to work with the Card object. Because all Card objects will have the same properties, it might be handy to have a function that prints out the properties in a neat format. Let's call this function PrintCard.

Your PrintCard function will be used as a method for Card objects, so you don't need to ask for parameters. Instead, you can use the this keyword again to refer to the current object's properties. Here is a function definition for the PrintCard() function:

```
function PrintCard() {
   line1 = "Name: " + this.name + "<br>\n";
   line2 = "Address: " + this.address + "<br>\n";
   line3 = "Work Phone: " + this.workphone + "<br>\n";
   line4 = "Home Phone: " + this.homephone + "<hr>\n";
   document.write(line1, line2, line3, line4);
}
```

This function simply reads the properties from the current object (this), prints each one with a caption, and skips to a new line.

You now have a function that prints a card, but it isn't officially a method of the Card object. The last thing you need to do is make PrintCard part of the function definition for Card objects. Here is the modified function definition:

```
function Card(name,address,work,home) {
   this.name = name;
   this.address = address;
   this.workphone = work;
   this.homephone = home;
   this.PrintCard = PrintCard;
}
```

The added statement looks just like another property definition, but it refers to the PrintCard function. This will work so long as the PrintCard function is defined with its own function definition. Methods are essentially properties that define a function rather than a simple value.

> The previous example uses lowercase names such as workphone for properties, and an uppercase name (PrintCard) for the method. You can use any case for property and method names, but this is one way to make it clear that PrintCard is a method rather than an ordinary property.

*Did you Know?*

# Creating an Object Instance

Now let's use the object definition and method you just created. To use an object definition, you create a new object. This is done with the new keyword. This is the same keyword you've already used to create Date and Array objects.

The following statement creates a new Card object called tom:

```
tom = new Card("Tom Jones", "123 Elm Street", "555-1234", "555-9876");
```

As you can see, creating an object is easy. All you do is call the `Card()` function (the object definition) and give it the required attributes, in the same order as the definition.

After this statement executes, a new object is created to hold Tom's information. This is called an *instance* of the `Card` object. Just as there can be several string variables in a program, there can be several instances of an object you define.

Rather than specify all the information for a card with the new keyword, you can assign them after the fact. For example, the following script creates an empty `Card` object called `holmes`, and then assigns its properties:

```
holmes = new Card();
holmes.name = "Sherlock Holmes";
holmes.address = "221B Baker Street";
holmes.workphone = "555-2345";
holmes.homephone = "555-3456";
```

After you've created an instance of the `Card` object using either of these methods, you can use the `PrintCard()` method to display its information. For example, this statement displays the properties of the `tom` card:

```
tom.PrintCard();
```

# Extending Built-in Objects

JavaScript includes a feature that enables you to extend the definitions of built-in objects. For example, if you think the `String` object doesn't quite fit your needs, you can extend it, adding a new property or method. This might be very useful if you were creating a large script that used many strings.

You can add both properties and methods to an existing object by using the `prototype` keyword. (A *prototype* is another name for an object's definition, or constructor function.) The `prototype` keyword enables you to change the definition of an object outside its constructor function.

As an example, let's add a method to the `String` object definition. You will create a method called `heading`, which converts a string into an HTML heading. The following statement defines a string called `title`:

```
title = "Fred's Home Page";
```

This statement would output the contents of the `title` string as an HTML level 1 header:

```
document.write(title.heading(1));
```

Listing 7.4 adds a heading method to the String object definition that will display the string as a heading, and then displays three headings using the method.

**LISTING 7.4**    Adding a Method to the String Object

```
<html>
<head><title>Test of heading method</title>
</head>
<body>
<script LANGUAGE="JavaScript" type="text/javascript">
function addhead (level) {
   html = "H" + level;
   text = this.toString();
   start = "<" + html + ">";
   stop = "</" + html + ">";
   return start + text + stop;
}
String.prototype.heading = addhead;
document.write ("This is a heading 1".heading(1));
document.write ("This is a heading 2".heading(2));
document.write ("This is a heading 3".heading(3));
</script>
</body>
</html>
```

First, you define the addhead() function, which will serve as the new string method. It accepts a number to specify the heading level. The start and stop variables are used to store the HTML "begin header" and "end header" tags, such as <h1> and </h1>.

After the function is defined, use the prototype keyword to add it as a method of the String object. You can then use this method on any String object or, in fact, any JavaScript string. This is demonstrated by the last three statements, which display quoted text strings as level 1, 2, and 3 headers.

## Try It Yourself                                                   ▼

### Storing Data in Objects

Now you've created a new object to store business cards and a method to print them out. As a final demonstration of objects, properties, functions, and methods, you will now use this object in a web page to display data for several cards.

Your script will need to include the function definition for PrintCard, along with the function definition for the Card object. You will then create three cards and print them out in the body of the document. We will use separate HTML and JavaScript files for this example. Listing 7.5 shows the complete script.

▼

**LISTING 7.5**    An Example Script That Uses the Card Object

```
// define the functions
function PrintCard() {
line1 = "<b>Name: </b>" + this.name + "<br>\n";
line2 = "<b>Address: </b>" + this.address + "<br>\n";
line3 = "<b>Work Phone: </b>" + this.workphone + "<br>\n";
line4 = "<b>Home Phone: </b>" + this.homephone + "<hr>\n";
document.write(line1, line2, line3, line4);
}
function Card(name,address,work,home) {
   this.name = name;
   this.address = address;
   this.workphone = work;
   this.homephone = home;
   this.PrintCard = PrintCard;
}
// Create the objects
sue = new Card("Sue Suthers", "123 Elm Street", "555-1234", "555-9876");
phred = new Card("Phred Madsen", "233 Oak Lane", "555-2222", "555-4444");
henry = new Card("Henry Tillman", "233 Walnut Circle", "555-1299", "555-1344");
// And print them
 sue.PrintCard();
 phred.PrintCard();
 henry.PrintCard();
```

Notice that the `PrintCard()` function has been modified slightly to make things look good with the captions in boldface. To use this script, save it as `cardtest.js`. Next, you'll need to include the script in a simple HTML document. Listing 7.6 shows the HTML document for this example.

**LISTING 7.6**    The HTML File for the Card Object Example

```
<html>
<head>
<title>JavaScript Business Cards</title>
</head>
<body>
<h1>JavaScript Business Card Test</h1>
<p>Script begins here.</p><hr>
<script language="JavaScript" type="text/javascript"
   src="cardtest.js">
</script>
<p>End of script.</p>
</body>
</html>
```

To test the script, save the HTML document in the same directory as the `cardtest.js` file you created earlier, and then load the HTML document into a browser. The browser's display of this example is shown in Figure 7.2.

**By the Way**

This example isn't a very sophisticated database because you have to include the data for each person in the HTML document. However, an object like this could be used to store a database record retrieved from a database server with thousands of records.

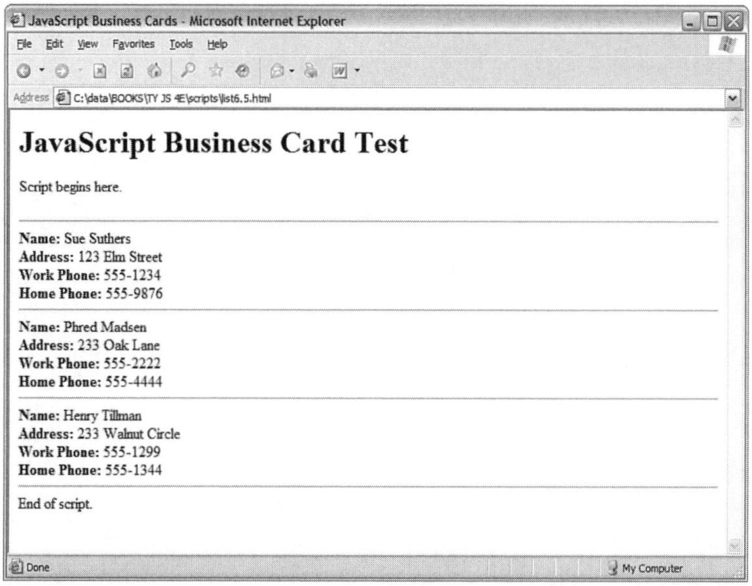

**FIGURE 7.2**
Internet Explorer displays the output of the business card example.

# Summary

In this chapter, you've looked at two important features of JavaScript. First, you learned how to use functions to group JavaScript statements, and how to call functions and use the values they return.

You also learned about JavaScript's object-oriented features—defining objects with constructor functions, creating object instances, and working with properties, property values, and methods.

In the next chapter, you'll look at two more features you'll use in almost every script—conditions to let your scripts evaluate data, and loops to repeat sections of code.

# CHAPTER 8

# Controlling Flow with Conditions and Loops

---

## What You'll Learn in This Chapter:

▶ The if Statement

▶ Using Shorthand Conditional Expressions

▶ Testing Multiple Conditions with if and else

▶ Using Multiple Conditions with switch

▶ Using for Loops

▶ Using while Loops

▶ Using do...while Loops

▶ Working with Loops

▶ Looping Through Object Properties

Statements in a JavaScript program generally execute in the order in which they appear, one after the other. Because this isn't always practical, most programming languages provide *flow control* statements that let you control the order in which code is executed. Functions, which you learned about in the previous chapter, are one type of flow control—although a function might be defined first thing in your code, its statements can be executed anywhere in the script.

In this chapter, you'll look at two other types of flow control in JavaScript: conditions, which allow a choice of different options depending on a value, and loops, which allow repetitive statements.

# The `if` **Statement**

One of the most important features of a computer language is the capability to test and compare values. This allows your scripts to behave differently based on the values of variables, or based on input from the user.

The `if` statement is the main conditional statement in JavaScript. This statement means much the same in JavaScript as it does in English—for example, here is a typical conditional statement in English:

*If the phone rings, answer it.*

This statement consists of two parts: a condition (*If the phone rings*) and an action (*answer it*). The `if` statement in JavaScript works much the same way. Here is an example of a basic `if` statement:

```
if (a == 1) window.alert("Found a 1!");
```

This statement includes a condition (if a equals 1) and an action (display a message). This statement checks the variable a and, if it has a value of 1, displays an alert message. Otherwise, it does nothing.

If you use an `if` statement like the preceding example, you can use a single statement as the action. You can also use multiple statements for the action by enclosing them in braces ({}), as shown here:

```
if (a == 1) {
   window.alert("Found a 1!");
   a = 0;
}
```

This block of statements checks the variable a once again. If it finds a value of 1, it displays a message and sets a back to 0.

## Conditional Operators

The action part of an `if` statement can include any of the JavaScript statements you've already learned (and any others, for that matter), but the condition part of the statement uses its own syntax. This is called a *conditional expression*.

A conditional expression usually includes two values to be compared (in the preceding example, the values were a and 1). These values can be variables, constants, or even expressions in themselves.

> Either side of the conditional expression can be a variable, a constant, or an expression. You can compare a variable and a value, or compare two variables. (You can compare two constants, but there's usually no reason to.)

**By the Way**

Between the two values to be compared is a *conditional operator*. This operator tells JavaScript how to compare the two values. For instance, the == operator is used to test whether the two values are equal. A variety of conditional operators is available:

▶ ==—Is equal to

▶ !=—Is not equal to

▶ <—Is less than

▶ >—Is greater than

▶ >=—Is greater than or equal to

▶ <=—Is less than or equal to

> Be sure not to confuse the equality operator (==) with the assignment operator (=), even though they both might be read as "equals." Remember to use = when *assigning* a value to a variable, and == when *comparing* values. Confusing these two is one of the most common mistakes in JavaScript programming.

**By the Way**

## Combining Conditions with Logical Operators

Often, you'll want to check a variable for more than one possible value, or check more than one variable at once. JavaScript includes *logical operators*, also known as Boolean operators, for this purpose. For example, the following two statements check different conditions and use the same action:

```
if (phone == "") window.alert("error!");
if (email == "") window.alert("error!");
```

Using a logical operator, you can combine them into a single statement:

```
if (phone == "" || email == "") window.alert("Something's Missing!");
```

This statement uses the logical Or operator (||) to combine the conditions. Translated to English, this would be, "If the phone number is blank or the email address is blank, display an error message."

An additional logical operator is the And operator, &&. Consider this statement:

```
if (phone == "" && email == "") window.alert("Both are Missing!");
```

This statement uses && (And) instead of ¦¦ (Or), so the error message will only be displayed if *both* the email address and phone number variables are blank. (In this particular case, Or is a better choice.)

**Did you Know?**

> If the JavaScript interpreter discovers the answer to a conditional expression before reaching the end, it does not evaluate the rest of the condition. For example, if the first of two conditions separated by the && operator is false, the second is not evaluated. You can take advantage of this to improve the speed of your scripts.

The third logical operator is the exclamation mark (!), which means Not. It can be used to invert an expression—in other words, a true expression would become false, and a false one would become true. For example, here's a statement that uses the Not operator:

```
if (!($phone == "")) alert("phone is OK");
```

In this statement, the ! (Not) operator inverts the condition, so the action of the if statement is executed only if the phone number variable is *not* blank. The extra parentheses are necessary because all JavaScript conditions must be in parentheses. You could also use the != (Not equal) operator to simplify this statement:

```
if ($phone != "") alert("phone is OK");
```

As with the previous statement, this alerts you if the phone number field is not blank.

**Did you Know?**

> The logical operators are powerful, but it's easy to accidentally create an impossible condition with them. For example, the condition (a < 10 && a > 20) might look correct at first glance. However, if you read it out loud, you get "If a is less than 10 and a is greater than 20"—an impossibility in our universe. In this case, Or (¦¦) should have been used.

## The `else` **Keyword**

An additional feature of the `if` statement is the `else` keyword. Much like its English equivalent, `else` tells the JavaScript interpreter what to do if the condition isn't true. The following is a simple example of the `else` keyword in action:

```
if (a == 1) {
   alert("Found a 1!");
   a = 0;
}
else {
   alert("Incorrect value: " + a);
}
```

This is a modified version of the previous example. This displays a message and resets the variable a if the condition is met. If the condition is not met (if a is not 1), a different message is displayed.

> Like the `if` statement, `else` can be followed either by a single action statement or by a number of statements enclosed in braces.

**By the Way**

# Using Shorthand Conditional Expressions

In addition to the `if` statement, JavaScript provides a shorthand type of conditional expression that you can use to make quick decisions. This uses a peculiar syntax that is also found in other languages, such as C. A conditional expression looks like this:

```
variable = (condition) ? (true action) : (false action);
```

This assigns one of two values to the variable: one if the condition is true, and another if it is false. Here is an example of a conditional expression:

```
value = (a == 1) ? 1 : 0;
```

This statement might look confusing, but it is equivalent to the following `if` statement:

```
if (a == 1)
   value = 1;
else
   value = 0;
```

In other words, the value after the question mark (?) will be used if the condition is true, and the value after the colon (:) will be used if the condition is false. The colon represents the `else` portion of this statement and, like the `else` portion of the `if` statement, is optional.

These shorthand expressions can be used anywhere JavaScript expects a value. They provide an easy way to make simple decisions about values. As an example, here's an easy way to display a grammatically correct message about a variable:

```
document.write("Found " + counter + ((counter == 1) ? " word." : " words."));
```

This will print the message Found 1 word if the counter variable has a value of 1, and Found 2 words if its value is 2 or greater. This is one of the most common uses for a conditional expression.

# Testing Multiple Conditions with `if` and `else`

You can now create an example script using `if` and `else`. In a previous chapter you created a simple script that displays the current date and time. This example will use conditions to display a greeting that depends on the time: "Good morning," "Good Afternoon," "Good Evening," or "Good Day." To accomplish this, you can use a combination of several `if` statements:

```
if (hours < 10) document.write("Good morning.");
else if (hours >= 14 && hours <= 17) document.write("Good afternoon.");
else if (hours >= 17) document.write("Good evening.");
else document.write("Good day.");
```

The first statement checks the hours variable for a value less than 10—in other words, it checks whether the current time is before 10:00 a.m. If so, it displays the greeting "Good morning."

The second statement checks whether the time is between 2:00 p.m. and 5:00 p.m. and, if so, displays "Good afternoon." This statement uses `else if` to indicate that this condition will only be tested if the previous one failed—if it's morning, there's no need to check whether it's afternoon. Similarly, the third statement checks for times after 5:00 p.m. and displays "Good evening."

The final statement uses a simple `else`, meaning it will be executed if none of the previous conditions matched. This covers the times between 10:00 a.m. and 2:00 p.m. (neglected by the other statements) and displays "Good day."

## The HTML File

To try this example in a browser, you'll need an HTML file. We will keep the JavaScript code separate, so Listing 8.1 is the complete HTML file. Save it as `timegreet.html` but don't load it into the browser until you've prepared the JavaScript file in the next section.

**LISTING 8.1** The HTML File for the Time and Greeting Example

```
<html>
<head><title>if statement example</title></head>
<body>
<h1>Current Date and Time</h1>
<p>
<script language="JavaScript" type="text/javascript"
 src = "timegreet.js">
</script>
</p>
</body>
</html>
```

## The JavaScript File

Listing 8.2 shows the complete JavaScript file for the time greeting example. This uses the built-in `Date` object functions to find the current date and store it in `hours`, `mins`, and `secs` variables. Next, `document.write` statements display the current time, and the `if` and `else` statements introduced earlier display an appropriate greeting.

**LISTING 8.2** A Script to Display the Current Time and a Greeting

```
// Get the current date
now = new Date();
// Split into hours, minutes, seconds
hours = now.getHours();
mins = now.getMinutes();
secs = now.getSeconds();
// Display the time
document.write("<h2>");
document.write(hours + ":" + mins + ":" + secs);
document.write("</h2>");
// Display a greeting
document.write("<p>");
if (hours < 10) document.write("Good morning.");
else if (hours >= 14 && hours <= 17) document.write("Good afternoon.");
else if (hours > 17) document.write("Good evening.");
else document.write("Good day.");
document.write("</p>");
```

To try this example, save this file as `timegreet.js` (or download it from this book's website) and then load the `timegreet.html` file into your browser. Figure 8.1 shows the results of this script.

**FIGURE 8.1**
The output of the time greeting example, as shown by Internet Explorer.

# Using Multiple Conditions with `switch`

In the previous example, you used several `if` statements in a row to test for different conditions. Here is another example of this technique:

```
if (button=="next") window.location="next.html";
else if (button=="previous") window.location="prev.html";
else if (button=="home") window.location="home.html";
else if (button=="back") window.location="menu.html";
```

Although this is a compact way of doing things, this method can get messy if each `if` statement has its own block of code with several statements. As an alternative, JavaScript includes the `switch` statement, which enables you to combine several tests of the same variable or expression into a single block of statements. The following shows the same example converted to use `switch`:

```
switch(button) {
    case "next":
        window.location="next.html";
        break;
    case "previous":
        window.location="prev.html";
        break;
case "home":
        window.location="home.html";
        break;
case "back":
        window.location="menu.html";
        break;
default:
        window.alert("Wrong button.");
}
```

The switch statement has several components:

▶ The initial switch statement. This statement includes the value to test (in this case, button) in parentheses.

▶ Braces ({ and }) enclose the contents of the switch statement, similar to a function or an if statement.

▶ One or more case statements. Each of these statements specifies a value to compare with the value specified in the switch statement. If the values match, the statements after the case statement are executed. Otherwise, the next case is tried.

▶ The break statement is used to end each case. This skips to the end of the switch. If break is not included, statements in multiple cases might be executed whether they match or not.

▶ Optionally, the default case can be included and followed by one or more statements that are executed if none of the other cases were matched.

> You can use multiple statements after each case statement within the switch structure. You don't need to enclose them in braces. If the case matches, the JavaScript interpreter executes statements until it encounters a break or the next case.

**By the Way**

# Using for **Loops**

The for keyword is the first tool to consider for creating loops. A for loop typically uses a variable (called a *counter* or an *index*) to keep track of how many times the loop has executed, and it stops when the counter reaches a certain number. A basic for statement looks like this:

```
for (var = 1; var < 10; var++) {
```

There are three parameters to the for loop, separated by semicolons:

▶ The first parameter (var = 1 in the example) specifies a variable and assigns an initial value to it. This is called the *initial expression* because it sets up the initial state for the loop.

▶ The second parameter (var < 10 in the example) is a condition that must remain true to keep the loop running. This is called the *condition* of the loop.

▶ The third parameter (var++ in the example) is a statement that executes with each iteration of the loop. This is called the *increment expression* because it is typically used to increment the counter. The increment expression executes at the end of each loop iteration.

After the three parameters are specified, a left brace ({) is used to signal the beginning of a block. A right brace (}) is used at the end of the block. All the statements between the braces will be executed with each iteration of the loop.

The parameters for a for loop may sound a bit confusing, but once you're used to it, you'll use for loops frequently. Here is a simple example of this type of loop:

```
for (i=0; i<10; i++) {
    document.write("This is line " + i + "<br>");
}
```

These statements define a loop that uses the variable i, initializes it with the value of zero, and loops as long as the value of i is less than 10. The increment expression, i++, adds one to the value of i with each iteration of the loop. Because this happens at the end of the loop, the output will list the numbers zero through nine.

When a loop includes only a single statement between the braces, as in this example, you can omit the braces if you want. The following statement defines the same loop without braces:

```
for (i=0; i<10; i++)
    document.write("This is line " + i + "<br>");
```

It's a good style convention to use braces with all loops whether they contain one statement or many. This makes it easy to add statements to the loop later without causing syntax errors.

The loop in this example contains a document.write statement that will be repeatedly executed. To see just what this loop does, you can add it to a <script> section of an HTML document as shown in Listing 8.3.

**LISTING 8.3    A Loop Using the** for **Keyword**

```
<html>
<head>
<title>Using a for Loop</title>
</head>
<body>
<h1>"for" Loop Example</h1>
<p>The following is the output of the
<b>for</b> loop:</p>
```

**LISTING 8.3**    Continued

```
<script language="JavaScript" type="text/javascript">
for (i=1;i<10;i++) {
   document.write("This is line " + i + "<br>");
}
</script>
</body>
</html>
```

This example displays a message with the loop's counter during each iteration. The output of Listing 8.3 is shown in Figure 8.2.

Notice that the loop was only executed nine times. This is because the conditional is i<10. When the counter (i) is incremented to 10, the expression is no longer true. If you need the loop to count to 10, you can change the conditional; either i<=10 or i<11 will work fine.

---

You might notice that the variable name i is often used as the counter in loops. This is a programming tradition that began with an ancient language called Forth. There's no need for you to follow this tradition, but it is a good idea to use one consistent variable for counters. (To learn more about Forth, see the Forth Interest Group's website at www.forth.org.)

**By the Way**

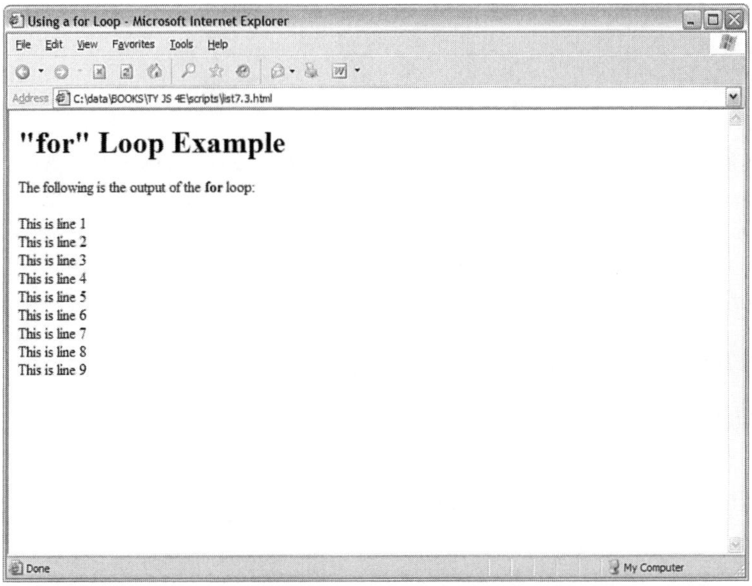

---

![Using a for Loop - Microsoft Internet Explorer. Address: C:\data\BOOKS\TY JS 4E\scripts\list7.3.html. Page heading "for" Loop Example. The following is the output of the for loop: This is line 1 through This is line 9.]

**FIGURE 8.2**
The results of the for loop example.

The structure of the `for` loop in JavaScript is based on Java, which in turn is based on C. Although it is traditionally used to count from one number to another, you can use just about any statement for the initialization, condition, and increment. However, there's usually a better way to do other types of loops with the `while` keyword, described in the next section.

# Using `while` Loops

Another keyword for loops in JavaScript is `while`. Unlike `for` loops, `while` loops don't necessarily use a variable to count. Instead, they execute as long as a condition is true. In fact, if the condition starts out as false, the statements won't execute at all.

The `while` statement includes the condition in parentheses, and it is followed by a block of statements within braces, just like a `for` loop. Here is a simple `while` loop:

```
while (total < 10) {
n++;
total += values[n];
}
```

This loop uses a counter, n, to iterate through the `values` array. Rather than stopping at a certain count, however, it stops when the total of the values reaches 10.

You might have noticed that you could have done the same thing with a `for` loop:

```
for (n=0;total < 10; n++) {
total += values[n];
}
```

As a matter of fact, the `for` loop is nothing more than a special kind of `while` loop that handles an initialization and an increment for you. You can generally use `while` for any loop. However, it's best to choose whichever type of loop makes the most sense for the job, or that takes the least amount of typing.

# Using `do...while` Loops

JavaScript 1.2 introduced a third type of loop: the do...while loop. This type of loop is similar to an ordinary `while` loop, with one difference: The condition is tested at the *end* of the loop rather than the beginning. Here is a typical do...while loop:

```
do {
n++;
total += values[n];
}
while (total < 10);
```

As you've probably noticed, this is basically an upside-down version of the previous `while` example. There is one difference: With the do loop, the condition is tested at the end of the loop. This means that the statements in the loop will always be executed at least once, even if the condition is never true.

> As with the `for` and `while` loops, the do loop can include a single statement without braces, or a number of statements enclosed in braces.

**By the Way**

# Working with Loops

Although you can use simple `for` and `while` loops for straightforward tasks, there are some considerations you should make when using more complicated loops. In the next sections, we'll look at infinite loops and the `break` and `continue` statements, which give you more control over your loops.

## Creating an Infinite Loop

The `for` and `while` loops give you quite a bit of control over the loop. In some cases, this can cause problems if you're not careful. For example, look at the following loop code:

```
while (i < 10) {
n++;
values[n] = 0;
}
```

There's a mistake in this example. The condition of the `while` loop refers to the `i` variable, but that variable doesn't actually change during the loop. This creates an *infinite loop*. The loop will continue executing until the user stops it, or until it generates an error of some kind.

Infinite loops can't always be stopped by the user, except by quitting the browser—and some loops can even prevent the browser from quitting, or cause a crash.

Obviously, infinite loops are something to avoid. They can also be difficult to spot because JavaScript won't give you an error that actually tells you there is an infinite loop. Thus, each time you create a loop in a script, you should be careful to make sure there's a way out.

> Depending on the browser version in use, an infinite loop might even make the browser stop responding to the user. Be sure you provide an escape route from infinite loops, and save your script before you test it just in case.

**By the Way**

Occasionally, you might want to create an infinite loop deliberately. This might include situations when you want your program to execute until the user stops it, or if you are providing an escape route with the break statement, which is introduced in the next section. Here's an easy way to create an infinite loop:

```
while (true) {
```

Because the value true is the conditional, this loop will always find its condition to be true.

## Escaping from a Loop

There is one way out of an infinite loop. You can use the break statement during a loop to exit it immediately and continue with the first statement after the loop. Here is a simple example of the use of break:

```
while (true) {
n++;
if (values[n] == 1) break;
}
```

Although the while statement is set up as an infinite loop, the if statement checks the corresponding value of an array. If it finds a value of 1, it exits the loop.

When the JavaScript interpreter encounters a break statement, it skips the rest of the loop and continues the script with the first statement after the right brace at the loop's end. You can use the break statement in any type of loop, whether infinite or not. This provides an easy way to exit if an error occurs, or if another condition is met.

## Continuing a Loop

One more statement is available to help you control the execution of statements in a loop. The continue statement skips the rest of the loop but, unlike break, it continues with the next iteration of the loop. Here is a simple example:

```
for (i=1; i<21; i++) {
   if (score[i]==0) continue;
   document.write("Student number ",i, " Score: ", score[i], "\n");
}
```

This script uses a for loop to print out scores for 20 students, stored in the score array. The if statement is used to check for scores with a value of 0. The script assumes that a score of 0 means that the student didn't take the test, so it continues the loop without printing that score.

# Looping Through Object Properties

A third type of loop is available in JavaScript. The for...in loop is not as flexible as an ordinary for or while loop. Instead, it is specifically designed to perform an operation on each property of an object.

For example, the navigator object contains properties that describe the user's browser. You can use for...in to display this object's properties:

```
for (i in navigator) {
document.write("property: " + i);
document.write(" value: " + navigator[i] + "<br>");
}
```

Like an ordinary for loop, this type of loop uses an index variable (i in the example). For each iteration of the loop, the variable is set to the next property of the object. This makes it easy when you need to check or modify each of an object's properties.

## Try It Yourself ▼

### Working with Arrays and Loops

To apply your knowledge of loops, you will now create a script that deals with arrays using loops. As you progress through this script, try to imagine how difficult it would be without JavaScript's looping features.

This simple script will prompt the user for a series of names. After all of the names have been entered, it will display the list of names in a numbered list. To begin the script, initialize some variables:

```
names = new Array();
i = 0;
```

The names array will store the names the user enters. You don't know how many names will be entered, so you don't need to specify a dimension for the array. The i variable will be used as a counter in the loops.

Next, use the prompt statement to prompt the user for a series of names. Use a loop to repeat the prompt for each name. You want the user to enter at least one name, so a do loop is ideal:

```
do {
    next = prompt("Enter the Next Name", "");
    if (next > " ") names[i] = next;
    i = i + 1;
    }
    while (next > " ");
```

**Did you Know?**

> If you're interested in making your scripts as short as possible, remember that you could use the increment (++) operator to combine the i = i + 1 statement with the previous statement: names[i++]=1.

This loop prompts for a string called next. If a name was entered and isn't blank, it's stored as the next entry in the names array. The i counter is then incremented. The loop repeats until the user doesn't enter a name or clicks Cancel in the prompt dialog.

Next, your script can display the number of names that was entered:

```
document.write("<h2>" + (names.length) + " names entered.</h2>");
```

This statement displays the length property of the names array, surrounded by level 2 header tags for emphasis.

Next, the script should display all the names in the order they were entered. Because the names are in an array, the for...in loop is a good choice:

```
document.write("<ol>");
for (i in names) {
    document.write("<li>" + names[i] + "<br>");
}
document.write("</ol>");
```

Here you have a for...in loop that loops through the names array, assigning the counter i to each index in turn. The script then prints the name with a <li> tag as an item in an ordered list. Before and after the loop, the script prints beginning and ending <ol> tags.

You now have everything you need for a working script. Listing 8.4 shows the HTML file for this example, and Listing 8.5 shows the JavaScript file.

**LISTING 8.4    A Script to Prompt for Names and Display Them (HTML)**

```
<html>
<head>
<title>Loops Example</title>
</head>
<body>
<h1>Loop Example</h1>
<p>Enter a series of names. I will then
display them in a nifty numbered list.</p>
<script language="JavaScript" type="text/javascript"
src="loops.js">
</script>
</body>
</html>
```

**LISTING 8.5**    A Script to Prompt for Names and Display Them (JavaScript)

```
// create the array
names = new Array();
i = 0;
// loop and prompt for names
do {
    next = window.prompt("Enter the Next Name", "");
    if (next > " ") names[i] = next;
    i = i + 1;
    } while (next > " ");
document.write("<h2>" + (names.length) + " names entered.</h2>");
// display all of the names
document.write("<ol>");
for (i in names) {
    document.write("<li>" + names[i] + "<br>");
}
document.write("</ol>");
```

To try this example, save the JavaScript file as loops.js and then load the HTML document into a browser. You'll be prompted for one name at a time. Enter several names, and then click Cancel to indicate that you're finished. Figure 8.3 shows what the final results should look like in a browser.

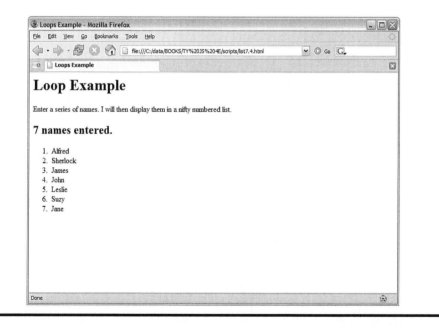

**FIGURE 8.3**
The output of the names example, as shown by Firefox.

# Summary

In this chapter, you've learned two ways to control the flow of your scripts. First, you learned how to use the `if` statement to evaluate conditional expressions and react to them. You also learned a shorthand form of conditional expression using the ? operator, and the `switch` statement for working with multiple conditions.

You also learned about JavaScript's looping capabilities using `for`, `while`, and other loops, and how to control loops further using the `break` and `continue` statements. Lastly, you looked at the `for...in` loop for working with each property of an object.

In the next chapter, you'll look at JavaScript's built-in functions, another essential tool for creating your own scripts. You'll also learn about third-party libraries that enable you to create complex effects with simple scripts.

# CHAPTER 9

# Using Built-In Functions and Libraries

## What You'll Learn in This Chapter:

▶ Using the Math Object
▶ Working with Math Functions
▶ Using the with Keyword
▶ Working with Dates
▶ Using Third-Party Libraries
▶ Other Libraries

In this chapter, you'll learn the basics of objects in JavaScript and the details of using the Math and Date objects. You'll also look at some third-party libraries, which enable you to achieve amazing JavaScript effects with a few lines of code.

## Using the Math Object

The Math object is a built-in JavaScript object that includes math constants and functions. You don't need to create a Math object; it exists automatically in any JavaScript program. The Math object's properties represent mathematical constants, and its methods are mathematical functions.

## Rounding and Truncating

Three of the most useful methods of the Math object enable you to round decimal values up and down:

▶ Math.ceil() rounds a number up to the next integer.

▶ Math.floor() rounds a number down to the next integer.

▶ Math.round() rounds a number to the nearest integer.

All of these take the number to be rounded as their single parameter. You might notice one thing missing: the capability to round to a decimal place, such as for dollar amounts. Fortunately, you can easily simulate this. Here is a simple function that rounds numbers to two decimal places:

```
function round(num) {
   return Math.round(num * 100) / 100;
}
```

This function multiplies the value by 100 to move the decimal, and then rounds the number to the nearest integer. Finally, the value is divided by 100 to restore the decimal to its original position.

## Generating Random Numbers

One of the most commonly used methods of the Math object is the Math.random() method, which generates a random number. This method doesn't require any parameters. The number it returns is a random decimal number between zero and one.

You'll usually want a random number between one and a value. You can do this with a general-purpose random number function. The following is a function that generates random numbers between one and the parameter you send it:

```
function rand(num) {
   return Math.floor(Math.random() * num) + 1;
}
```

This function multiplies a random number by the value specified in the num parameter, and then converts it to an integer between one and the number by using the Math.floor() method.

## Other Math **Functions**

The Math object includes many functions beyond those you've looked at here. For example, Math.sin() and Math.cos() calculate sines and cosines. The Math object also includes properties for various mathematical constants, such as Math.PI.

# Working with Math Functions

The Math.random method generates a random number between 0 and 1. However, it's very difficult for a computer to generate a truly random number. (It's also hard for a human being to do so—that's why dice were invented.)

Today's computers do reasonably well at generating random numbers, but just how good is JavaScript's Math.random function? One way to test it is to generate many random numbers and calculate the average of all of them.

In theory, the average should be somewhere near .5, halfway between 0 and 1. The more random values you generate, the closer the average should get to this middle ground.

As an example of the use of the Math object's methods, you can create a script that tests JavaScript's random number function. To do this, you'll generate 5,000 random numbers and calculate their average.

Rather than typing it in, you can download and try this chapter's example at this book's website.

*Did you Know?*

In case you skipped Chapter 8, "Controlling Flow with Conditions and Loops," and are getting out your calculator, don't worry—you'll use a loop to generate the random numbers. You'll be surprised how fast JavaScript can do this.

To begin your script, you will initialize a variable called total. This variable will store a running total of all of the random values, so it's important that it starts at 0:

```
total = 0;
```

Next, begin a loop that will execute 5,000 times. Use a for loop because you want it to execute a fixed number of times:

```
for (i=1; i<=5000; i++) {
```

Within the loop, you will need to create a random number and add its value to total. Here are the statements that do this and continue with the next iteration of the loop:

```
num = Math.random();
total += num;
}
```

Depending on the speed of your computer, it might take a few seconds to generate those 5,000 random numbers. Just to be sure something is happening, the script will display a status message after each 1,000 numbers:

```
if (i % 1000 == 0)
   document.write("Generated " + i + " numbers...<br>");
```

**By the Way**

> The % symbol in the previous code is the *modulo operator*, which gives you the remainder after dividing one number by another. Here it is used to find even multiples of 1,000.

The final part of your script will calculate the average by dividing total by 5,000. Your script can also round the average to three decimal places, using the trick you learned earlier in this chapter:

```
average = total / 5000;
average = Math.round(average * 1000) / 1000;
document.write("<H2>Average of 5000 numbers: " + average + "</H2>");
```

To test this script and see just how random those numbers are, combine the complete script with an HTML document and <script> tags. Listing 9.1 shows the complete random number testing script.

**LISTING 9.1    A Script to Test JavaScript's Random Number Function**

```
<html>
<head>
<title>Math Example</title>
</head>
<body>
<h1>Math Example</h1>
<p>How random are JavaScript's random numbers?
Let's generate 5000 of them and find out.</p>
<script language="JavaScript" type="text/javascript">
total = 0;
for (i=1; i<=5000; i++) {
    num = Math.random();
    total += num;
    if (i % 1000 == 0)
       document.write("Generated " + i + " numbers...<br>");
}
```

**LISTING 9.1**    Continued

```
average = total / 5000;
average = Math.round(average * 1000) / 1000;
document.write("<H2>Average of 5000 numbers: " + average + "</H2>");
</script>
</body>
</html>
```

To test the script, load the HTML document into a browser. After a short delay, you should see a result. If it's close to `.5`, the numbers are reasonably random. My result was `.502`, as shown in Figure 9.1.

> The average you've used here is called an *arithmetic mean*. This type of average isn't a perfect way to test randomness. Actually, all it tests is the distribution of the numbers above and below `.5`. For example, if the numbers turned out to be 2,500 `.4`s and 2,500 `.6`s, the average would be a perfect `.5`—but they wouldn't be very random numbers. (Thankfully, JavaScript's random numbers don't have this problem.)

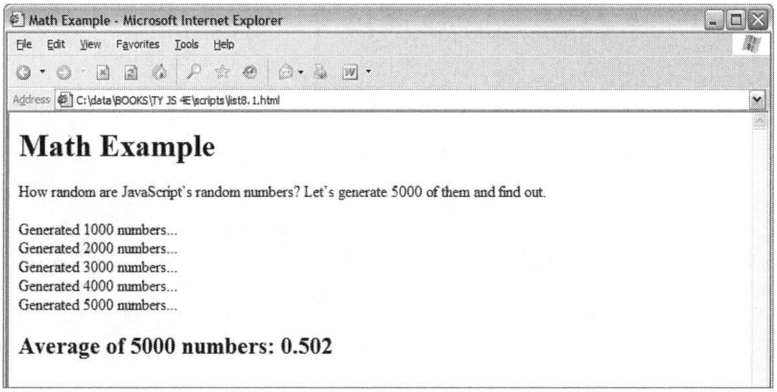

**By the Way**

**FIGURE 9.1**
The random number testing script in action.

# Using the with Keyword

The with keyword is one you haven't seen before. You can use it to make JavaScript programming easier—or at least easier to type.

The with keyword specifies an object, and it is followed by a block of statements enclosed in braces. For each statement in the block, any properties you mention without specifying an object are assumed to be for that object.

As an example, suppose you have a string called `lastname`. You can use `with` to perform string operations on it without specifying the name of the string every time:

```
with (lastname) {
    window.alert("length of last name: " + length);
    capname = toUpperCase();
}
```

In this example, the `length` property and the `toUpperCase` method refer to the `lastname` string, although it is only specified once with the `with` keyword.

Obviously, the `with` keyword only saves a bit of typing in situations like this. However, you might find it more useful when you're dealing with a DOM object throughout a large procedure, or when you are using a built-in object, such as the `Math` object, repeatedly.

# Working with Dates

The `Date` object is a built-in JavaScript object that enables you to conveniently work with dates and times. You can create a `Date` object anytime you need to store a date, and use the `Date` object's methods to work with the date.

You encountered one example of a `Date` object in a previous chapter. The `Date` object has no properties. To set or obtain values from a `Date` object, you must use the methods described in the next section.

JavaScript dates are stored as the number of milliseconds since midnight, January 1, 1970. This date is called the *epoch*. Dates before 1970 weren't allowed in early versions, but are now represented by negative numbers.

## Creating a Date **Object**

You can create a `Date` object using the `new` keyword. You can also optionally specify the date to store in the object when you create it. You can use any of the following formats:

```
birthday = new Date();
birthday = new Date("June 20, 2003 08:00:00");
birthday = new Date(6, 20, 2003);
birthday = new Date(6, 20, 2003, 8, 0, 0);
```

You can choose any of these formats, depending on which values you wish to set. If you use no parameters, as in the first example, the current date is stored in the object. You can then set the values using the set methods, described in the next section.

# Setting Date Values

A variety of set methods enable you to set components of a Date object to values:

▶ setDate() sets the day of the month.

▶ setMonth() sets the month. JavaScript numbers the months from 0 to 11, starting with January (0).

▶ setFullYear() sets the year.

▶ setTime() sets the time (and the date) by specifying the number of milliseconds since January 1, 1970.

▶ setHours(), setMinutes(), and setSeconds() set the time.

As an example, the following statement sets the year of a Date object called holiday to 2003:

```
holiday.setFullYear(2003);
```

# Reading Date Values

You can use the get methods to get values from a Date object. This is the only way to obtain these values, because they are not available as properties. Here are the available get methods for dates:

▶ getDate() gets the day of the month.

▶ getMonth() gets the month.

▶ getFullYear() gets the year.

▶ getTime() gets the time (and the date) as the number of milliseconds since January 1, 1970.

▶ getHours(), getMinutes(), getSeconds(), and getMilliseconds() get the components of the time.

Along with `setFullYear` and `getFullYear`, which require four-digit years, JavaScript includes `setYear` and `getYear` methods, which use two-digit year values. You should always use the four-digit version to avoid Year 2000 issues.

## Working with Time Zones

Finally, a few functions are available to help your `Date` objects work with local time values and time zones:

▶ `getTimeZoneOffset()` gives you the local time zone's offset from UTC (Coordinated Universal Time, based on the old Greenwich Mean Time standard). In this case, *local* refers to the location of the browser. (Of course, this only works if the user has set his or her system clock accurately.)

▶ `toUTCString()` converts the `date` object's time value to text, using UTC. This method was introduced in JavaScript 1.2 to replace the `toGMTString` method, which still works but should be avoided.

▶ `toLocalString()` converts the `date` object's time value to text, using local time.

Along with these basic functions, JavaScript 1.2 and later include UTC versions of several of the functions described previously. These are identical to the regular commands, but work with UTC instead of local time:

▶ `getUTCDate()` gets the day of the month in UTC time.

▶ `getUTCDay()` gets the day of the week in UTC time.

▶ `getUTCFullYear()` gets the four-digit year in UTC time.

▶ `getUTCMonth()` returns the month of the year in UTC time.

▶ `getUTCHours()`, `getUTCMinutes()`, `getUTCSeconds()`, and `getUTCMilliseconds()` return the components of the time in UTC.

▶ `setUTCDate()`, `setUTCFullYear()`, `setUTCMonth()`, `setUTCHours()`, `setUTCMinutes()`, `setUTCSeconds()`, and `setUTCMilliseconds()` set the time in UTC.

## Converting Between Date Formats

Two special methods of the `Date` object allow you to convert between date formats. Instead of using these methods with a `Date` object you created, you use them with the built-in object `Date` itself. These include the following:

▶ `Date.parse()` converts a date string, such as `June 20, 1996`, to a `Date` object (number of milliseconds since 1/1/1970).

▶ `Date.UTC()` does the opposite. It converts a `Date` object value (number of milliseconds) to a UTC (GMT) time.

# Using Third-Party Libraries

When you use JavaScript's built-in `Math` and `Date` functions, JavaScript does most of the work—you don't have to figure out how to convert dates between formats or calculate a cosine. Third-party libraries are not included with JavaScript, but they serve a similar purpose—enabling you to do complicated things with only a small amount of code.

Using one of these libraries is usually as simple as copying one or more files to your site and including a `<script>` tag in your document to load the library. Several popular JavaScript libraries are discussed in the following sections. More detailed descriptions, including the use of these libraries for Ajax applications, are given towards the end of this book.

## Prototype

Prototype, created by Sam Stephenson, is a JavaScript library that simplifies tasks such as working with DOM objects, dealing with data in forms, and remote scripting (AJAX). By including a single `prototype.js` file in your document, you have access to many improvements to basic JavaScript.

Adding Prototype to your pages requires only one file, `prototype.js`, and one `<script>` tag:

```
<script type="text/javascript" src="prototype.js"> </script>
```

See Chapter 25 for a discussion on Prototype.

## Script.aculo.us

The code for a task like on-page animation can be complex, but you can also include effects in your pages using a prebuilt library. This enables you to use impressive effects with only a few lines of code.

Script.aculo.us by Thomas Fuchs is one such library. It includes functions to simplify drag-and-drop tasks, such as rearranging lists of items. It also includes a number of Combination Effects, which enable you to use highlighting and animated transitions within your pages. For example, a new section of the page can be briefly highlighted in yellow to get the user's attention, or a portion of the page can fade out or slide off the screen.

After you've included the appropriate files, using effects is as easy as using any of JavaScript's built-in methods. For example, the following statements use Script.aculo.us to fade out an element of the page with the id value `test`:

```
obj = document.getElementById("test");
new Effect.Fade(obj);
```

Script.aculo.us is built on the Prototype framework described in the previous section, and includes all of the functions of Prototype, so you could also simplify this further by using the $ function:

```
new Effect.Fade($("test"));
```

See Chapter 27 for more on using the Script.aculo.us library.

# Other Libraries

There are many more JavaScript libraries out there, and more are appearing all of the time as JavaScript is taken more seriously as an application language. Here are some more libraries you might want to explore:

► Dojo (http://www.dojotoolkit.org/) is an open-source toolkit that adds power to JavaScript to simplify building applications and user interfaces. It adds features ranging from extra string and math functions to animation and Ajax.

► The Yahoo! UI Library (http://developer.yahoo.net/yui/) was developed by Yahoo! and made available to everyone under an open-source license. It includes features for animation, DOM features, event management, and easy-to-use user interface elements such as calendars and sliders.

▶ MochiKit (http://mochikit.com/) is a lightweight library that adds features for working with the DOM, CSS colors, string formatting, and Ajax. It also supports a nice logging mechanism for debugging your scripts.

---

Prototype, Script.aculo.us, Dojo, and MochiKit are among the selection of frameworks supplied on the CD that accompanies this book.

**On the CD**

# Summary

In this chapter, you learned some specifics about the `Math` and `Date` objects built into JavaScript, and learned more than you ever wanted to know about random numbers. You also learned about third-party libraries that can simplify your scripting.

This concludes Part II of the book. In Part III, "Introducing Ajax," you'll begin to use your JavaScript knowledge to build a working Ajax application.

# PART III

# Introducing Ajax

# CHAPTER 10

# The Heart of Ajax—the XMLHTTPRequest **Object**

---

## *What You'll Learn in This Chapter:*

▶ **Introducing** XMLHTTPRequest
▶ **Creating the** XMLHTTPRequest **Object**

In this chapter you will learn how to create an instance of the XMLHTTPRequest object regardless of which browser your user may have. The object's properties and methods will be introduced.

Chapter 3, "Anatomy of an Ajax Application," introduced the building blocks of an Ajax application and discussed how these pieces fit together.

This chapter examines the object at the heart of every Ajax application—the XMLHTTPRequest object.

> You have already met JavaScript objects in Chapter 7, "Using Functions and Objects." The XMLHTTPRequest object, after it has been created, becomes a further such object within the page's object hierarchy and has its own properties and methods.

**By the** Way

## **Introducing** XMLHTTPRequest

XMLHTTPRequest is supported by virtually all modern browsers, including Microsoft's Internet Explorer 5+ and a variety of non-Microsoft browsers, including Mozilla, Firefox, Konqueror, Opera, and Safari, and is supported on a wide range of platforms, including Microsoft Windows, UNIX/Linux, and Mac OS X.

> Some browsers may require attention to their security settings to allow the XMLHTTPRequest object to operate correctly. See your browser's documentation for details.

The purpose of the XMLHTTPRequest object is to allow JavaScript to formulate HTTP requests and submit them to the server. Traditionally programmed web applications normally make such requests *synchronously*, in conjunction with a user-initiated event such as clicking on a link or submitting a form, resulting in a new or updated page being served to the browser.

Using XMLHTTPRequest, however, you can have your page make such calls *asynchronously* in the background, allowing you to continue using the page without the interruption of a browser refresh and the loading of a new or revised page.

This capability underpins all Ajax applications, making the XMLHTTPRequest object the key to Ajax programming.

> Although the object's name begins with *XML*, in fact, any type of document may be returned from the server; ASCII text, HTML, and XML are all popular choices, and we will encounter all of these in the course of the book.

# Creating the XMLHTTPRequest Object

You cannot make use of the XMLHTTPRequest until you have created an instance of it. Creating an instance of an object in JavaScript is usually just a matter of making a call to a method known as the object's constructor. In the case of XMLHTTPRequest, however, you must change this routine a little to cater to the peculiarities of different browsers, as you see in the following section.

## Different Rules for Different Browsers

Microsoft first introduced the XMLHTTPRequest object, implementing it in Internet Explorer 5 as an *ActiveX object*.

> ActiveX is a proprietary Microsoft technology for enabling active objects into web pages. Among the available web browsers, it is currently only supported in Microsoft's Internet Explorer. Internet Explorer uses its built-in XML parser, MSXML, to create the XMLHTTPRequest object.

Most other browser developers have now included into their products an equivalent object, but implemented as a native object in the browser's JavaScript interpreter.

Because you don't know in advance which browser, version, or operating system your users will have, your code must adapt its behavior on-the-fly to ensure that the instance of the object will be created successfully.

For the majority of browsers that support XMLHTTPRequest as a native object (Mozilla, Opera, and the rest), creating an instance of this object is straightforward. The following line creates an XMLHTTPRequest object called request:

```
var request = new XMLHTTPRequest();
```

Here we have declared a variable request and assigned to it the value returned from the statement new XMLHTTPRequest(), which is invoking the constructor method for the XMLHTTPRequest object.

To achieve the equivalent result in Microsoft Internet Explorer, you need to create an ActiveX object. Here's an example:

```
var request = new ActiveXObject("Microsoft.XMLHTTP");
```

Once again, this assigns the name request to the new object.

To complicate matters a little more, some versions of Internet Explorer have a different version of MSXML, the Microsoft XML parser, installed; in those cases you need to use the following instruction:

```
var request = new ActiveXObject("Msxml2.XMLHTTP");
```

## A Solution for All Browsers

You need, therefore, to create a script that will correctly create an instance of a XMLHTTPRequest object regardless of which browser you are using (provided, of course, that the browser supports XMLHTTPRequest).

A good solution to this problem is to have your script try in turn each method of creating an instance of the object, until one such method succeeds. Have a look at Listing 10.1, in which such a strategy is used.

**LISTING 10.1**    Using Object Detection for a Cross-Browser Solution

```
function getXMLHTTPRequest()
{
var request = false;
try
  {
```

**LISTING 10.1**    Continued

```
   request = new XMLHttpRequest(); /* e.g. Firefox */
  }
catch(err1)
  {
  try
    {
    vrequest = new ActiveXObject("Msxml2.XMLHTTP");
  /* some versions IE */
    }
  catch(err2)
    {
    try
      {
      request = new ActiveXObject("Microsoft.XMLHTTP");
  /* some versions IE */
      }
    catch(err3)
      {
      request = false;
      }
    }
  }
return request;
}
```

Listing 10.1 uses the JavaScript statements try and catch. The try statement allows us to attempt to run a piece of code. If the code runs without errors, all is well; however, should an error occur we can use the catch statement to intervene before an error message is sent to the user and determine what the program should then do about the error.

**By the Way**

> Note the syntax:
>
> ```
>     catch(identifier)
> ```
>
> Here identifier is an object created when an error is caught. It contains information about the error; for instance, if you wanted to alert the user to the nature of a JavaScript runtime error, you could use a code construct like this:
>
> ```
>     catch(err)
>       {
>       alert(err.description);
>       }
> ```
>
> to open a dialog containing details of the error.

An alternative, and equally valid, technique would be to detect which type of browser is in use by testing which objects are defined in the browser. Listing 10.2 shows this technique.

**LISTING 10.2** Using Browser Detection for a Cross-Browser Solution

```
function getXMLHTTPRequest()
{
var request = false;
if(window.XMLHTTPRequest)
   {
   request = new XMLHTTPRequest();
   } else {
   if(window.ActiveXObject)
     {
     try
        {
        request = new ActiveXObject("Msml2.XMLHTTP");
        }
     catch(err1)
        {
        try
           {
              request =
➥new ActiveXObject("Microsoft.XMLHTTP");
           }
        catch(err2)
           {
           request = false;
           }
        }
     }
   }
return request;
}
```

In this example we've used the test

```
if(window.XMLHTTPRequest) { … }
```

to determine whether XMLHTTPRequest is a native object of the browser in use; if so, we use the constructor method

```
request = new XMLHTTPRequest();
```

to create an instance of the XMLHTTPRequest object; otherwise, we try creating a suitable ActiveX object as in the first example.

Whatever method you use to create an instance of the XMLHTTPRequest object, you should be able to call this function like this:

```
var myRequest = getXMLHTTPRequest();
```

> JavaScript also makes available a `navigator` object that holds information about the browser being used to view the page. Another method we could have used to branch our code is to use this object's `appName` property to find the name of the browser:
>
>     var myBrowser = navigator.appName;
>
> This would return "Microsoft Internet Explorer" for IE.

## Methods and Properties

Now that we have created an instance of the `XMLHTTPRequest` object, let's look at some of the object's properties and methods, listed in Table 10.1.

**TABLE 10.1**   `XMLHTTPRequest` **Objects and Methods**

| Properties | Description |
|---|---|
| onreadystatechange | Determines which event handler will be called when the object's `readyState` property changes |
| readyState | Integer reporting the status of the request:<br>0 = uninitialized<br>1 = loading<br>2 = loaded<br>3 = interactive<br>4 = completed |
| responseText | Data returned by the server in text string form |
| responseXML | Data returned by the server expressed as a document object |
| status | HTTP status code returned by server |
| statusText | HTTP reason phrase returned by server |
| **Methods** | **Description** |
| abort() | Stops the current request |
| getAllResponseHeaders() | Returns all headers as a string |
| getResponseHeader(x) | Returns the value of header x as a string |
| open('method','URL','a') | Specifies the HTTP method (for example, GET or POST), the target URL, and whether the request should be handled asynchronously (If yes, a='true'—the default; if no, a='false'.) |
| send(content) | Sends the request, optionally with POST data |
| setRequestHeader('x','y') | Sets a parameter and value pair x=y and assigns it to the header to be sent with the request |

Over the next few chapters we'll examine how these methods and properties are used to create the functions that form the building blocks of Ajax applications.

For now, let's examine just a few of these methods.

## The open() Method

The open() method prepares the XMLHTTPRequest object to communicate with the server. You need to supply at least the two mandatory arguments to this method:

▶ First, specify which HTTP method you intend to use, usually GET or POST.

▶ Next, the destination URL of the request is included as the second argument. If making a GET request, this URL needs to be suitably encoded with any parameters and their values as part of the URL.

For security reasons, the XMLHTTPRequest object is allowed to communicate only with URLs within its own domain. An attempt to connect to a remote domain results in a "permission denied" error message.

> A common mistake is to reference your domain as mydomain.com in a call made from www.mydomain.com. The two will be regarded as different by the JavaScript interpreter, and connection will not be allowed.

**Watch Out!**

Optionally you may include a third argument to the send request, a Boolean value to declare whether the request is being sent in asynchronous mode. If set to false, the request will not be sent in asynchronous mode, and the page will be effectively locked until the request is completed. The default value of true will be assumed if the parameter is omitted, and requests will then be sent asynchronously.

> A Boolean data type has only two possible values, 1 (or true) and 0 (or false).

**By the Way**

## The send() Method

Having prepared the XMLHTTPRequest using the open() method, you can send the request using the send() method. One argument is accepted by the send() function.

If your request is a GET request, the request information will be encoded into the destination URL, and you can then simply invoke the send() method using the argument null:

```
objectname.send(null);
```

However, if you are making a POST request, the content of the request (suitably encoded) will be passed as the argument.

```
objectname.setRequestHeader('Content-Type',
➥'application/x-www-form-urlencoded');
objectname.send(var1=value1&var2=value2);
```

In this case we use the setRequestHeader method to indicate what type of content we are including.

# Summary

This chapter introduced the XMLHTTPRequest object, the driving force behind any Ajax application, and illustrated how an instance of such an object is created both for Internet Explorer and for other, non-Microsoft browsers. We also briefly examined some of the object's properties and methods.

Following chapters will show how more of the object's methods and properties are used.

# CHAPTER 11

# Talking with the Server

---

## *What You'll Learn in This Chapter:*

▶ Sending the Server Request
▶ Monitoring Server Status
▶ The Callback Function

In this chapter you'll learn how to use the properties and methods of the XMLHTTPRequest object to allow the object to send requests to and receive data from the server.

## Sending the Server Request

Chapter 10, "The XMLHTPPRequest Object," discussed at some length the JavaScript XMLHTTPRequest object and how an instance of it may be created in various different browsers.

Now that we have our XMLHTTPRequest object, let's consider how to create and send server requests, and what messages we might expect to receive back from the server.

We're going to jump right in and first write some code using what you learned in Chapter 10 to create an XMLHTTPRequest object called myRequest. We'll then write a JavaScript function called callAjax() to send an asynchronous request to the server using that object. Afterward we'll break down the code line by line to see what it's doing.

Listing 11.1 shows our prototype function to prepare and send an Ajax request using this object.

**LISTING 11.1**   Sending a Server Request

```
function getXMLHTTPRequest()
{
var req = false;
try
  {
   req = new XMLHttpRequest(); /* e.g. Firefox */
  }
catch(err1)
  {
  try
    {
     req = new ActiveXObject("Msxml2.XMLHTTP");
  /* some versions IE */
    }
  catch(err2)
    {
    try
      {
       req = new ActiveXObject("Microsoft.XMLHTTP");
  /* some versions IE */
      }
      catch(err3)
        {
         req = false;
        }
    }
  }
return req;
}

var myRequest = getXMLHTTPRequest();

function callAjax() {
// declare a variable to hold some information
// to pass to the server
var lastname = 'Smith';
// build the URL of the server script we wish to call
var url = "myserverscript.php?surname=" + lastname;
// ask our XMLHTTPRequest object to open a
// server connection
myRequest.open("GET", url, true);
// prepare a function responseAjax() to run when
// the response has arrived
myRequest.onreadystatechange = responseAjax;
// and finally send the request
myRequest.send(null);
}
```

**Did you Know?**

Remember that, as you learned in Chapter 4, "Creating Simple Scripts in JavaScript" lines starting with // are treated as comments by JavaScript. You may use lines like these to document your code or add other useful notes, and your browser's JavaScript interpreter will ignore them when executing code instructions.

First, we need to create an instance of an XMLHTTPRequest object and call it myRequest. You'll no doubt recognize the code for this from Chapter 10.

Next we'll look at the function callAjax().

The first line simply declares a variable and assigns a value to it:

```
var lastname = 'Smith';
```

This is the piece of data that our function intends to send to the server, as the value of a variable called surname that is required by our server-side script. In reality, of course, the value of such data would usually be obtained dynamically by handling a page event such as a mouse click or a keyboard entry, but for now this will serve as a simple example.

The server request we intend to make is a GET request, so we must construct a suitable target URL having our parameter and value pairs suitably coded on the end; the next line carries this out:

```
var url = "myserverscript.php?surname=" + lastname;
```

We dealt briefly with the open() method in Chapter 10. We use it in the next line to prepare our server request:

```
myRequest.open("GET", url, true);
```

This line specifies that we are preparing a GET request and passes to it the destination URL complete with the appended content of the GET request.

The third parameter, true, indicates that we want our request to be handled asynchronously. In this case it could have been omitted because the default value of true is assumed in such cases. However, it does no harm to include it for clarity.

Next, we need to tell our XMLHTTPRequest object myRequest what it should do with the "progress reports" it will receive from the server. The XMLHTTPRequest object has a property onreadystatechange that contains information about what JavaScript function should be called whenever the server status changes, and in the next line

```
myRequest.onreadystatechange = responseAjax;
```

we assign the function responseAjax() to do this job. We will write this function later in the chapter.

## Dealing with the Browser Cache

All browsers maintain a so-called *cache* of visited web pages, a local record of page contents stored on the hard disk of the browser's computer. When you request a particular web page, the browser first tries to load the page from its cache, rather than submitting a new HTTP request.

> This appears to be more of a problem with IE than with the non-Microsoft browsers. Only GET requests are affected; POST requests are not cached.

Although this can sometimes be advantageous in terms of page load times, it creates a difficulty when trying to write Ajax applications. Ajax is all about talking to the server, not reloading information from cache; so when you make an asynchronous request to the server, a new HTTP request must be generated every time.

It is possible to add HTTP headers to the data returned by server-side routines, intended to tell the browser not to cache a particular page. Examples include

```
"Pragma: no-cache"
```

and

```
"Cache-Control: must-revalidate"
```

among others.

Unfortunately such strategies vary widely in their effectiveness. Different browsers have different cache handling strategies and support different header declarations, making it difficult to ensure that pages are not cached.

A commonly used trick to work around this problem involves the adding of a parameter with a random and meaningless value to the request data. In the case of a GET request, this necessitates adding a further parameter and value pair to the end of the URL.

If the random part of the URL is different each time, this effectively "fools" the browser into believing that it is to send the asynchronous request to an address not previously visited. This results in a new HTTP request being sent on every occasion.

Let's see how to achieve this. As you learned in Chapter 9, in JavaScript you can generate random numbers using the Math.random() method of the native Math() object. Listing 11.2 contains a couple of changes to the callAjax() function.

**LISTING 11.2**    Dealing with the Browser Cache

```
function getXMLHTTPRequest()
{
var req = false;
try
  {
   req = new XMLHttpRequest(); /* e.g. Firefox */
  }
catch(err1)
  {
  try
    {
     req = new ActiveXObject("Msxml2.XMLHTTP");
  /* some versions IE */
    }
  catch(err2)
    {
    try
      {
        req = new ActiveXObject("Microsoft.XMLHTTP");
  /* some versions IE */
      }
      catch(err3)
        {
         req = false;
        }
    }
  }
return req;
}

var myRequest = getXMLHTTPRequest();

function callAjax() {
// declare a variable to hold some information
// to pass to the server
var lastname = 'Smith';
// build the URL of the server script we wish to call
var url = "myserverscript.php?surname=" + lastname;
// generate a random number
var myRandom=parseInt(Math.random()*99999999);
// ask our XMLHTTPRequest object to open
// a server connection
myRequest.open("GET", url + "&rand=" + myRandom, true);
// prepare a function responseAjax() to run when
// the response has arrived
myRequest.onreadystatechange = responseAjax;
// and finally send the request
myRequest.send(null);
}
```

You can see from Listing 11.2 that the script will now generate a destination URL for our Ajax request that looks something like this:

```
myserverscript.php?surname=Smith&rand=XXXX
```

where XXXX will be some random number, thereby preventing the page from being returned from cache and forcing a new HTTP request to be sent to the server.

> Some programmers prefer to add the current timestamp rather than a random number. This is a string of characters derived from the current date and time, and has been discussed in detail elsewhere in the book. In the following example, the JavaScript `Date()` and `getTime()` methods of the native `Date()` object are used:
>
> ```
> myRand= new Date().getTime();
> ```

# Monitoring Server Status

The `XMLHTTPRequest` object contains mechanisms by which we can stay informed of the progress of our Ajax request and determine when the information returned by the server is ready to use in our application.

Let's now have a look at the relevant properties.

## The `readyState` Property

The `readyState` property of the `XMLHTTPRequest` object gives you information from the server about the current state of a request you have made. This property is monitored by the `onreadystatechange` property, and changes in the value of `readyState` cause `onreadystatechange` to become true and therefore cause the appropriate function (`responseAjax()` in our example) to be executed.

**Did you Know?**

> The function called on completion of the server request is normally referred to as the *callback function*.

`readyState` can take the following values:

       0 = uninitialized

       1 = loading

       2 = loaded

       3 = interactive

       4 = completed

When a server request is first made, the value of readyState is set to zero, meaning uninitialized.

As the server request progresses, data begins to be loaded by the server into the XMLHTTPRequest object, and the value of the readyState property changes accordingly, moving to 1 and then 2.

An object readyState value of 3, interactive, indicates that the object is sufficiently progressed so that certain interactivity with it is possible, though the process is not yet fully complete.

When the server request has completed fully and the object is available for further processing, the value of readyState changes finally to 4.

> Not all of the possible values may exist for any given object. The object may "skip" certain states if they bear no relevance to the object's content type.

**Did you Know?**

In most practical cases, you should look for the readyState property to achieve a value of 4, at which point you can be assured that the server has finished its task and the XMLHTTPRequest object is ready for use.

## Server Response Status Codes

In addition to the readyState property, you have a further means to check that an asynchronous request has executed correctly: the HTTP server response status code.

HTTP responses were discussed in Chapter 1. If you refer to Table 1.1 you'll see that a response status code of 200 corresponds to an OK message from the server.

We'll see how to test for this as we further develop our callback function.

# The Callback Function

By now, then, you have learned how to create an instance of an XMLHTTPRequest object, declare the identity of a callback function, and prepare and send an asynchronous server request. You also know which property tells you when the server response is available for use.

Let's look at our callback function, responseAjax().

First, note that this function is called every time there is a change in the value of the onreadystatechange property. Usually, then, when this function is called, it is required to do absolutely nothing because the value of the `readyState` property has not yet reached 4 and we therefore know that the server request has not completed its processing.

We can achieve this simply by using a JavaScript `if` statement:

```
function responseAjax() {
    // we are only interested in readyState of 4,
    // i.e. "completed"
    if(myRequest.readyState == 4) {
        … program execution statements …
    }
}
```

In addition to checking that the server request has completed, we also want to check the HTTP response status code to ensure that it is equal to 200, indicating a successful response to our asynchronous HTTP request.

Referring quickly back to Table 10.1, we can see that our `XMLHTTPRequest` object `myRequest` has two properties that report the HTTP status response. These are

```
myRequest.status
```

which contains the status response code, and

```
myRequest.statusText
```

containing the reason phrase.

We can employ these properties by using a further loop:

```
function responseAjax() {
    // we are only interested in readyState of 4,
    // i.e. "loaded"
    if(myRequest.readyState == 4) {
        // if server HTTP response is "OK"
        if(myRequest.status == 200) {
            … program execution statements …
        } else {
            // issue an error message for any
            // other HTTP response
            alert("An error has occurred: "
➡+ myRequest.statusText);
        }
    }
}
```

This code introduces an `else` clause into our `if` statement. Any server status response other than 200 causes the contents of this `else` clause to be executed, opening an alert dialog containing the text of the reason phrase returned from the server.

# Using the Callback Function

So how do we go about calling our `callAjax()` callback function from our HTML page? Let's see an example. Here's the code for a simplified form in an HTML page:

```
<form name='form1'>
Name: <input type='text' name='myname'><br>
Tel: <input type='text' name='telno'><br>
<input type='submit'>
</form>
```

We'll launch the function using the `onBlur` event handler of a text input field in a form:

```
<form name='form1'>
Name: <input type='text' name='myname'
➥onBlur='callAjax()'><br>
Tel: <input type='text' name='telno'><br>
<input type='submit'>
</form>
```

The `onBlur` event handler is activated when the user leaves the field in question. In this case, when the user leaves the field, `callAjax()` will be executed, creating an instance of the `XMLHTTPRequest` object and making an asynchronous server request to

```
myserverscript.php?surname=Smith
```

That doesn't sound very useful. However, what if we were to now make a slight change to the code of `callAjax()`?

```
function callAjax() {
// declare a variable to hold some
// information to pass to the server
var lastname = document.form1.myname.value;
.....
```

Now we can see that, as the user leaves the form field `myname`, the value she had typed into that field would be passed to the server via our asynchronous request. Such a call may, for example, check a database to verify the existence of the named person, and if so return information to populate other fields on the form.

The result, so far as the user is concerned, is that she sees the remaining fields magically populated with data before submitting—or even completing—the form.

How we might use the returned data to achieve such a result is discussed in Chapter 12, "Using the Returned Data."

# Summary

This chapter looked at the ways in which our XMLHTTPRequest object can communicate with the server, including sending asynchronous requests, monitoring the server status, and executing a callback function.

In Chapter 12, you will see how Ajax applications can deal with the data returned by the server request.

# CHAPTER 12

# Using the Returned Data

## What You'll Learn in This Chapter:

▶ The responseText and responseXML Properties
▶ Parsing responseXML
▶ Providing User Feedback

In this chapter you will learn how to process the information returned from the server in response to an Ajax request.

## The responseText and responseXML Properties

Chapter 11, "Talking with the Server," discussed the server communications that allow you to send and monitor asynchronous server requests. The final piece of the Ajax jigsaw is the information returned by the server in response to a request.

This chapter discusses what forms that information can take, and how you can process it and use it in an application. We will use two of the XMLHTTPRequest object's properties, namely responseText and responseXML.

Table 10.1 listed several properties of the XMLHTTPRequest object that we have yet to describe. Among these are the responseText and responseXML properties.

Chapter 10 discussed how we could use the readyState property of the XMLHTTPRequest object to determine the current status of the XMLHTTPRequest call. By the time our server request has completed, as detected by the condition myRequest.readyState == 4 for our XMLHTTPRequest object myRequest, then the two properties responseText and responseXML will respectively contain text and XML representations of the data returned by the server.

In this chapter you'll see how to access the information contained in these two properties and apply each in an Ajax application.

## The responseText **Property**

The responseText property tries to represent the information returned by the server
as a text string.

**Did you
Know?**

> If the XMLHTTPRequest call fails with an error, or has not yet been sent,
> responseText will have a value null. Flip back to Chapter 6, "Using Variables,
> Strings, and Arrays," if you need to remind yourself about null values.

Let's look again at the callback function prototype:

```
function responseAjax() {
  // we are only interested in readyState of 4, i.e. "loaded"
  if(myRequest.readyState == 4) {
     // if server HTTP response is "OK"
     if(myRequest.status == 200) {
         … program execution statements …
     } else {
        // issue an error message for any other HTTP response
        alert("An error occurred: " + myRequest.statusText);
     }
  }
}
```

Let's add a program statement to the branch of the if statement that is executed on
success, as in Listing 12.1.

**LISTING 12.1    Displaying the Value of responseText**

```
function responseAjax() {
   // we are only interested in readyState of 4,
   // i.e. "completed"
   if(myRequest.readyState == 4) {
      // if server HTTP response is "OK"
      if(myRequest.status == 200) {
         alert("The server said: "
+ myRequest.responseText);
      } else {
         // issue an error message for
         // any other HTTP response
         alert("An error has occurred: "
+ myRequest.statusText);
      }
   }
}
```

In this simple example, our script opens an alert dialog to display the text returned by the server. The line

```
alert("The server said: " + myRequest.responseText);
```

takes the text returned by the server-side routine and appends it to the string `"The server said: "` before presenting it in a JavaScript alert dialog.

Let's look at an example using a simple PHP file on the server:

```
<?php echo "Hello Ajax caller!"; ?>
```

> We'll be looking in detail at PHP in Part IV. For now, all you really need to know is that PHP's `echo()` command asks the server to output whatever is enclosed between the parentheses.

 **By the Way**

A successful `XMLHTTPRequest` call to this file would result in the `responseText` property containing the string `Hello Ajax caller!`, causing the callback function to produce the dialog shown in Figure 12.1.

**FIGURE 12.1**
Output generated by Listing 12.1.

> The `responseText` property is read-only, so there's no point in trying to manipulate its value until that value has first been copied into another variable.

**Did you Know?**

Because the `responseText` contains a simple text string, we can manipulate it using any of JavaScript's methods relating to strings, some of which were introduced in Chapter 6. Table 12.1 includes some of the available methods.

**TABLE 12.1**  Some JavaScript String Manipulation Methods

| Method | Description |
|---|---|
| `charAt(number)` | Selects the single character at the specified position within the string |
| `indexOf(substring)` | Finds the position where the specified substring starts |
| `lastIndexOf(substring)` | Finds the last occurrence of the substring within the string |
| `substring(start,end)` | Gets the specified part of the string |
| `toLowerCase()` | Converts the string to lowercase |
| `toUpperCase()` | Converts the string to uppercase |

We'll be looking at how `responseText` may be used in real situations in Chapter 19, "Returning Data as Text."

## The `responseXML` **Property**

Now suppose that the PHP script we used on the server in the previous example had instead looked like Listing 12.2. Once again, we won't worry too much about the nuts-and-bolts of the PHP commands, as we'll be looking at PHP in detail in Part IV of the book.

**LISTING 12.2    A Server-Side Script to Return XML**

```php
<?php
header('Content-Type: text/xml');
echo "<?xml version=\"1.0\" ?><greeting>
➥Hello Ajax caller!</greeting>";
?>
```

Remember reading about HTTP headers, way back in Chapter 1? The first line inside the `<?php` and `?>` delimiters uses PHP's `header` instruction to add an HTTP header to the returned data. The header returned is the parameter and value pair

```
Content-Type: text/xml
```

which announces to our `XMLHTTPRequest` object to expect that the following data from the server will be formatted as XML.

The next line is another PHP echo statement that outputs this simple, but complete, XML document:

```
<?xml version="1.0" ?>
<greeting>
Hello Ajax caller!
</greeting>
```

When the server call is completed, we now find this XML document loaded into the `responseXML` property of our `XMLHTTPRequest` object.

***Did you Know?***

> It is important to note that the `responseXML` property does not contain just a string that forms a text representation of the XML document, as was the case with the `responseText` property; instead, the entire data and hierarchical structure of the XML document has been stored as a DOM-compatible object.

We can now access the content of the XML document via JavaScript's DOM methods and properties.

## The getElementsByTagName() **Method**

This useful method allows you to build a JavaScript array of all the elements having a particular tagname. You can then access elements of that array using normal JavaScript statements. Here's an example:

```
var myElements = object.getElementsByTagName('greeting');
```

This line creates the array myElements and populates it with all the elements with tagname greeting. As with any other array, you can find out the length of the array (that is, the number of elements having the declared tagname) by using the length property:

```
myElements.length
```

You can access a particular element individually if you want; the first occurring element with tagname greeting can be accessed as myElements[0], the second (if there is a second) as myElements[1], and so:

```
var theElement = myElements[0];
```

You could also access these individual array elements directly:

```
var theElement = object.getElementsByTagName('greeting')[0];
```

*Did you Know?*

# Parsing responseXML

Listing 12.3 gives an example of how we can use getElementsByTagName to return the text of our greeting in an alert dialog.

**LISTING 12.3**   Parsing responseXML using getElementsByTagName()

```
function responseAjax() {
    // we are only interested in readyState
    // of 4, i.e. "completed"
    if(myRequest.readyState == 4) {
        // if server HTTP response is "OK"
        if(myRequest.status == 200) {
            var greetNode = http.responseXML
➥.getElementsByTagName("greeting")[0];
            var greetText = greetNode.childNodes[0]
➥.nodeValue;
            alert("Greeting text: " + greetText);
        } else {
            // issue an error message for
            // any other HTTP response
            alert("An error has occurred: "
➥+ myRequest.statusText);
        }
    }
}
```

After the usual checks on the values of the `readyState` and `status` properties, the code locates the required element from `responseXML` using the `getElementsByTagName()` method and then uses `childNodes[0].nodeValue` to extract the text content from this element, finally displaying the returned text in a JavaScript alert dialog.

Figure 12.2 shows the alert dialog, showing the text string recovered from the `<greeting>` element of the XML document.

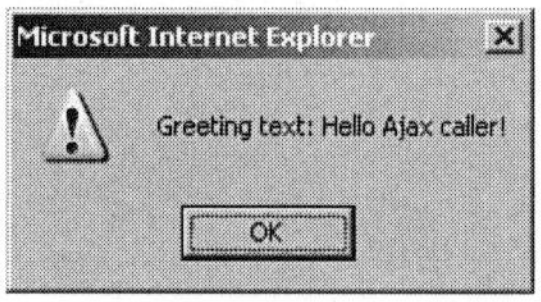

**FIGURE 12.2**
Displaying the
returned
greeting.

## Providing User Feedback

In web pages with traditional interfaces, it is clear to the user when the server is busy processing a request; the interface is effectively unusable while a new page is being prepared and served.

The situation is a little different in an Ajax application. Because the interface remains usable during an asynchronous HTTP request, it may not be apparent to the user that new information is expected from the server. Fortunately there are some simple ways to warn that a server request is in progress.

Recall that our callback function is called each time the value of `readyState` changes, but that we are only really interested in the condition `myRequest.readyState == 4`, which indicates that the server request is complete.

Let's refer again to Listing 12.3. For all values of `readyState` other than 4, the function simply terminates having done nothing. We can use these changes to the value of `readyState` to indicate to the user that a server request is progressing but has not yet completed. Consider the following code:

```
function responseAjax() {
    if(myRequest.readyState == 4) {
        if(myRequest.status == 200) {
            … [success - process the server response]  …
        } else {
            … [failed - report the HTTP error]  …
        }
    } else {      // if readyState has changed
                  // but readyState <> 4
        … [do something here to provide user feedback] …
    }
}
```

A commonly used way to do this is to modify the contents of a page element to show something eye-catching, such as a flashing or animated graphic, while a request is being processed and then remove it when processing is complete.

## The `getElementById()` Method

JavaScript's `getElementById()` method allows you to locate an individual document element by its `id` value. You can use this method in your user feedback routine to temporarily change the contents of a particular page element to provide the visual clue that a server request is in progress.

**Did you Know?**

> Elements within a page that have had `id` values declared are expected to each have a unique `id` value. This allows you to identify a unique element. Contrast this with the `class` attribute, which can be applied to any number of separate elements in a page and is more commonly used to set the display characteristics of a group of objects.

Suppose that we have, say, a small animated graphic file `anim.gif` that we want to display while awaiting information from the server. We want to display this graphic inside a `<div>` element within the HTML page. We begin with this `<div>` element empty:

```
<div id="waiting"></div>
```

Now consider the code of the callback function:

```
function responseAjax() {
    if(myRequest.readyState == 4) {
        document.getElementById('waiting').innerHTML = '';
        if(myRequest.status == 200) {
                ... [success - process the server response]   ...
        } else {
                ... [failed - report the HTTP error]   ...
        }
    } else {      // if readyState has changed
                  // but readyState <> 4
            document.getElementById('waiting')
.innerHTML = '<img src="anim.gif">';
    }
}
```

On each change in value of the property `readyState`, the callback function checks for the condition `readyState == 4`. Whenever this condition fails to be met, the `else` condition of the outer loop uses the `innerHTML` property to ensure that the page element with id `waiting` (our `<div>` element) contains an image whose source is the animated GIF. As soon as the condition `readyState == 4` is met, and we therefore know that the server request has concluded, the line

```
document.getElementById('waiting').innerHTML = '';
```

once more erases the animation.

We'll see this technique in action in Chapter 13, "Our First Ajax Application," when we create a complete Ajax application.

# Summary

This chapter examined the last link in the Ajax chain: how to deal with server responses containing both text and XML information.

We also introduced a further JavaScript DOM method, `getElementsByTagName()`.

In the next chapter, the last in Part III, we use this knowledge along with that gained from earlier chapters, to construct a complete and working Ajax application.

# CHAPTER 13

# Our First Ajax Application

---

## What You'll Learn in This Chapter:

▶ Constructing the Ajax Application
▶ The HTML Document
▶ Adding JavaScript
▶ Putting It All Together

In this chapter you will learn how to construct a complete and working Ajax application using the techniques discussed in previous chapters.

# Constructing the Ajax Application

The previous chapters have introduced all the techniques involved in the design and coding of a complete Ajax application. In this chapter, we're going to construct just such an application.

Our first application will be simple in function, merely returning and displaying the time as read from the server's internal clock; nevertheless it will involve all the basic steps required for any Ajax application:

▶ An HTML document forming the basis for the application

▶ JavaScript routines to create an instance of the XMLHTTPRequest object and construct and send asynchronous server calls

▶ A simple server-side routine (in PHP) to configure and return the required information

▶ A callback function to deal with the returned data and use it in the application

Let's get to it, starting with the HTML file that forms the foundation for our application.

# The HTML Document

Listing 13.1 shows the code for our HTML page.

**LISTING 13.1**    The HTML Page for Our Ajax Application

```
<!DOCTYPE HTML PUBLIC "-//W3C//DTD HTML 4.01
➥Transitional//EN"
"http://www.w3.org/TR/html4/loose.dtd">
<html>
<head>
<title>Ajax Demonstration</title>
<style>
.displaybox {
width:150px;
background-color:#ffffff;
border:2px solid #000000;
padding:10px;
font:24px normal verdana, helvetica, arial, sans-serif;
}
</style>
</head>
<body style="background-color:#cccccc;
➥text-align:center">

<h1>Ajax Demonstration</h1>
<h2>Getting the server time without page refresh</h2>
<form>
<input type="button" value="Get Server Time" />
</form>
<div id="showtime" class="displaybox"></div>

</body>
</html>
```

This is a simple HTML layout, having only a title, subtitle, button, and <div> element, plus some style definitions.

> In HTML the <div> … </div> element stands for division and can be used to allow a number of page elements to be grouped together and manipulated in a block.

Figure 13.1 shows what the HTML page looks like.

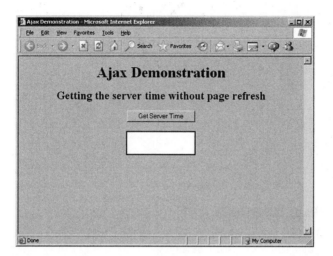

**FIGURE 13.1**
The HTML file of
Listing 13.1.

# Adding JavaScript

We can now add our JavaScript routines to the HTML page. We'll do so by adding them inside a `<script>` … `</script>` container to the `<head>` section of the page.

---

Alternatively we could have added the routines in an external JavaScript file (ajax.js, say) and called this file from our document by using a statement like:

```
<script language="JavaScript" type="text/javascript"
➥src="ajax.js"></script>
```

in the `<head>` section of the document.

*Did you Know?*

---

## The XMLHTTPRequest **Object**

First, let's add our function to create our XMLHTTPRequest object:

```
function getXMLHTTPRequest() {
try {
req = new XMLHttpRequest();
} catch(err1) {
  try {
  req = new ActiveXObject("Msxml2.XMLHTTP");
  } catch (err2) {
    try {
    req = new ActiveXObject("Microsoft.XMLHTTP");
```

```
    } catch (err3) {
      req = false;
    }
  }
}
return req;
}
```

It's now a simple matter to create our XMLHTTPRequest object, which on this occasion we're going to call http:

```
var http = getXMLHTTPRequest();
```

## The Server Request

Now we need a function to construct our server request, define a callback function, and send the request to the server. This is the function that will be called from an event handler in the HTML page:

```
function getServerTime() {
  var myurl = 'telltimeXML.php';
  myRand = parseInt(Math.random()*999999999999999);
  // add random number to URL to avoid cache problems
  var modurl = myurl+"?rand="+myRand;
  http.open("GET", modurl, true);
  // set up the callback function
  http.onreadystatechange = useHttpResponse;
  http.send(null);
}
```

Once again we have added a parameter with a random value to the URL to avoid any cache problems. Our callback function is named useHttpResponse and is called each time a change is detected in the value of http's readyState property.

## Our PHP Server-Side Script

Before explaining the operation of the callback function, we need to refer to the code of the simple PHP server routine telltimeXML.php, shown in Listing 13.2.

### LISTING 13.2    telltimeXML.php

```
<?php
header('Content-Type: text/xml');
echo "<?xml version=\"1.0\" ?><clock1><timenow>"
➥.date('H:i:s')."</timenow></clock1>";
?>
```

This short program reports the server time using PHP's date() function.

**By the Way**

It's not vitally important that you understand PHP's date() function in order to follow this script—but in case you're curious, it will be fully explained in Chapter 14, "Getting to Know PHP." Feel free to skip forward a little to read about it if you want to, and then return here.

The argument passed to this function defines how the elements of the date and time should be formatted. Here we've ignored the date-related elements completely and asked for the time to be returned as Hours:Minutes:Seconds using the 24-hour clock.

Our server script returns an XML file in the following format:

```
<?xml version="1.0" ?>
<clock1>
    <timenow>
    XX:XX:XX
    </timenow>
</clock1>
```

with XX:XX:XX replaced by the current server time. We will use the callback function to extract this time information and display it in the <div> container of the HTML page.

## The Callback Function

Here is the code for the callback function useHttpResponse:

```
function useHttpResponse() {
   if (http.readyState == 4) {
    if(http.status == 200) {
       var timeValue = http.responseXML
➥.getElementsByTagName("timenow")[0];
       document.getElementById('showtime').innerHTML
➥ = timeValue.childNodes[0].nodeValue;
    }
  } else {
  document.getElementById('showtime').innerHTML
➥ = '<img src="anim.gif">';
  }
}
```

Once again we have used the getElementByTagname method, this time to select the <timenow> element of the XML data, which we have stored in a variable timeValue. However, on this occasion we're not going to display the value in an alert dialog as we did in Chapter 12, "Using the Returned Data."

This time we want instead to use the information to update the contents of an element in the HTML page. Note from Listing 13.1 how the <div> container is defined in our HTML page:

```
<div id="showtime" class="displaybox"></div>
```

In addition to the class declaration (which is used in the <style> definitions to affect how the <div> element is displayed), we see that there is also defined an id (identity) for the container, with a value set to showtime.

Currently the <div> contains nothing. We want to update the content of this container to show the server time information stored in timeValue. We do so by selecting the page element using JavaScript's getElementById() method, which we met in Chapter 12. We'll then use the JavaScript innerHTML property to update the element's contents:

```
document.getElementById('showtime').innerHTML
➥ = timeValue.childNodes[0].nodeValue;
```

## Employing Event Handlers

Finally, we must decide how the server requests will be triggered.  In this case we shall slightly edit the HTML document to use the onClick() event handler of the <button> object:

```
<input type="button" value="Get Server Time"
➥ onClick="getServerTime()">
```

This will correctly deal with the occasion when the Get Server Time button is clicked. It does, however, leave the <div> element empty when we first load the page.

To overcome this little problem, we can use the onLoad() event handler of the page's <body> element:

```
<body style="background-color:#cccccc"
➥ onLoad="getServerTime()">
```

This event handler fires as soon as the <body> area of the page has finished loading.

# Putting It All Together

Listing 13.3 shows the complete client-side code for our Ajax application.

### LISTING 13.3    The Complete Ajax Application

```
<html>
<head>
<title>Ajax Demonstration</title>
<style>
.displaybox {
width:150px;
background-color:#ffffff;
border:2px solid #000000;
```

## LISTING 13.3   Continued

```
padding:10px;
font:24px normal verdana, helvetica, arial, sans-serif;
}
</style>
<script language="JavaScript" type="text/javascript">
function getXMLHTTPRequest() {
try {
req = new XMLHttpRequest();
} catch(err1) {
  try {
  req = new ActiveXObject("Msxml2.XMLHTTP");
  } catch (err2) {
    try {
    req = new ActiveXObject("Microsoft.XMLHTTP");
    } catch (err3) {
      req = false;
    }
  }
}
return req;
}

var http = getXMLHTTPRequest();

function getServerTime() {
  var myurl = 'telltimeXML.php';
  myRand = parseInt(Math.random()*999999999999999);
  var modurl = myurl+"?rand="+myRand;
  http.open("GET", modurl, true);
  http.onreadystatechange = useHttpResponse;
  http.send(null);
}

function useHttpResponse() {
   if (http.readyState == 4) {
    if(http.status == 200) {
       var timeValue = http.responseXML
➥.getElementsByTagName("timenow")[0];
       document.getElementById('showtime').innerHTML
➥ = timeValue.childNodes[0].nodeValue;
    }
  } else {
  document.getElementById('showtime').innerHTML
➥ = '<img src="anim.gif">';
  }
}
</script>
</head>
<body style="background-color:#cccccc"
➥ onLoad="getServerTime()">
<center>
<h1>Ajax Demonstration</h1>
<h2>Getting the server time without page refresh</h2>
<form>
<input type="button" value="Get Server Time"
➥ onClick="getServerTime()">
```

**LISTING 13.3    Continued**

```
</form>
<div id="showtime" class="displaybox"></div>
</center>
</body>
</html>
```

Loading the page into our browser, we can see that the server time is displayed in the <div> container, indicating that the onLoad event handler for the <body> of the page has fired when the page has loaded.

## User Feedback

Note also that we have provided user feedback via the line

```
document.getElementById('showtime').innerHTML
➥ = '<img src="anim.gif">';
```

which executes on each change to the value readyState until the condition

```
readyState == 4
```

is satisfied. This line loads into the time display element an animated GIF with a rotating pattern, indicating that a server request is in progress, as shown in Figure 13.2. This technique was described in more detail in Chapter 12.

> If you have a fast server and a good Internet connection, it may be difficult to see this user feedback in action because the time display is updated virtually instantaneously. To demonstrate the operation of the animated GIF image, we can slow down the server script to simulate the performance of a more complex script and/or an inferior connection, by using PHP's sleep() command:
>
> ```
> <?php
> header('Content-Type: text/xml');
> sleep(3);
> echo "<?xml version=\"1.0\" ?><clock1><timenow>"
> ➥.date('H:i:s')."</timenow></clock1>";
> ?>
> ```
>
> The line
>
> ```
> sleep(x);
> ```
>
> forces the server to pause program execution for x seconds.

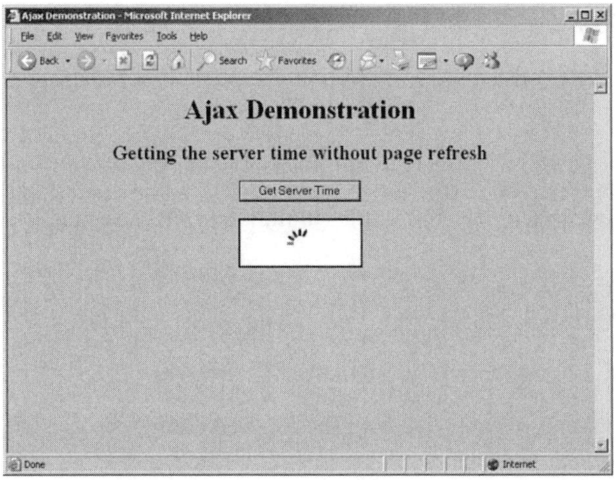

FIGURE 13.2
An animated
image provides
user feedback.

Now, each time we click on the Get Server Time button, the time display is updated. Figure 13.3 shows the completed application.

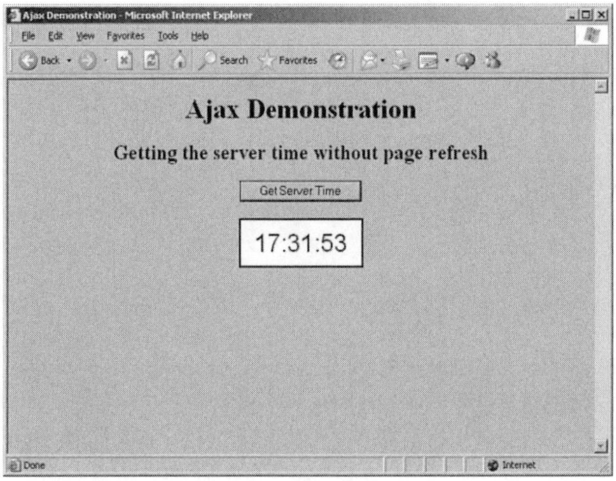

FIGURE 13.3
Our completed
Ajax application.

# Summary

In this chapter, we constructed a simple yet complete Ajax application that does the following:

- ▶ Creates an instance of the `XMLHTTPRequest` object

- ▶ Reacts to JavaScript event handlers built into an HTML page

- ▶ Constructs and sends asynchronous server requests

- ▶ Parses XML received from the server using JavaScript DOM methods

- ▶ Provides user feedback that a request is in progress

- ▶ Updates the displayed page with the received data

That completes Part III of the book, "Introducing Ajax." There's a lot more Ajax to come later in the book, but first we'll look in detail at PHP in Part IV "Server-side Scripting with PHP."

# PART IV

# Server-side Scripting with PHP

# CHAPTER 14

# Getting to Know PHP

---

## *What You'll Learn in This Chapter:*

▶ PHP Basics
▶ Your First PHP Script

In this chapter you will find out what PHP is all about and see what it is able to do.

# PHP Basics

PHP is hugely popular, and rightly so. Even if you haven't come across an existing user singing its praises, you've almost certainly used a website that runs on PHP. This chapter clarifies what PHP does, how it works, and what it is capable of.

PHP is a programming language that was designed for creating dynamic websites. It slots into your web server and processes instructions contained in a web page before that page is sent through to your web browser. Certain elements of the page can therefore be generated on-the-fly so that the page changes each time it is loaded. For instance, you can use PHP to show the current date and time at the top of each page in your site, as you'll see later in this chapter.

The name PHP is a recursive acronym that stands for *PHP: Hypertext Preprocessor*. It began life called PHP/FI, the "FI" part standing for *Forms Interpreter*. Though the name was shortened a while back, one of PHP's most powerful features is how easy it becomes to process data submitted in HTML forms. PHP can also talk to various database systems, giving you the ability to generate a web page based on a SQL query.

For example, you could enter a search keyword into a form field on a web page, query a database with this value, and produce a page of matching results. You will have seen this kind of application many times before, at virtually any online store as well as many websites that do not sell anything, such as search engines.

The PHP language is flexible and fairly forgiving, making it easy to learn even if you have not done any programming in the past. If you already know another language, you will almost certainly find similarities here. In fact, many of the JavaScript programming concepts introduced in Part II of the book—numbers, strings, arrays, objects, and so on— will crop up again in our discussions about PHP, often with only minor changes of syntax.

## Server-Side Scripting

The most important concept to learn when starting out with PHP is where exactly it fits into the grand scheme of things in a web environment. When you understand this, you will understand what PHP can and cannot do.

The PHP module attaches to your web server, telling it that files with a particular extension should be examined for PHP code. Any PHP code found in the page is executed—with any PHP code replaced by the output it produces—before the web page is sent to the browser.

> The usual web server configuration is that `somefile.php` will be interpreted by PHP, whereas `somefile.html` will be passed straight through to the web browser, without PHP getting involved.

The only time the PHP interpreter is called upon to do something is when a web page is loaded. This could be when you click a link, submit a form, or just type in the URL of a web page. When the web browser has finished downloading the page, PHP plays no further part until your browser requests another page.

Because it is only possible to check the values entered in an HTML form when the submit button is clicked, PHP cannot be used to perform client-side validation—in other words, to check that the value entered in one field meets certain criteria before allowing you to proceed to the next field. Client-side validation can be done using JavaScript, a language that runs inside the web browser itself, and JavaScript and PHP can be used together if that is the effect you require.

The beauty of PHP is that it does not rely on the web browser at all; your script will run the same way whatever browser you use. When writing server-side code, you do not need to worry about JavaScript being enabled or about compatibility with older browsers beyond the ability to display HTML that your script generates or is embedded in.

The CD accompanying this book includes the powerful and convenient XAMPP package. If you would like your own server environment for your PHP experiments, rather than using hosted web space, you can use this package to install the Apache web server, fully configured with PHP interpreter and other tools, on your own PC or on another PC on your network.

*On the CD*

# PHP Tags

Consider the following extract from a PHP-driven web page that displays the current date:

```
Today is <?php echo date('j F Y');?>
```

The <?php tag tells PHP that everything that follows is program code rather than HTML, until the closing ?> tag. In this example, the echo command tells PHP to display the next item to screen; the following date command produces a formatted version of the current date, containing the day, month, and year.

The semicolon character is used to indicate the end of a PHP command. In the previous examples, there is only one command, and the semicolon is not actually required, but it is good practice to always include it to show that a command is complete.

*By the Way*

In this book PHP code appears inside tags that look like <?php ... ?>. Other tag styles can be used, so you may come across other people's PHP code beginning with tags that look like <? (the short tag), <% (the ASP tag style) or <SCRIPT LANGUAGE="php"> (the script tag).

Of the different tag styles that can be used, only the full <?php tag and the script tag are always available. The others are turned off or on by using a PHP configuration setting.

It is good practice to always use the <?php tag style so your code will run on any system that has PHP installed, with no additional configuration needed. If you are tempted to use <? as a shortcut, know that any time you move your code to another web server, you need to be sure it will understand this tag style.

*Did you Know?*

Anything that is not enclosed in PHP tags is passed straight through to the browser, exactly as it appears in the script. Therefore, in the previous example, the text Today is appears before the generated date when the page is displayed.

# Your First PHP Script

Before you go any further, you need to make sure you can create and run PHP scripts as you go through the examples in this book. This could be on your own machine, and you can find instructions for installing a PHP environment, along with the XAMPP software, on the accompanying CD. Also, many web hosting companies include PHP in their packages, and you may already have access to a suitable piece of web space.

Go ahead and create a new file called time.php that contains Listing 14.1, in a location that can be accessed by a PHP-enabled web server. This is a slight variation on the date example shown previously.

**LISTING 14.1**    Displaying the System Date and Time

```
The time is
<?php echo date('H:i:s');?>
and the date is
<?php echo date('j F Y');?>
```

When you enter the URL to this file in your web browser, you should see the current date and time, according to the system clock on your web server, displayed.

**Watch Out!**

If you are running PHP from your local PC, PHP code in a script will be executed only if it is accessed through a web server that has the PHP module enabled. If you open a local script directly in the web browser—for instance, by double-clicking or dragging and dropping the file into the browser—it will be treated as HTML only.

**Did you Know?**

If you were using a default Apache installation in Windows, you would create time.php in the folder C:\Program Files\Apache Group\Apache\htdocs, and the correct URL would be http://localhost/time.php. If you have loaded the XAMPP software from the CD accompanying this book, refer to the XAMPP documentation to find the location of your web folder.

If you entered Listing 14.1 exactly as shown, you might notice that the actual output produced could be formatted a little better—there is no space between the time and the word *and*. Any line in a script that only contains code inside PHP tags will not take up a line of output in the generated HTML.

Full details of how to use PHP's date format can be found at
http://es2.php.net/date

*Did you*
*Know?*

If you use the View Source option in your web browser, you can see the exact output produced by your script, which should look similar to the following:

```
The time is
15:33:09and the date is
13 October 2004
```

If you insert a space character after ?>, that line now contains non-PHP elements, and the output is spaced correctly.

## The echo **Command**

While PHP is great for embedding small, dynamic elements inside a web page, in fact the whole page could consist of a set of PHP instructions to generate the output if the entire script were enclosed in PHP tags.

The echo command is used to send output to the browser. Listing 14.1 uses echo to display the result of the date command, which returns a string that contains a formatted version of the current date. Listing 14.2 does the same thing but uses a series of echo commands in a single block of PHP code to display the date and time.

**LISTING 14.2**    Using echo **to Send Output to the Browser**

```
<?php
echo "The time is ";
echo date('H:i:s');
echo " and the date is ";
echo date('j F Y');
?>
```

The non-dynamic text elements you want to output are contained in quotation marks. Either double quotes (as used in Listing 14.2) or single quotes (the same character used for an apostrophe) can be used to enclose text strings, although you

will see an important difference between the two styles in Chapter 15, "Variables."
The following statements are equally valid:

```
echo "The time is ";
echo 'The time is ';
```

Notice that space characters are used in these statements inside the quotation marks
to ensure that the output from `date` is spaced away from the surrounding text. In
fact the output from Listing 14.2 is slightly different from that for Listing 14.1, but in
a web browser you will need to use View Source to see the difference. The raw output
from Listing 14.2 is as follows:

```
The time is 15:59:50 and the date is 13 October 2004
```

There are no line breaks in the page source produced this time. In a web browser,
the output looks just the same as for Listing 14.1 because in HTML all whitespace,
including carriage returns and multiple space or tab characters, is displayed as a
single space in a rendered web page.

A newline character inside a PHP code block does not form part of the output. Line
breaks can be used to format the code in a readable way, but several short commands could appear on the same line of code, or a long command could span several lines—that's why you use the semicolon to indicate the end of a command.

Listing 14.3 is identical to Listing 14.2 except that the formatting makes this script
almost unreadable.

**LISTING 14.3    A Badly Formatted Script That Displays the Date and Time**

```
<?php echo "The time is ";   echo date('H:i:s'); echo
" and the date is "
; echo date(
'j F Y'
);
?>
```

If you wanted to send an explicit newline character to the web browser, you could
use the character sequence \n. There are several character sequences like this
that have special meanings. Refer to the PHP documentation for details.

# Comments

Another way to make sure your code remains readable is by adding comments to it. A *comment* is a piece of free text that can appear anywhere in a script and is completely ignored by PHP. The different comment styles supported by PHP are shown in Table 4.1.

**TABLE 14.1　Comment Styles in PHP**

| Comment | Description |
|---|---|
| // or # | Single-line comment. Everything to the end of the current line is ignored. |
| /* ... */ | Single- or multiple-line comment. Everything between /* and */ is ignored. |

Listing 14.4 produces the same formatted date and time as Listings 14.1, 14.2, and 14.3, but it contains an abundance of comments. Because the comments are just ignored by PHP, the output produced consists of only the date and time.

> Refer to Chapter 4, "Creating Simple Scripts in JavaScript," to see how comments are dealt with in JavaScript. Very similar, isn't it? JavaScript does not support single-line comments delimited by #, but otherwise the use of comments is the same in JavaScript and in PHP.

**By the Way**

**LISTING 14.4　Using Comments in a Script**

```php
<?php
/* time.php
   This script prints the current date
   and time in the web browser
*/

echo "The time is ";
echo date('H:i:s');  // Hours, minutes, seconds

echo " and the date is ";
echo date('j F Y');  // Day name, month name, year
?>
```

Listing 14.4 includes a header comment block that contains the filename and a brief description, as well as inline comments that show what each date command will produce.

▼    **Try It Yourself**

### Using PHP's Date and Time Functions

Go back to the simple PHP scripts we used in Chapters 12 and 13, and check out the details of how they work by referring to this chapter.

Then try changing the date and time formats of the returned data, and see what results you get from your simple Ajax application.

▲    Add some comments to your PHP code, using the comment syntax styles explained in this chapter, to explain the changes you made.

# Summary

In this chapter you have learned how PHP works in a web environment, and you have seen what a simple PHP script looks like. In the next chapter you will learn how to use variables.

# CHAPTER 15

# Variables

---

## *What You'll Learn in This Chapter:*

- ▶ Understanding Variables
- ▶ Data Types
- ▶ Working with Numbers
- ▶ Numeric Data Types
- ▶ Numeric Functions
- ▶ Working with Strings
- ▶ Formatting Strings
- ▶ String Functions
- ▶ Working with Arrays
- ▶ Array Functions
- ▶ Date Formats
- ▶ Working with Timestamps

In this chapter you will learn how to assign values to variables in PHP and use them in some simple expressions. We shall also discuss PHP's data formats, and have a brief look at manipulating times and dates.

## Understanding Variables

In PHP, a variable name is always prefixed with a dollar sign. For instance, you could have a variable called number that holds the value 5 or a variable called name that holds the value Chris. The following PHP code declares variables with those names and values:

```
$number = 5;
$name = "Chris";
```

> Unlike in some programming languages, in PHP variables do not need to be declared before they can be used. You can assign a value to a new variable name any time you want to start using it.

Variables can be used in place of fixed values throughout the PHP language. The following example uses echo to display the value stored in a variable in the same way that you would display a piece of fixed text:

```
$name = "Chris";
echo "Hello, ";
echo $name;
```

The output produced is

```
Hello, Chris
```

## Naming Variables

Variable names can contain only letters, numbers, and the underscore character, and each must begin with a letter or underscore.

> Variable names in PHP are case-sensitive. For example, $name is a different variable than $Name, and the two could store different values in the same script.

> Using the underscore character is a handy way to give a variable a name that is made up of two or more words. For example $first_name and $date_of_birth are more readable for having underscores in place.
>
> Another popular convention for combining words is to capitalize the first letter of each word—for example, $FirstName and $DateOfBirth. If you prefer this style, feel free to use it in your scripts but remember that the capitalization does matter.

## Expressions

When a variable assignment takes place, the value given does not have to be a fixed value. It could be an *expression*—two or more values combined using an *operator* to produce a result. It should be fairly obvious how the following example works, but the following text breaks it down into its components:

```
$sum = 16 + 30;
echo $sum;
```

To show that variables can be used in place of fixed values, you can perform the same addition operation on two variables:

```
$a = 16;
$b = 30;
$sum = $a + $b;
echo $sum;
```

The values of $a and $b are added together, and once again, the output produced is 46.

## Variables in Strings

You have already seen that text strings need to be enclosed in quotation marks and learned that there is a difference between single and double quotes.

The difference is that a dollar sign in a double-quoted string indicates that the current value of that variable should become part of the string. In a single-quoted string, on the other hand, the dollar sign is treated as a literal character, and no reference is made to any variables.

The following examples should help explain this. In the following example, the value of variable $name is included in the string:

```
$name = "Chris";
echo "Hello, $name";
```

This code displays Hello, Chris.

In the following example, this time the dollar sign is treated as a literal, and no variable substitution takes place:

```
$name = 'Chris';
echo 'Hello, $name';
```

This code displays Hello, $name.

You could correct this by using the *concatenation* operator, the period symbol, which can be used to join two or more strings together, as shown in the following example:

```
echo 'Hello, '.$name;
```

# Data Types

Every variable that holds a value also has a data type that defines what kind of value it is holding. The basic data types in PHP are shown in Table 15.1.

**TABLE 15.1**    PHP Data Types

| Data Type | Description |
|---|---|
| Boolean | A truth value; can be either TRUE or FALSE. |
| Integer | A number value; can be a positive or negative whole number. |
| Double (or float) | A floating-point number value; can be any decimal number. |
| String | An alphanumeric value; can contain any number of ASCII characters. |

When you assign a value to a variable, the data type of the variable is also set. PHP determines the data type automatically, based on the value you assign. If you want to check what data type PHP thinks a value is, you can use the gettype function.

Running the following code shows that the data type of a decimal number is double:

```
$value = 7.2;
echo gettype($value);
```

The complementary function to gettype is settype, which allows you to override the data type of a variable. If the stored value is not suitable to be stored in the new type, it will be modified to the closest value possible.

# Working with Numbers

As you would expect, PHP includes all the basic arithmetic operators.

## Arithmetic Operators

Addition is performed with the plus symbol (+). This example adds 6 and 12 together and displays the result:

```
echo 6 + 12;
```

Subtraction is performed with the minus symbol:

```
echo 24 - 5;
```

The minus symbol can also be used to negate a number (for example, –20).

Multiplication is performed with the asterisk symbol:

```
echo 4 * 9;
```

Division is performed with the forward slash symbol:

```
echo 48 / 12;
```

Modulus is performed by using the percent symbol (%). This example displays 3—the remainder of 21 divided by 6:

```
echo 21 % 6;
```

The modulus operator can be used to test whether a number is odd or even by using $number % 2. The result will be 0 for all even numbers and 1 for all odd numbers (because any odd number divided by 2 has a remainder of 1).

## Incrementing and Decrementing

In PHP you can increment or decrement a number by using a double plus (++) or double minus (- -)symbol. The following statements both add one to $number:

```
$number++;
```

```
++$number;
```

The operator can be placed on either side of a variable, and its position determines at what point the increment takes place.

This statement subtracts one from $countdown before displaying the result:

```
echo --$countdown;
```

However, the following statement displays the current value of $countdown before decrementing it:

```
echo $countdown--;
```

The increment and decrement operators are commonly used in loops, which we shall discuss in the next chapter.

## Compound Operators

Compound operators provide a handy shortcut when you want to apply an arithmetic operation to an existing variable. The following example uses the compound addition operator to add six to the current value of $count:

```
$count += 6;
```

The effect of this is to take the initial value of $count, add six to it, and then assign it back to $count. In fact, the operation is equivalent to doing the following:

```
$count = $count + 6;
```

All the basic arithmetic operators have corresponding compound operators, as shown in Table 15.2.

**TABLE 15.2** Compound Operators

| Operator | Equivalent To |
| --- | --- |
| $a += $b | $a = $a + $b; |
| $a -= $b | $a = $a - $b; |
| $a *= $b | $a = $a * $b; |
| $a /= $b | $a = $a / $b; |
| $a %= $b | $a = $a % $b; |

# Numeric Data Types

You have already seen that PHP assigns a data type to each value and that the numeric data types are integer and double, for whole numbers.

To check whether a value is either of these types, you use the is_float and is_int functions. Likewise, to check for either numeric data type in one operation, you can use is_numeric.

> If you want to check that both the values and data types are the same in a condition, you use the triple equals comparison operator (===).

# Numeric Functions

Let's take a look at some of the numeric functions available in PHP.

## Rounding Numbers

There are three different PHP functions for rounding a decimal number to an integer.

You use `ceil` or `floor` to round a number up or down to the nearest integer, respectively. For example, `ceil(1.3)` returns 2, whereas `floor(6.8)` returns 6.

To round a value to the nearest whole number, you use `round`. A fractional part under .5 will be rounded down, whereas .5 or higher will be rounded up. For example, `round(1.3)` returns 1, whereas `round(1.5)` returns 2.

The `round` function can also take an optional precision argument. The following example displays a value rounded to two decimal places:

```
$score = 0.535;
echo round($score, 2);
```

The value displayed is `0.54`; the third decimal place being 5 causes the final digit to be rounded up.

# Random Numbers

You use `rand` to generate a random integer, using your system's built-in random number generator. The `rand` function optionally takes two arguments that specify the range of numbers from which the random number will be picked.

The following statement picks a random number between 1 and 10 and displays it:

```
echo rand(1, 10);
```

You can put this command in a script and run it a few times to see that the number changes each time it is run.

There is really no such thing as a computer-generated random number. In fact, numbers are actually picked from a very long sequence that has very similar properties to true random numbers. To make sure you always start from a different place in this sequence, you have to *seed* the random number generator by calling the `srand` function; no arguments are required.

# Mathematical Functions

PHP includes many mathematical functions, including trigonometry, logarithms, and number base conversions. As you will rarely need to use these in a web environment, those functions are not covered in this book.

To find out about a function that performs a specific mathematical purpose, refer to the online manual at www.php.net/manual/en/ref.math.php.

# Working with Strings

A *string* is a collection of characters that is treated as a single entity. In PHP, strings are enclosed in quotation marks, and you can declare a string type variable by assigning it a string that is contained in either single or double quotes.

The following examples are identical; both create a variable called $phrase that contains the phrase shown:

```
$phrase = "The sky is falling";
$phrase = 'The sky is falling';
```

## Escaping Characters with Backslash

Double quotes can be used within single-quoted strings and vice versa. For instance, these string assignments are both valid:

```
$phrase = "It's time to party!";
$phrase = 'So I said, "OK"';
```

However, if you want to use the same character within a quoted string, you must escape that quote by using a backslash. The following examples demonstrate this:

```
$phrase = 'It\'s time to party!";
$phrase = "So I said, \"OK\"";
```

In the previous examples, if the backslash were not used, PHP would mismatch the quotes, and an error would result.

You can send the common nonprintable ASCII characters by using standard escape characters. A newline is \n, tab is \t, and so on. Refer to man ascii on your system or www.ascii.cl for a comprehensive list.

## Concatenation

You have already seen how strings can be joined using the period symbol as a concatenation operator. A compound version of this operator, .=, can be used to append a string to an existing variable.

The following example builds up a string in stages and then displays the result:

```
$phrase = "I want ";
$phrase .= "to teach ";
$phrase .= "the world ";
$phrase .= "to sing";
echo $phrase;
```

The phrase appears as expected. Note the use of spaces after teach and world to ensure that the final string is correctly spaced.

## Comparing Strings

You can compare string values simply by using the standard comparison operators. To check whether two strings are equal, you use the double equals (==) sign:

```
if ($password == "letmein")
  echo "You have a guessable password";
```

# Formatting Strings

PHP provides a powerful way of creating formatted strings, using the printf and sprintf functions. If you have used this function in C, these will be quite familiar to you, although the syntax in PHP is a little different.

## Using printf

You use printf to display a formatted string. At its very simplest, printf takes a single string argument and behaves the same as echo:

```
printf("Hello, world");
```

The power of printf, however, lies in its ability to substitute values into placeholders in a string. Placeholders are identified by the percent character (%), followed by a format specification character.

The following example uses the simple format specifier %f to represent a float number.

```
$price = 5.99;
printf("The price is %f", $price);
```

The second argument to printf is substituted in place of %f, so the following output is produced:

```
The price is 5.99
```

There is actually no limit to the number of substitution arguments in a printf statement, as long as there are an equivalent number of placeholders in the string to be displayed. The following example demonstrates this by adding in a string item:

```
$item = "The Origin of Species";
$price = 5.99;
printf("The price of %s is %f", $item, $price);
```

Table 15.3 shows the format characters that can be used with the printf function in PHP to indicate different types of values.

**TABLE 15.3**    `printf` Format Characters

| Character | Meaning |
|---|---|
| b | A binary (base 2) number |
| c | The ASCII character with the numeric value of the argument |
| d | A signed decimal (base 10) integer |
| e | A number displayed in scientific notation (for example, 2.6e+3) |
| u | An unsigned decimal integer |
| f | A floating-point number |
| o | An octal (base 8) number |
| s | A string |
| x | A hexadecimal (base 16) number with lowercase letters |
| X | A hexadecimal (base 16) number with uppercase letters |

The precision specifier is used with a floating-point number to specify the number of decimal places to display. The most common usage is with currency values, to ensure that the two cent digits always appear, even in a whole dollar amount.

The precision value follows the optional width specifier and is indicated by a period followed by the number of decimal places to display. The following example uses `%.2f` to display a currency value with no width specifier:

```
$price = 6;
printf("The price is %.2f", $price);
```

The price is correctly formatted as follows:

```
The price is 6.00
```

With floats, the width specifier indicates only the width of the number before the decimal point. For example, `%6.2f` will actually be nine characters long, with the period and two decimal places.

## **Using** sprintf

The `sprintf` function is used to assign formatted strings to variables. The syntax is the same as for `printf`, but rather than being output as the result, the formatted value is returned by the function as a string.

For example, to assign a formatted price value to a new variable, you could do the following:

```
$new_price = sprintf("%.2f", $price);
```

All the format specifier rules that apply to `printf` also apply to `sprintf`.

# String Functions

Let's take a look at some of the other string functions available in PHP. The full list of string functions can be found in the online manual, at www.php.net/manual/en/ref.strings.php.

## Capitalization

You can switch the capitalization of a string to all uppercase or all lowercase by using `strtoupper` or `strtolower`, respectively.

The following example demonstrates the effect this has on a mixed-case string:

```
$phrase = "I love PHP";
echo strtoupper($phrase) . "<br>";
echo strtolower($phrase) . "<br>";
```

The result displayed is as follows:

```
I LOVE PHP
i love php
```

## Dissecting a String

The `substr` function allows you to extract a substring by specifying a start position within the string and a length argument. The following example shows this in action:

```
$phrase = "I love PHP";
echo substr($phrase, 3, 5);
```

This call to `substr` returns the portion of $phrase from position 3 with a length of 5 characters. Note that the position value begins at zero, not one, so the actual substring displayed is `ove P`.

If the length argument is omitted, the value returned is the substring from the position given to the end of the string. The following statement produces `love PHP` for $phrase:

```
echo substr($phrase, 2);
```

If you need to know how long a string is, you use the `strlen` function:

```
echo strlen($phrase);
```

To find the position of a character or a string within another string, you can use strpos. The first argument is often known as the *haystack*, and the second as the *needle*, to indicate their relationship.

The following example displays the position of the @ character in an email address:

```
$email = "chris@lightwood.net";
echo strpos($email, "@");
```

Remember that the character positions in a string are numbered from the left, starting from zero, so the above expression would output '5'.

The `strstr` function extracts a portion of a string from the position at which a character or string appears up to the end of the string. This is a convenience function that saves your using a combination of `strpos` and `substr`.

The following two statements are equivalent:

```
$domain = strstr($email, "@");
```

```
$domain = strstr($email, strpos($email, "@"));
```

# Working with Arrays

An *array* is a variable type that can store and index a set of values. An array is useful when the data you want to store has something in common or is logically grouped into a set.

## Creating and Accessing Arrays

The following PHP statement declares an array called $temps and assigns it 12 values that represent the temperatures for January through December:

```
$temps = array(38, 40, 49, 60, 70, 79,
               84, 83, 76, 65, 54, 42);
```

The array $temps that is created contains 12 values that are indexed with numeric key values from 0 to 11. To reference an indexed value from an array, you suffix the variable name with the index key. To display March's temperature, for example, you would use the following:

```
echo $temps[2];
```

By the Way

Because index values begin at zero by default, the value for March—the third month—is contained in the second element of the array.

The square brackets syntax can also be used to assign values to array elements. To set a new value for November, for instance, you could use the following:

```
$temps[10] = 56;
```

By the Way

The array function is a shortcut function that quickly builds an array from a supplied list of values, rather than adding each element in turn.

If you omit the index number when assigning an array element, the next highest index number will automatically be used. Starting with an empty array $temps, the following code would begin to build the same array as before:

```
$temps[] = 38;
$temps[] = 40;
$temps[] = 49;
...
```

In this example, the value 38 would be assigned to $temps[0], 40 to $temps[1], and so on. If you want to make sure that these assignments begin with $temps[0], it's a good idea to initialize the array first to make sure there is no existing data in that array. You can initialize the $temps array with the following command:

```
$temps = array();
```

## Looping Through an Array

You can easily loop through every element in an array by using a loop construct to perform another action for each value in the array.

By using a while loop, you can find all the index keys and their values from an array—similar to using the print_r function—as follows:

```
while (list($key, $value) = each($temps)) {
  echo "Key $key has value $val <br>";
}
```

For each element in the array, the index key value will be stored in $key and the value in $value.

PHP also provides another construct for traversing arrays in a loop, using a foreach construct. Whether you use a while or foreach loop is a matter of preference; you should use whichever you find easiest to read.

The `foreach` loop equivalent to the previous example is as follows:

```
foreach($temps as $key => $value) {
  ...
}
```

## Associative Arrays

The array examples so far in this chapter have used numeric keys. An *associative* array allows you to use textual keys so that the indexes can be more descriptive.

To assign a value to an array by using an associative key and to reference that value, you simply use a textual key name enclosed in quotes, as in the following examples:

```
$temps["jan"] = 38;
echo $temps["jan"];
```

To define the complete array of average monthly temperatures in this way, you can use the `array` function as before, but you indicate the key value as well as each element. You use the => symbol to show the relationship between a key and its value:

```
$temps = array("jan" => 38, "feb" => 40, "mar" => 49,
               "apr" => 60, "may" => 70, "jun" => 79,
               "jul" => 84, "aug" => 83, "sep" => 76,
               "oct" => 65, "nov" => 54, "dec" => 42);
```

The elements in an associative array are stored in the order in which they are defined (you will learn about sorting arrays later in this chapter), and traversing this array in a loop will find the elements in the order defined. You can call `print_r` on the array to verify this. The first few lines of output are as follows:

```
Array
(
    [jan] => 38
    [feb] => 40
    [mar] => 49
...
```

## Array Functions

You have already seen the `array` function used to generate an array from a list of values. Now let's take a look at some of the other functions PHP provides for manipulating arrays.

There are many more array functions in PHP than this book can cover. If you need to perform a complex array operation that you have not learned about, refer to the online documentation at www.php.net/ref.array.

## Looking Inside Arrays

The count function returns the number of elements in an array. It takes a single array argument. For example, the following statement shows that there are 12 values in the $temps array:

```
echo count($temps);
```

To find out whether a value exists within an array without having to write a loop to search through every value, you can use in_array or array_search. The first argument is the value to search for, and the second is the array to look inside:

```
if (in_array("PHP", $languages)) {
  ...
}
```

The difference between these functions is the return value. If the value exists within the array, array_search returns the corresponding key, whereas in_array returns only a Boolean result.

> Somewhat confusingly, the order of the *needle* and *haystack* arguments to in_array and array_search is opposite that of string functions, such as strpos and strstr.

**Watch**
*Out!*

# Date Formats

PHP does not have a native date data type, so in order to store date values in a script, you must first decide on the best way to store these values.

## Do-It-Yourself Date Formats

Although you often see dates written in a structured format, such as 05/03/1974 or 2001-12-31, these are not ideal formats for working with date values. However, the latter of these two is more suitable than the first because the order of its components is from most significant (the year) to the least significant (the day), so values can be compared using the usual PHP operators.

As a string, 2002-01-01 is greater than 2001-12-31, but because comparisons are performed more efficiently on numbers than on strings, this could be written better as just 20020201, where the format is YYYYMMDD. This format can be extended to include a time portion—again, with the most significant elements first—as YYYYM-MDDHHMMSS, for example.

However, date arithmetic with this format is nearly impossible. While you can add one to 20040501, for instance, and find the next day in that month, simply adding one to 20030531 would result in a nonsense date of May 32.

## UNIX Timestamp Format

The UNIX timestamp format is an integer representation of a date and time. It is a value that counts the number of seconds since midnight on January 1, 1970 and was discussed briefly in Chapter 9.

Right now, we have a 10-digit date and time timestamp. To find the current timestamp, you use the `time` function:

```
echo time();
```

The UNIX timestamp format is useful because it is very easy to perform calculations on because you know that the value always represents a number of seconds. For example, you can just add 3,600 to a timestamp value to increase the time by one hour or add 86,400 to add one day—because there are 3,600 seconds in an hour and 86,400 seconds in a day.

One drawback, however, is that the UNIX timestamp format cannot handle dates prior to 1970. Although some systems may be able to use a negative timestamp value to count backward from the Epoch, this behavior cannot be relied on.

Timestamps are good for representing contemporary date values, but they may not always be suitable for handling dates of birth or dates of historical significance. You should consider what values you will be working with when deciding whether a timestamp is the correct format to use.

# Working with Timestamps

There are times when using your own date format is beneficial, but in most cases a timestamp is the best choice. Let's look at how PHP interacts with the timestamp date format.

## Formatting Dates

In Chapter 14, "Getting to Know PHP," you used the `date` function to display the current date by passing a format string as the argument, such as in the following example:

```
echo date("j F Y H:i:s");
```

The date displayed looks something like this:

```
12 November 2004 10:23:55
```

The optional second argument to date is a timestamp value of the date that you want to display. For example, to display the date when a timestamp first requires a 10-digit number, you could use the following:

```
echo date("j F Y H:I:s", 1000000000);
```

The list of format codes for the date function is shown in Table 15.4.

**TABLE 15.4**    Format Codes for date

| Code | Description |
| --- | --- |
| a | Lowercase am or pm |
| A | Uppercase AM or PM |
| d | Two-digit day of month, 01–31 |
| D | Three-letter day name, Mon–Sun |
| F | Full month name, January–December |
| g | 12-hour hour with no leading zero, 1–12 |
| G | 24-hour hour with no leading zero, 0–23 |
| h | 12-hour hour with leading zero, 01–12 |
| H | 24-hour hour with leading zero, 00–23 |
| I | Minutes with leading zero, 00–59 |
| j | Day of month with no leading zero, 1–31 |
| l | Full day name, Monday–Sunday |
| m | Month number with leading zeros, 01–12 |
| M | Three-letter month name, Jan–Dec |
| n | Month number with no leading zeros, 1–12 |
| s | Seconds with leading zero, 00–59 |
| S | Ordinal suffix for day of month, st, nd, rd, or th |
| w | Number of day of week, 0–6, where 0 is Sunday |
| W | Week number, 0–53 |
| y | Two-digit year number |
| Y | Four-digit year number |
| z | Day of year, 0–365 |

## Creating Timestamps

Don't worry; you don't have to count from January 1, 1970, each time you want to calculate a timestamp. The PHP function `mktime` returns a timestamp based on given date and time values.

The arguments, in order, are the hour, minute, second, month, day, and year. The following example would assign $timestamp the timestamp value for 8 a.m. on December 25, 2001:

```
$timestamp = mktime(8, 0, 0, 12, 25, 2001);
```

The UNIX timestamp format counts from January 1, 1970, at midnight GMT. The `mktime` function returns a timestamp relative to the time zone in which your system operates. For instance, `mktime` would return a timestamp value 3,600 higher when running on a web server in Texas than on a machine in New York with the same arguments.

The `mktime` function is forgiving if you supply it with nonsense arguments, such as a day of the month that doesn't exist. For instance, if you try to calculate a timestamp for February 29 in a non-leap year, the value returned will actually represent March 1, as the following statement confirms:

```
echo date("d/m/Y", mktime(12, 0, 0, 2, 29, 2003));
```

You can exploit this behavior as a way of performing date and time arithmetic. Consider the following example, which calculates and displays the date and time 37 hours after midday on December 30, 2001:

```
$time = mktime(12 + 37, 0, 0, 12, 30, 2001);
echo date("d/m/Y H:i:s", $time);
```

By simply adding a constant to one of the arguments in `mktime`, you can shift the timestamp value returned by that amount. The date and time display as follows:

```
01/01/2002 01:00:00
```

The value returned in this example has correctly shifted the day, month, year, and hour values, taking into account the number of days in December and that December is the last month of the year.

## Converting Other Date Formats to Timestamps

If you have a date stored in a format like DD-MM-YYYY, it's a fairly simple process to convert this to a timestamp by breaking up the string around the hyphen character. The explode function takes a delimiter argument and a string and returns an array that contains each part of the string that was separated by the given delimiter.

The following example breaks a date in this format into its components and builds a timestamp from those values:

```
$date = "03-05-1974";
$parts = explode("/", $date);
$timestamp = mktime(12, 0, 0,
                $parts[1], $parts[0], $parts[2]);
```

For many date formats, there is an even easier way to create a timestamp—using the function strtotime. The following examples all display the same valid time-stamp from a string date value:

```
$timestamp = strtotime("3 May 04");
$timestamp = strtotime("3rd May 2004");
$timestamp = strtotime("May 3, 2004");
$timestamp = strtotime("3-may-04");
$timestamp = strtotime("2004-05-03");
$timestamp = strtotime("05/03/2004");
```

Note that in the last examples, the date format given is MM/DD/YYYY, not DD/MM/YYYY. You can find the complete list of formats that are acceptable to strto-time at www.gnu.org/software/tar/manual/html_chapter/tar_7.html.

# Summary

In this chapter you have learned about variables in PHP, and about the data for-mats that can be stored within them, and also how to store and manipulate date and time values in PHP. In the next chapter you will learn about classes in PHP, and you will discover how to use third-party library classes that you download.

# CHAPTER 16

# Flow Control

## What You'll Learn on This Chapter:

▶ Conditional Statements
▶ Loops

In this chapter you will learn about the conditional and looping constructs that allow you to control the flow of a PHP script.

In this chapter we'll look at two types of flow control: conditional statements, which tell your script to execute a section of code only if certain criteria are met, and loops, which indicate a block of code that is to be repeated a number of times.

## Conditional Statements

A conditional statement in PHP begins with the keyword if, followed by a condition in parentheses. The following example checks whether the value of the variable $number is less than 10, and the echo statement displays its message only if this is the case:

```
$number = 5;
if ($number < 10) {
  echo "$number is less than ten";
}
```

The condition $number < 10 is satisfied if the value on the left of the < symbol is smaller than the value on the right. If this condition holds true, then the code in the following set of braces will be executed; otherwise, the script jumps to the next statement after the closing brace.

**By the Way**

Every conditional expression evaluates to a Boolean value, and an `if` statement simply acts on a TRUE or FALSE value to determine whether the next block of code should be executed. Any zero value in PHP is considered FALSE, and any nonzero value is considered TRUE.

As it stands, the previous example will be TRUE because 5 is less than 10, so the statement in braces is executed, and the corresponding output is displayed. Now, if you change the initial value of $number to 10 or higher and rerun the script, the condition fails, and no output is produced.

Braces are used in PHP to group blocks of code together. In a conditional statement, they surround the section of code that is to be executed if the preceding condition is true.

**Did you Know?**

You will come across three types of brackets when writing PHP scripts. The most commonly used terminology for each type is parentheses (( )), braces ({ }), and square brackets ([ ]).

Braces are not required after an `if` statement. If they are omitted, the following single statement is executed if the condition is true. Any subsequent statements are executed, regardless of the status of the conditional.

**Did you Know?**

Although how your code is indented makes no difference to PHP, it is customary to indent blocks of code inside braces with a few space characters to visually separate that block from other statements.

Even if you only want a condition or loop to apply to one statement, it is still useful to use braces for clarity. It is particularly important in order to keep things readable when you're nesting multiple constructs.

## Conditional Operators

PHP allows you to perform a number of different comparisons, to check for the equality or relative size of two values. PHP's conditional operators are shown in Table 16.1.

**TABLE 16.1**  Conditional Operators in PHP

| Operator | Description |
|----------|-------------|
| == | Is equal to |
| === | Is identical to (is equal and is the same data type) |
| != | Is not equal to |
| !== | Is not identical to |
| < | Is less than |
| <= | Is less than or equal to |
| > | Is greater than |
| >= | Is greater than or equal to |

---

> Be careful when comparing for equality to use a double equals symbol (==). A single = is always an assignment operator and, unless the value assigned is zero, your condition will always return true—and remember that TRUE is any nonzero value. Always use == when comparing two values to avoid headaches.

**Watch Out!**

## Logical Operators

You can combine multiple expressions to check two or more criteria in a single conditional statement. For example, the following statement checks whether the value of $number is between 5 and 10:

```
$number = 8;
if ($number >= 5 and $number <= 10) {
  echo "$number is between five and ten";
}
```

The keyword and is a *logical operator,* which signifies that the overall condition will be true only if the expressions on either side are true. That is, $number has to be both greater than or equal to 5 and less than or equal to 10.

Table 16.2 shows the logical operators that can be used in PHP.

**TABLE 16.2**   Logical Operators in PHP

| Operator | Name | Description |
|---|---|---|
| ! *a* | NOT | True if *a* is not true |
| *a* && *b* | AND | True if both *a* and *b* are true |
| *a* ¦¦ *b* | OR | True if either *a* or *b* is true |
| *a* and *b* | AND | True if both *a* and *b* are true |
| *a* xor *b* | XOR | True if *a* or *b* is true, but not both |
| *a* or *b* | OR | True if either *a* or *b* is true |

You may have noticed that there are two different ways of performing a logical AND or OR in PHP. The difference between and and && (and between or and ¦¦) is the precedence used to evaluate expressions.

Table 16.2 lists the highest-precedence operators first. The following conditions, which appear to do the same thing, are subtly but significantly different:

```
a or b and c
a ¦¦ b and c
```

In the former condition, the and takes precedence and is evaluated first. The overall condition is true if *a* is true or if both *b* and *c* are true.

In the latter condition, the ¦¦ takes precedence, so *c* must be true, as must either *a* or *b*, to satisfy the condition.

## Multiple Condition Branches

By using an else clause with an if statement, you can specify an alternate action to be taken if the condition is not met. The following example tests the value of $number and displays a message that says whether it is greater than or less than 10:

```
$number = 16;
if ($number < 10) {
  echo "$number is less than ten";
}
else {
  echo "$number is more than ten";
}
```

The else clause provides an either/or mechanism for conditional statements. To add more branches to a conditional statement, the elseif keyword can be used to add a further condition that is checked only if the previous condition in the statement fails.

The following example uses the date function to find the current time of day—
date("H") gives a number between 0 and 23 that represents the hour on the
clock—and displays an appropriate greeting:

```
$hour = date("H");
if ($hour < 12) {
  echo "Good morning";
}
elseif ($hour < 17) {
  echo "Good afternoon";
}
else {
  echo "Good evening";
}
```

This code displays Good morning if the server time is between midnight and 11:59,
Good afternoon from midday to 4:59 p.m., and Good evening from 5 p.m.
onward.

Notice that the elseif condition only checks that $hour is less than 17 (5 p.m.). It
does not need to check that the value is between 12 and 17 because the initial if
condition ensures that PHP will not get as far as the elseif if $hour is less than 12.

The code in the else clause is executed if all else fails. For values of $hour that are
17 or higher, neither the if nor the elseif condition will be true.

> In PHP you can also write elseif as two words: else if. The way PHP interprets
> this variation is slightly different, but its behavior is exactly the same.

**By the Way**

# **The** switch **Statement**

An if statement can contain as many elseif clauses as you need, but including
many of these clauses can often create cumbersome code, and an alternative is
available. switch is a conditional statement that can have multiple branches in a
much more compact format.

The following example uses a switch statement to check $name against two lists to
see whether it belongs to a friend:

```
switch ($name) {
  case "Damon":
  case "Shelley":
    echo "Welcome, $name, you are my friend";
    break;
  case "Adolf":
  case "Saddam":
    echo "You are no friend of mine, $name";
```

```
    break;
  default:
    echo "I do not know who you are, $name";
}
```

Each case statement defines a value for which the next block of PHP code will be
executed. If you assign your first name to $name and run this script, you will be
greeted as a friend if your name is Damon or Shelley, and you will be told that you
are not a friend if your name is either Adolf or Saddam. If you have any other
name, the script will tell you it does not know who you are.

There can be any number of case statements preceding the PHP code to which they
relate. If the value that is being tested by the switch statement (in this case $name)
matches any one of them, any subsequent PHP code will be executed until a break
command is reached.

**Watch
Out!**

> The break statement is important in a switch statement. When a case state-
> ment has been matched, any PHP code that follows will be executed—even if
> there is another case statement checking for a different value. This behavior can
> sometimes be useful, but mostly it is not what you want—so remember to put a
> break after every case.

Any other value for $name will cause the default code block to be executed. As with
an else clause, default is optional and supplies an action to be taken if nothing
else is appropriate.

# Loops

PHP offers three types of loop constructs that all do the same thing—repeat a section
of code a number of times—in slightly different ways.

## The while Loop

The while keyword takes a condition in parentheses, and the code block that follows is repeated while that condition is true. If the condition is false initially, the
code block will not be repeated at all.

**By the
Way**

> The repeating code must perform some action that affects the condition in such a
> way that the loop condition will eventually no longer be met; otherwise, the loop
> will repeat forever.

The following example uses a while loop to display the square numbers from 1 to 10:

```
$count = 1;
while ($count <= 10) {
  $square = $count * $count;
  print "$count squared is $square <br>";
  $count++;
}
```

The counter variable $count is initialized with a value of 1. The while loop calculates the square of that number and displays it, then adds one to the value of $count. The ++ operator adds one to the value of the variable that precedes it.

The loop repeats while the condition $count <= 10 is true, so the first 10 numbers and their squares are displayed in turn, and then the loop ends.

## The do **Loop**

The do loop is very similar to the while loop except that the condition comes after the block of repeating code. Because of this variation, the loop code is always executed at least once—even if the condition is initially false.

The following do loop is equivalent to the previous example, displaying the numbers from 1 to 10, with their squares:

```
$count = 1;
do {
  $square = $count * $count;
  print "$count squared is $square <br>";
  $count++;
} while ($count <= 10);
```

## The for **Loop**

The for loop provides a compact way to create a loop. The following example performs the same loop as the previous two examples:

```
for ($count = 1; $count <= 10; $count++) {
  $square = $count * $count;
  print "$count squared is $square <br>";
}
```

As you can see, using for allows you to use much less code to do the same thing as with while and do.

A `for` statement has three parts, separated by semicolons:

- ▶ The first part is an expression that is evaluated once when the loop begins. In the preceding example, you initialized the value of `$count`.

- ▶ The second part is the condition. While the condition is true, the loop continues repeating. As with a `while` loop, if the condition is false to start with, the following code block is not executed at all.

- ▶ The third part is an expression that is evaluated once at the end of each pass of the loop. In the previous example, `$count` is incremented after each line of the output is displayed.

## Nesting Conditions and Loops

So far you have only seen simple examples of conditions and loops. However, you can nest these constructs within each other to create some quite complex rules to control the flow of a script.

**Did you Know?**

The more complex the flow control in your script is, the more important it becomes to indent your code to make it clear which blocks of code correspond to which constructs.

## Breaking Out of a Loop

You have already learned about using the keyword `break` in a `switch` statement. You can also use `break` in a loop construct to tell PHP to immediately exit the loop and continue with the rest of the script.

The `continue` keyword is used to end the current pass of a loop. However, unlike with `break`, the script jumps back to the top of the same loop and continues execution until the loop condition fails.

# Summary

In this chapter you have learned how to vary the flow of your PHP script by using conditional statements and loops. In the next chapter you will see how to create reusable functions from blocks of PHP code.

# CHAPTER 17

# Functions

## What You'll Learn in This Chapter:

▶ Using Functions
▶ Arguments and Return Values
▶ Using Library Files

In this chapter you will learn how frequently used sections of code can be turned into reusable functions.

# Using Functions

A *function* is used to make a task that might consist of many lines of code into a routine that can be called using a single instruction.

PHP contains many functions that perform a wide range of useful tasks. Some are built in to the PHP language; others are more specialized and are available only if certain extensions are activated when PHP is installed.

The online PHP manual (www.php.net) is an invaluable reference. As well as documentation for every function in the language, the manual pages are also annotated with user-submitted tips and examples, and you can even submit your own comments if you want.

To quickly pull up the PHP manual page for any function, use this shortcut: www.php.net/ *function_name*.

You have already used the date function to generate a string that contains a formatted version of the current date. Let's take a closer look at how that example from Chapter 14, "Getting to Know PHP," works. The example looked like this:

```
echo date('j F Y');
```

The online PHP manual gives the prototype for date as follows:

```
string date (string format [, int timestamp])
```

This means that date takes a string argument called format and, optionally, the integer timestamp. It returns a string value. This example sends j F Y to the function as the format argument, but timestamp is omitted. The echo command displays the string that is returned.

**By the Way**

> Every function has a prototype that defines how many arguments it takes, the arguments' data types, and what value is returned. Optional arguments are shown in square brackets ([ ]).

## Defining Functions

In addition to the built-in functions, PHP allows you to define your own. There are advantages to using your own function. Not only do you have to type less when the same piece of code has to be executed several times but a custom-defined function also makes your script easier to maintain. If you want to change the way a task is performed, you only need to update the program code once—in the function definition—rather than fix it every place it appears in your script.

**Did you Know?**

> Grouping tasks into functions is the first step toward *modularizing* your code— something that is especially important to keep your scripts manageable as they grow in size and become more complex.

The following is a simple example that shows how a function is defined and used in PHP:

```
function add_tax($amount) {
  $total = $amount * 1.09;
  return $total;
}

$price = 16.00;
echo "Price before tax: $price <br>";
echo "Price after tax: ";
echo add_tax($price);
```

The `function` keyword defines a function called `add_tax` that will execute the code block that follows. The code that makes up a function is always contained in braces. Putting `$amount` in parentheses after the function name stipulates that `add_tax` takes a single argument that will be stored in a variable called `$amount` inside the function.

The first line of the function code is a simple calculation that multiplies `$amount` by 1.09—which is equivalent to adding 9% to that value—and assigns the result to `$total`. The `return` keyword is followed by the value that is to be returned when the function is called from within the script.

Running this example produces the following output:

```
Price before tax: 16
Price after tax: 17.44
```

This is an example of a function that you might use in many places in a web page; for instance, on a page that lists all the products available in an online store, you would call this function once for each item that is displayed to show the after-tax price. If the rate of tax changes, you only need to change the formula in `add_tax` to alter every price displayed on that page.

# Arguments and Return Values

Every function call consists of the function name followed by a list of arguments in parentheses. If there is more than one argument, the list items are separated with commas. Some functions do not require any arguments at all, but a pair of parentheses is still required—even if there are no arguments contained in them.

The built-in function `phpinfo` generates a web page that contains a lot of information about the PHP module. This function does not require any arguments, so it can be called from a script that is as simple as

```
<?php phpinfo();?>
```

If you create this script and point a web browser at it, you will see a web page that contains system information and configuration settings.

## Returning Success or Failure

Because `phpinfo` generates its own output, you do not need to prefix it with `echo`, but, for the same reason, you cannot assign the web page it produces to a variable. In fact, the return value from `phpinfo` is the integer value 1.

By the Way

> Functions that do not have an explicit return value usually use a return code to indicate whether their operation has completed successfully. A zero value (FALSE) indicates failure, and a nonzero value (TRUE) indicates success.

The following example uses the `mail` function to attempt to send an email from a PHP script. The first three arguments to `mail` specify the recipient's email address, the message subject, and the message body. The return value of `mail` is used in an `if` condition to check whether the function was successful:

```
if (mail("chris@lightwood.net", "Hello", "This is a test email")) {
  echo "Email was sent successfully";
}
else {
  echo "Email could not be sent";
}
```

If the web server that this script is run on is not properly configured to send email, or if there is some other error when trying to send, `mail` will return zero, indicating that the email could not be sent. A nonzero value indicates that the message was handed off to your mail server for sending.

By the Way

> Although you will not always need to test the return value of every function, you should be aware that every function in PHP does return some value.

## Default Argument Values

The `mail` function is an example of a function that takes multiple arguments; the recipient, subject, and message body are all required. The prototype for `mail` also specifies that this function can take an optional fourth argument, which can contain additional mail headers.

Calling `mail` with too few arguments results in a warning. For instance, a script that contains the following:

```
mail("chris@lightwood.net", "Hello");
```

will produce a warning similar to this:

```
Warning: mail() expects at least 3 parameters, 2 given in
/home/chris/mail.php on line 3
```

However, the following two calls to `mail` are both valid:

```
mail("chris@lightwood.net", "Hello", "This is a test email");

mail("chris@lightwood.net", "Hello", "This is a test email",
    "Cc: editor@samspublishing.com");
```

To have more than one argument in your own function, you simply use a comma-separated list of variable names in the function definition. To make one of these arguments optional, you assign it a default value in the argument list, the same way you would assign a value to a variable.

The following example is a variation of add_tax that takes two arguments—the net amount and the tax rate to add on. $rate has a default value of 10, so it is an optional argument:

```
function add_tax_rate($amount, $rate=10) {
  $total = $amount * (1 + ($rate / 100));
  return($total);
}
```

Using this function, the following two calls are both valid:

```
add_tax_rate(16);
add_tax_rate(16, 9);
```

The first example uses the default rate of 10%, whereas the second example specifies a rate of 9% to be used—producing the same behavior as the original add_tax function example.

> All the optional arguments to a function must appear at the end of the argument list, with the required values passed in first. Otherwise, PHP will not know which arguments you are passing to the function.

**Watch Out!**

# Variable Scope

The reason values have to be passed in to functions as arguments has to do with *variable scope*—the rules that determine what sections of script are able to access which variables.

The basic rule is that any variables defined in the main body of the script cannot be used inside a function. Likewise, any variables used inside a function cannot be seen by the main script.

**By the Way**

Variables available within a function are said to be *local variables* or that their scope is local to that function. Variables that are not local are called *global variables*.

Local and global variables can have the same name and contain different values, although it is best to try to avoid this to make your script easier to read.

When called, add_tax calculates $total, and this is the value returned. However, even after add_tax is called, the local variable $total is undefined outside that function.

The following piece of code attempts to display the value of a global variable from inside a function:

```
function display_value() {
  echo $value;
}

$value = 125;
display_value();
```

If you run this script, you will see that no output is produced because $value has not been declared in the local scope.

To access a global variable inside a function, you must use the global keyword at the top of the function code. Doing so overrides the scope of that variable so that it can be read and altered within the function. The following code shows an example:

```
function change_value() {
  global $value;
  echo "Before: $value <br>";
  $value = $value * 2;
}
$value = 100;
display_value();
echo "After: $value <br>";
```

The value of $value can now be accessed inside the function, so the output produced is as follows:

```
Before: 100
After: 200
```

# Using Library Files

After you have created a function that does something useful, you will probably want to use it again in other scripts. Rather than copy the function definition into each script that needs to use it, you can use a library file so that your function needs to be stored and maintained in only one place.

Before you go any further, you should create a library file called `tax.php` that contains both the add_tax and add_tax_rate functions but no other PHP code.

> A library file needs to enclose its PHP code inside <?php tags just like a regular script; otherwise, the contents will be displayed as HTML when they are included in a script.

## Including Library Files

To incorporate an external library file into another script, you use the `include` keyword. The following includes `tax.php` so that add_tax can be called in that script:

```
include "tax.php";
$price = 95;
echo "Price before tax: $price <br>";
echo "Price after tax: ";
echo add_tax($price);
```

You can use the `include_once` keyword if you want to make sure that a library file is loaded only once. If a script attempts to define the same function a second time, an error will result. Using `include_once` helps to avoid this, particularly when files are being included from other library files. It is often useful to have a library file that includes several other files, each containing a few functions, rather than one huge library file.

> The `require` and `require_once` instructions work in a similar way to `include` and `include_once` but have subtly different behavior. In the event of an error, `include` generates a warning, but the script carries on running as best it can. A failure from a `require` statement causes the script to exit immediately.

**Did you Know?**

# Summary

In this chapter you have learned how to use functions to modularize your code. In the next chapter you will learn about ways to work with classes in PHP.

# CHAPTER 18

# Using Classes

In this chapter you will learn the basics of object-oriented PHP. You will see how a class is defined and how you can access methods and properties from third-party classes.

## Object-Oriented PHP

PHP can, if you want, be written in an object-oriented (OO) fashion. In PHP5, the OO functionality of the language has been enhanced considerably.

If you are familiar with other OO languages, such as C++ or Java, you may prefer the OO approach to programming PHP, whereas if you are used to other procedural languages, you may not want to use objects at all. There are, after all, many ways to solve the same problem.

If you are new to programming as well as to PHP, you probably have no strong feelings either way just yet. It's certainly true that OO concepts are easier to grasp if you have no programming experience at all than if you have a background in a procedural language, but even so OO methods are not something that can be taught in a brief chapter in this book!

The aim of this chapter is to introduce how a class is created and referenced in PHP so that if you have a preference for using objects, you can begin to develop scripts by using OO methods. Most importantly, however, you will be able to pick up and use some of the many freely available third-party class libraries that are available for PHP from resources such as those at www.phpclasses.org.

# What Is a Class?

A *class* is the template structure that defines an object. It can contain *functions*—also known as *class methods*—and *variables*—also known as *class properties* or *attributes*.

Each class consists of a set of PHP statements that define how to perform a task or set of tasks that you want to repeat frequently. The class can contain *private* methods, which are only used internally to perform the class's functions, and *public* methods, which you can use to interface with the class.

A good class hides its inner workings and includes only the public methods that are required to provide a simple interface to its functionality. If you bundle complex blocks of programming into a class, any script that uses that class does not need to worry about exactly how a particular operation is performed. All that is required is knowledge of the class's public methods.

Because there are many freely available third-party classes for PHP, in many situations, you need not waste time implementing a feature in PHP that is already freely available.

## When to Use Classes

At first, there may not appear to be any real advantage in using a class over using functions that have been modularized into an include file. OO is not necessarily a better approach to programming; rather, it is a different way of thinking. Whether you choose to develop your own classes is a matter of preference.

One of the advantages of OO programming is that it can allow your code to scale into very large projects easily. In OO programming, a class can inherit the properties of another and extend it; this means that functionality that has already been developed can be reused and adapted to fit a particular situation. This is called *inheritance*, and it is a key feature of OO development.

When you have completed this book, if you are interested in learning more about OO programming, take a look at *Sams Teach Yourself Object-Oriented Programming in 21 Days* by Anthony Sintes.

## What a Class Looks Like

A class is a grouping of various functions and variables—and that is exactly how it looks when written in PHP. A class definition looks very similar to a function definition; it begins with the keyword `class` and an identifier, followed by the class definition, contained in a pair of curly brackets ({}).

The following is a trivial example of a class to show how a class looks. This example contains just one property, myValue, and one method, myMethod (which does nothing):

```
class myClass {
  var $myValue;

  function myMethod() {
    return 0;
  }
}
```

If you are already familiar with OO programming and want to get a head start with OO PHP, you can refer to the online documentation at www.php.net/manual/en/language.oop5.php.

# Creating and Using Objects

To create an instance of an object from a class, you use the new keyword in PHP, as follows:

```
$myObject = new myClass;
```

In this example, myClass is the name of a class that must be defined in the script—usually in an include file—and $myObject becomes a myClass object.

> You can use the same class many times in the same script by simply creating new instances from that class but with new object names.

## Methods and Properties

The methods and properties defined in myClass can be referenced for $myObject. The following are generic examples:

```
$myObject->myValue = "555-1234";
$myObject->myMethod();
```

The arrow symbol (->)—made up of a hyphen and greater-than symbol—indicates a method or property of the given object. To reference the current object within the class definition, you use the special name $this.

The following example defines myClass with a method that references one of the object properties:

```
class myClass {
  var $myValue = "Jelly";
```

```
  function myMethod() {
    echo "myValue is " . $this->myValue . "<br>";
  }
}

$myObject = new myClass;
$myObject->myMethod();
$myObject->myValue = "Custard";
$myObject->myMethod();
```

This example makes two separate calls to myMethod. The first time it displays the default value of myValue; an assignment within the class specifies a default value for a property. The second call comes after that property has had a new value assigned. The class uses $this to reference its own property and does not care, or even know, that in the script its name is $myObject.

If the class includes a special method known as a *constructor*, arguments can be supplied in parentheses when an object is created, and those values are later passed to the constructor function. This is usually done to initialize a set of properties for each object instance, and it looks similar to the following:

```
$myObject = new myClass($var1, $var2);
```

## Using a Third-Party Class

The best way to learn how to work with classes is to use one. Let's take a look at a popular third-party class written by Manuel Lemos, which provides a comprehensive way to validate email addresses. You can download this class from www.phpclasses.org/browse/file/28.html and save the file locally as email_validation.php.

Manuel's class validates an email address not only by checking that its format is correct but also by performing a domain name lookup to ensure that it can be delivered. It even connects to the remote mail server to make sure the given mailbox actually exists.

**By the Way**

> If you are following this example on a Windows-based web server, you need to download an additional file, getmxrr.php, to add a suitable domain name lookup function to PHP. You can download this file from www.phpclasses.org/browse/file/2080.html.

The email_validation.php script defines a class called email_validation_class, so you first need to create a new instance of a validator object called $validator, as follows:

```
$validator = new email_validation_class;
```

You can set a number of properties for your new class. Some are required in order for the class to work properly, and others allow you to change the default behavior.

Each object instance requires you to set the properties that contain the mailbox and domain parts of a real email address, which is the address that will be given to the remote mail server when checking a mailbox. There are no default values for these properties; they always have to be set as follows:

```
$validator->localuser = "chris";
$validator->localhost = "lightwood.net";
```

The optional timeout property defines how many seconds to wait when connected to a remote mail server before giving up. Setting the debug property causes the text of the communication with the remote server to be displayed onscreen. You never need to do this, though, unless you are interested in what is going on. The following statements define a timeout of 10 seconds and turn on debug output:

```
$validator->timeout = 10;
$validator->debug = TRUE;
```

The full list of adjustable properties for a validator object is shown in Table 18.1.

**TABLE 18.1**  Properties of an email_validation_class Object

| Property | Description |
| --- | --- |
| timeout | Indicates the number of seconds before timing out when connecting to a destination mail server |
| data_timeout | Indicates the number of seconds before timing out while data is exchanged with the mail server; if zero, takes the value of timeout |
| localuser | Indicates the user part of the email address of the sending user |
| localhost | Indicates the domain part of the email address of the sending user |
| debug | Indicates whether to output the text of the communication with the mail server |
| html_debug | Indicates whether the debug output should be formatted as an HTML page |

The methods in email_validation_class are mostly private; you cannot call them directly, but the internal code is made up of a set of functions. If you examine email_validation.php, you will see function definitions, including Tokenize, GetLine, and VerifyResultLines, but none of these are useful outside the object itself.

The only public method in a validator object is named `ValidateEmailBox`, and when called, it initiates the email address validation of a string argument. The following example shows how `ValidateEmailBox` is called:

```
$email = "chris@datasnake.co.uk";
if ($validator->ValidateEmailBox($email)) {
  echo "$email is a valid email address";
}
else {
  echo "$email could not be validated";
}
```

The return value from `ValidateEmailBox` indicates whether the validation check is successful. If you have turned on the debug attribute, you will also see output similar to the following, in addition to the output from the script:

```
Resolving host name "mail.datasnake.co.uk"...
Connecting to host address "217.158.68.125"...
Connected.
S 220 mail.datasnake.co.uk ESMTP
C HELO lightwood.net
S 250 mail.datasnake.co.uk
C MAIL FROM: <chris@lightwood.net>
S 250 ok
C RCPT TO: <chris@datasnake.co.uk>
S 250 ok
C DATA
S 354 go ahead
This host states that the address is valid.
Disconnected.
```

# Summary

In this chapter you have learned about OO PHP and seen how to use classes in your own scripts.

Here we conclude Part IV of the book, in which we've discussed PHP in some detail. Next, in Part V "More Complex Ajax Technologies," we return to Ajax to explore some more challenging uses of the technology.

# PART V

# More Complex Ajax Technologies

# CHAPTER 19

# Returning Data as Text

---

## What You'll Learn in This Chapter:

▶ Getting More from the responseText Property

In this chapter you will learn some more techniques for using the responseText property to add functionality to Ajax applications.

## Getting More from the responseText Property

The chapters of Part III, "Introducing Ajax," discussed the individual components that make Ajax work, culminating in a complete Ajax application. In Part V, "More Complex Ajax Technologies," each chapter examines how you can extend what you know to develop more sophisticated Ajax applications.

For this chapter, we'll look a little more closely at the responseText property of the XMLHTTPRequest object and see how we can give our application some extra functionality via its use.

As you have seen in previous chapters, the XMLHTTPRequest object provides two properties that contain information received from the server, namely responseText and responseXML. The former presents the calling application with the server data in string format, whereas the latter provides DOM-compatible XML that can be parsed using JavaScript methods.

Although the responseXML property allows you to carry out some sophisticated programming tasks, much can be achieved just by manipulating the value stored in the responseText property.

## Returning Text

The term *text* is perhaps a little misleading. The `responseText` property contains a character string, the value of which you can assign to a JavaScript variable via a simple assignment statement:

```
var mytext = http.responseText;
```

There is no rule saying that the value contained in such a string must be legible text; in fact, the value can contain complete gibberish provided that the string contains only characters that JavaScript accepts in a string variable.

This fact allows a degree of flexibility in what sorts of information you can transfer using this property.

## Using Returned Text Directly in Page Elements

Perhaps the simplest example is to consider the use of the value held in `responseText` in updating the textual part of a page element, say a `<div>` container. In this case you may simply take the returned string and apply it to the page element in question.

Here's a simple example. The following is the HTML code for an HTML page that forms the basis for an Ajax application:

```
<html>
<head>
  <title>My Ajax Application</title>
</head>
<body>
Here is the text returned by the server:<br />
<div id="myPageElement"></div>
</body>
</html>
```

Clearly this is a simple page that, as it stands, would merely output the line "Here is the text returned by the server:" and nothing else.

Now suppose that we add to the page the necessary JavaScript routines to generate an instance of an `XMLHTTPRequest` object (in this case called `http`) and make a server request in response to the `onLoad()` event handler of the page's `<body>` element. Listing 19.1 shows the source code for the revised page.

**LISTING 19.1**   A Basic Ajax Application Using the responseText Property

```
<html>
<head>
<title>My Ajax Application</title>
<script Language="JavaScript">
function getXMLHTTPRequest() {
try {
req = new XMLHttpRequest();
} catch(err1) {
  try {
  req = new ActiveXObject("Msxml2.XMLHTTP");
  } catch (err2) {
    try {
    req = new ActiveXObject("Microsoft.XMLHTTP");
    } catch (err3) {
      req = false;
    }
  }
}
return req;
}

var http = getXMLHTTPRequest();

function getServerText() {
  var myurl = 'textserver.php';
  myRand = parseInt(Math.random()*999999999999999);
  var modurl = myurl+"?rand="+myRand;
  http.open("GET", modurl, true);
  http.onreadystatechange = useHttpResponse;
  http.send(null);
}

function useHttpResponse() {
   if (http.readyState == 4) {
    if(http.status == 200) {
      var mytext = http.responseText;
      document.getElementById('myPageElement')
➥.innerHTML = mytext;
    }
  } else {
  document. getElementById('myPageElement')
➥.innerHTML = "";
  }
}

</script>
</head>
<body onLoad="getServerText()">
Here is the text returned by the server:<br>
<div id="myPageElement"></div>
</body>
</html>
```

Most, and probably all, of this code will be familiar from previous chapters. The part that interests us here is the callback function useHttpResponse(), which contains these lines:

```
var mytext = http.responseText;
document.getElementById('myPageElement').innerHTML = mytext;
```

Here we have simply assigned the value received in responseText to become the content of our chosen <div> container.

Running the preceding code with the simple server-side script

```
<?php
echo "This is the text from the server";
?>
```

produces the screen display of Figure 19.1.

**FIGURE 19.1**
Displaying text
in a page
element via
responseText.

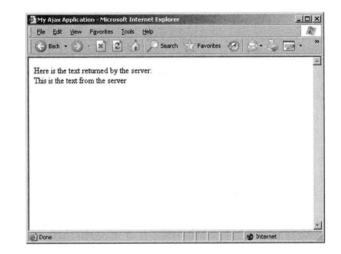

## Including HTML in responseText

Now let's modify the code from the preceding example.

As you know from previous chapters, HTML markup is entirely composed of tags written using text characters. If the value contained in the responseText property is to be used for modifying the display of the page from which the server request is being sent, there is nothing to stop us having our server script include HTML markup in the information it returns.

Suppose that we once again use the code of Listing 19.1 but with a modified server script:

```php
<?php
echo "<h3>Returning Formatted Text</h3>";
echo "<hr />";
echo "We can use HTML to <stroong>format</strong>
➡ text before we return it!";
?>
```

Figure 19.2 shows the resulting browser display.

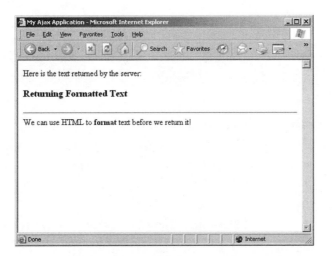

**FIGURE 19.2**
Display showing HTML formatted at the server.

As a slightly more involved example, consider the case where the server script generates more complex output. We want our application to take this server output and display it as the contents of a table.

This time we'll use our server-side PHP script to generate some tabular information:

```php
<?php
$days = array('Monday','Tuesday','Wednesday',
➡'Thursday','Friday','Saturday','Sunday');
echo "<table border='2'>";
echo "<tr><th>Day Number</th><th>Day Name</th></tr>";
for($i=0;$i<7;$i++)
{
  echo "<tr><td>".$i."</td><td>".$days[$i]."</td></tr>";
}
echo "</table>";
?>
```

Once again using the code of Listing 19.1 to call the server-side script via `XMLHTTPRequest`, we obtain a page as displayed in Figure 19.3.

**FIGURE 19.3**
Returning more
complex HTML.

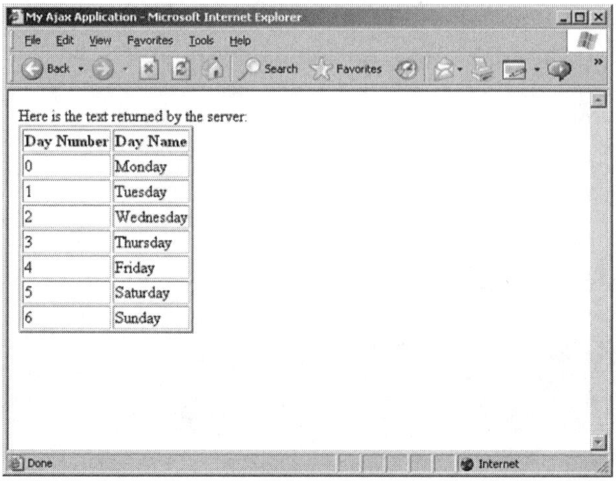

## More Complex Formatted Data

So far we have demonstrated ways to return text that may be directly applied to an element on a web page. So far, so good. However, if you are willing to do a little more work in JavaScript to manipulate the returned data, you can achieve even more.

Provided that the server returns a string value in the `responseText` property of the `XMLHTTPRequest` object, you can use any data format you may devise to encode information within it.

Consider the following server-side script, which uses the same data array as in the previous example:

```php
<?php
$days = array('Monday','Tuesday','Wednesday',
'Thursday','Friday','Saturday','Sunday');
$numdays = sizeof($days);
for($i=0;$i<($numdays - 1);$i++)
{
echo $days[$i]."¦";
}
echo $days[$numdays-1];
?>
```

**By the Way**

Note the use of the PHP `sizeof()` function to determine the number of items in the array. In PHP, as in JavaScript, array keys are numbered from 0 rather than 1.

The string returned in the `responseText` property now contains the days of the week, separated—or *delimited*—by the pipe character ¦. If we copy this string into a JavaScript variable `mystring`,

```
var mystring = http.responseText;
```

we will find that the variable `mystring` contains the string

```
Monday¦Tuesday¦Wednesday¦Thursday¦Friday¦Saturday¦Sunday
```

We may now conveniently divide this string into an array using JavaScript's `split()` method:

```
var results = http.responseText.split("¦");
```

> The JavaScript `split()` method slices up a string, making each cut wherever in the string it locates the character that it has been given as an argument. That character need not be a pipe; popular alternatives are commas or slashes.

*Did you Know?*

We now have a JavaScript array `results` containing our data:

```
results[0] = 'Monday'
results[1] = 'Tuesday'
etc…
```

Rather than simply displaying the received data, we now can use it in JavaScript routines in any way we want.

> For complex data formats, XML may be a better way to receive and handle data from the server. However, it is remarkable how much can be done just by using the `responseText` property.

*Did you Know?*

# Summary

With little effort, the `XMLHTTPRequest` object's `responseText` property can be persuaded to do more than simply return some text to display in a web page.

For all but the most complex data formats, it may prove simpler to manipulate `responseText` than to deal with the added complexity of XML.

In this chapter you saw several examples of this technique, ranging from the simple update of text content within a page element, to the manipulation of more complex data structures.

# CHAPTER 20

# AHAH—Asynchronous HTML and HTTP

---

## What You'll Learn in This Chapter:

▶ Introducing AHAH

▶ Creating a Small Library for AHAH

▶ Using myAHAHlib.js

In this chapter you will learn how to use AHAH (Asynchronous HTML and HTTP) to build Ajax-style applications without using XML.

## Introducing AHAH

You saw in Chapter 19, "Returning Data as Text," just how much can be achieved with an Ajax application without using any XML at all. Many tasks, from simply updating the text on a page to dealing with complicated data structures, can be carried out using only the text string whose value is returned in the XMLHTTPRequest object's responseText property.

It is possible to build complete and useful applications without any XML at all. In fact, the term *AHAH (Asynchronous HTML and HTTP)* has been coined for just such applications.

This chapter takes the concepts of Chapter 19 a little further, examining in more detail where—and how—AHAH can be applied.

By the Way

This technique, a kind of subset of Ajax, has been given various acronyms. These include AHAH (asynchronous HTML and HTTP), JAH (Just Asynchronous HTML), and HAJ (HTML And JavaScript). In this book we'll refer to it as AHAH.

## Why Use AHAH Instead of Ajax?

There is no doubt that XML is an important technology with diverse and powerful capabilities. For complex Ajax applications with sophisticated data structures it may well be the best—or perhaps the only—option. However, using XML can sometimes complicate the design of an application, including:

▶ Work involved in the design of custom schemas for XML data.

▶ Cross-browser compatibility issues when using JavaScript's DOM methods.

▶ Performance may suffer from having to carry out processor-intensive XML parsing.

Using AHAH can help you avoid these headaches, while offering a few more advantages, too:

▶ Easy reworking of some preexisting web pages.

▶ HTML can be easier to fault-find than XML.

▶ Use of CSS to style the returned information, rather than having to use XSLT.

By the Way

*XSLT* is a transformation language used to convert XML documents into other formats—for example, into HTML suitable for a browser to display.

In the following sections we'll package our AHAH scripts into a neat external JavaScript file that we can call from our applications.

# Creating a Small Library for AHAH

The Ajax applications examined in the last couple of chapters, although complete and functional, involved embedding a lot of JavaScript code into our pages. As you have seen, each application tends to contain similar functions:

▶ A method to create an instance of the XMLHTTPRequest object, configure it, and send it

▶ A callback function to deal with the returned text contained in the responseText property

You can abstract these functions into simple JavaScript function calls, especially in cases where you simply want to update a single page element with a new value returned from the server.

# Introducing myAHAHlib.js

Consider Listing 20.1; most of this code will be instantly recognizable to you.

**LISTING 20.1**   myAHAHlib.js

```
function callAHAH(url, pageElement, callMessage) {
    document.getElementById(pageElement)
➥.innerHTML = callMessage;
    try {
    req = new XMLHttpRequest(); /* e.g. Firefox */
    } catch(e) {
      try {
      req = new ActiveXObject("Msxml2.XMLHTTP");
  /* some versions IE */
      } catch (e) {
        try {
        req = new ActiveXObject("Microsoft.XMLHTTP");
  /* some versions IE */
        } catch (E) {
          req = false;
        }
      }
    }
    req.onreadystatechange
➥ = function() {responseAHAH(pageElement);};
    req.open("GET",url,true);
    req.send(null);
  }

function responseAHAH(pageElement) {
   var output = '';
   if(req.readyState == 4) {
      if(req.status == 200) {
         output = req.responseText;
         document.getElementById(pageElement)
➥.innerHTML = output;
      }
   }
 }
```

The function `callAHAH()` encapsulates the tasks of creating an instance of the `XMLHTTPRequest` object, declaring the callback function, and sending the request.

Note that instead of simply declaring

```
req.onreadystatechange = responseAHAH;
```

we instead used the JavaScript construct

```
req.onreadystatechange
➥ = function() {responseAHAH(pageElement);};
```

This type of declaration allows us to pass an argument to the declared function, in this case identifying the page element to be updated.

`callAHAH()` also accepts an additional argument, `callMessage`. This argument contains a string defining the content that should be displayed in the target element while we await the outcome of the server request. This provides a degree of feedback for the user, indicating that something is happening on the page. In practice this may be a line of text, such as

```
'Updating page; please wait a moment ….'
```

Once again, however, you may choose to embed some HTML code into this string. Using an animated GIF image within an `<img>` element provides an effective way of warning a user that a process is underway.

The callback function `responseAHAH()` carries out the specific task of applying the string returned in the `responseText` property to the `innerHTML` property of the selected page element `pageElement`:

```
output = req.responseText;
document.getElementById(pageElement).innerHTML = output;
```

This code has been packaged into a file named myAHAHlib.js, which you can call from an HTML page, thus making the functions available to your AHAH application. The next section shows some examples of its use.

# Using myAHAHlib.js

In Part II we encountered the concept of JavaScript functions being located in an external file that is referred to within our page.

That's how we'll use our new file myAHAHlib.js, using a statement in this form:

```
<SCRIPT language="JavaScript" SRC="myAHAHlib.js"></SCRIPT>
```

We will then be at liberty to call the functions within the script whenever we want.

The following is the skeleton source code of such an HTML page:

```
<html>
<head>
<title>Another Ajax Application</title>
<SCRIPT language="JavaScript" SRC="myAHAHlib.js"></SCRIPT>
</head>
<body>
<form>
<input type="button" onClick=
➥"callAHAH('serverscript.php?parameter=x',
➥'displaydiv', 'Please wait - page updating …')" >
This is the place where the server response
will be posted:<br>
<div id="displaydiv"></div>
</form>
</body>
</html>
```

In this simple HTML page, a button element is used to create the event that causes the `callAHAH()` method to be called. This method places the text string

```
'Please wait - page updating …'
```

in the `<div>` element having id `displaydiv` and sends the asynchronous server call to the URL `serverscript.php?parameter=x`.

When `responseAHAH()` detects that the server has completed its response, the `<div>` element's content is updated using the value stored in `responseText`; instead of showing the "please wait" message, the `<div>` now displays whatever text the server has returned.

## Applying myAHAHlib.js in a Project

We can demonstrate these techniques with a further simple Ajax application. This time, we'll build a script to grab the `'keywords'` metatag information from a user-entered URL.

By the Way

*Metatags* are optional HTML container elements in the `<head>` section of an HTML page. They contain data about the web page that is useful to search engines and indexes in deciding how the page's content should be classified. The `'keywords'` metatag, where present, typically contains a comma-separated list of words with meanings relevant to the site content. An example of a `'keywords'` metatag might look like this:

```
<meta name="keywords" content="programming, design,
➥ development, Ajax, JavaScript, XMLHTTPRequest, script">
```

Listing 20.2 shows the HTML code.

**LISTING 20.2**    `getkeywords.html`

```html
<html>
<head>
<title>A 'Keywords' Metatag Grabber</title>
<SCRIPT language="JavaScript" SRC="myAHAHlib.js">
</SCRIPT>
</head>
<body>
<script type="text/javascript" src="ahahLib.js">
</script>
<form>
<table>
<tr>
  <td>
    URL: http://
  </td>

  <td>
    <input type="text" id="myurl" name="myurl" size=30>
    <input type="button" onclick =
"callAHAH('keywords.php?url='+document
.getElementById('myurl').value,'displaydiv',
 'Please wait; loading content …')" value="Fetch">
  </td>
</tr>
<tr><td colspan=2 height=50 id="displaydiv"></td></tr>
</table>
</form>
</body>
</html>
```

Finally, consider the server-side script:

```php
<?php
$tags = @get_meta_tags('http://'.$url);
$result = $tags['keywords'];
if(strlen($result) > 0)
{
   echo $result;
} else {
   echo "No keywords metatag is available";
}
?>
```

We present the selected URL to the PHP method `get_meta_tags()` as an argument:

```php
$tags = @get_meta_tags('http://'.$url);
```

This method is specifically designed to parse the metatag information from HTML pages in the form of an associative array. In this script, the array is given the name $tags, and we can recover the 'keywords' metatag by examining the array entry $tags['keywords']; we can then check for the presence or absence of a 'keywords' metatag by measuring the length of the returned string using PHP's strlen() method.

**Did you Know?**

> The @ character placed before a PHP method tells the PHP interpreter not to output an error message if the method should encounter a problem during execution. We require it in this instance because not all web pages contain a 'keywords' metatag; in the cases where none exists, we would prefer the method to return an empty string so that we can add our own error handling.

When the file getkeywords.html is first loaded into the browser, we are presented with the display shown in Figure 20.1.

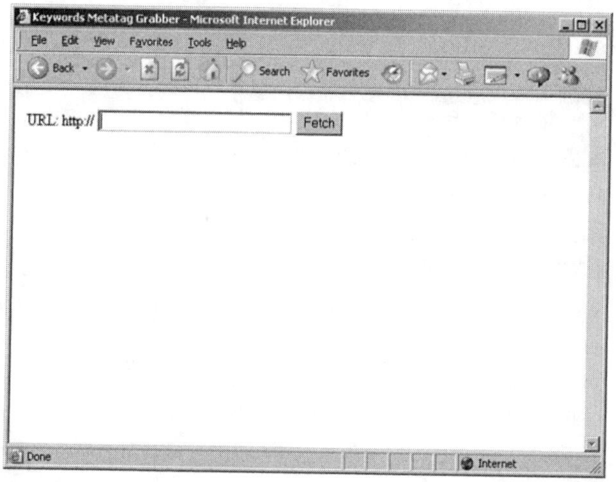

**FIGURE 20.1**
The browser display after first loading the application.

Here we are invited to enter a URL. When we then click on the Fetch button, callAHAH() is executed and sends our chosen URL as a parameter to the server-side script. At the same time, the message "Please wait; loading content ... " is placed in the <div> container. Although possibly only visible for a fraction of a second, we now have a display such as that shown in Figure 20.2.

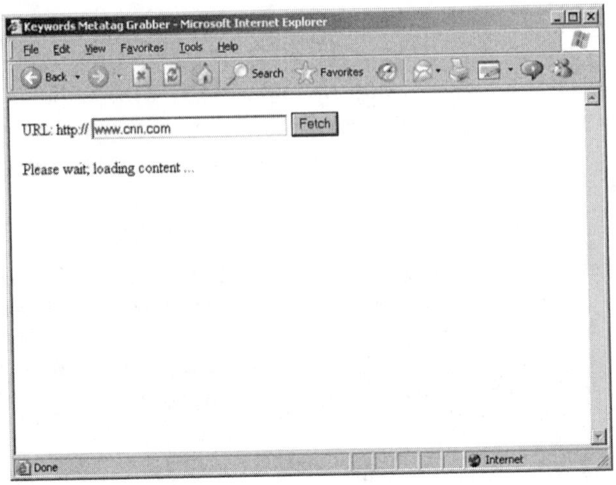

**FIGURE 20.2**
Awaiting
the server
response.

Finally, when the server call has concluded, the contents of the responseText property are loaded into the <div> container, producing the display of Figure 20.3.

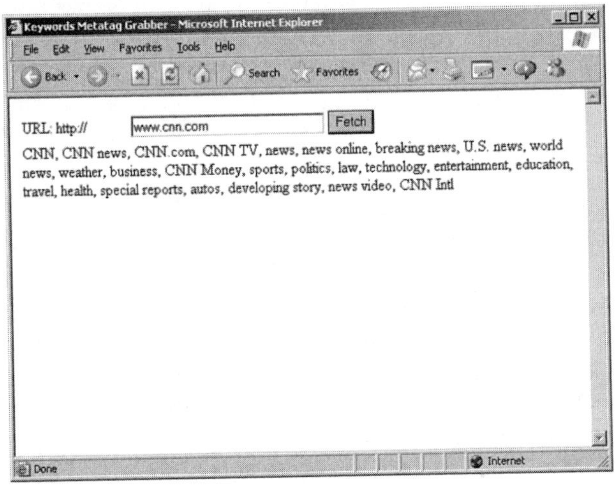

**FIGURE 20.3**
The keywords
are successfully
returned.

One option we haven't yet considered is the idea of passing back JavaScript code within `responseText`. Because JavaScript source code (like everything else in an HTML page) is made up of statements written in plain text, you can return JavaScript source from the server in the `responseText` property.

You can then execute this JavaScript code using JavaScript's `eval()` method:

```
eval(object.responseText);
```

Consider the situation where your server script returns the string:

```
"alert('Hello World!');"
```

In this case the `eval()` method would execute the content as a JavaScript statement, creating a dialog saying 'Hello World!' with an OK button.

*Did you Know?*

## Try It Yourself

### Extending the Library

As it stands, myAHAHlib.js is a simple implementation of AHAH. There are many ways it could be improved and extended, depending on how it is to be used. Rather than cover these in this chapter, we'll leave these for your own experimentation. Here's a few suggestions to get you started:

- ▶ Currently only GET requests are supported. How might the functions be modified to allow POST requests too?

- ▶ Much of the user feedback discussed in Chapter 13, "Our First Ajax Application," is not yet implemented in `responseAHAH()`.

- ▶ Is it possible for `callAHAH()` to be modified to accept an array of page elements for updating and (with the aid of a suitable server-side script) process them all at once?

# Summary

It will hopefully have become clear, in the course of this chapter and Chapter 19, that Ajax can achieve a lot of functionality without using any XML at all.

By carefully using combinations of client-side coding in JavaScript and server-side scripting in your chosen language, you can create data schemes of high complexity.

In simpler applications, where all you want to do is update the text of page elements, the XMLHTTPRequest object's functionality may be abstracted into a JavaScript function library and called from an HTML page via straightforward methods.

For some tasks, however, you need to leverage the power of XML. We'll look at this subject in Chapter 21, "Returning Data as XML."

# CHAPTER 21

# Returning Data as XML

## What You'll Learn in This Chapter:

▶ Adding the "x" to Ajax
▶ The `responseXML` **Property**
▶ Project—An RSS Headline Reader

In this chapter you will learn to use XML data returned from the server via the `responseXML` property of the `XMLHTTPRequest` object.

## Adding the "x" to Ajax

Chapter 19, "Returning Data as Text," and Chapter 20, "AHAH—Asynchronous HTML and HTTP," dealt at some length with the string value contained in `responseText` and looked at several techniques for using this information in applications. These examples ranged from simple updates of page element text to applications using more sophisticated data structures encoded into string values that can be stored and transferred in the `responseText` property.

The *x* in Ajax does, of course, stand for XML, and there are good reasons for using the power of XML in your applications. This is particularly true when you need to use highly structured information and/or perform complex translations between different types of data representation.

As discussed previously, the `XMLHTTPRequest` object has a further property called `responseXML`, which can be used to transfer information from the server via XML, rather than in text strings.

You saw in Chapter 13, "Our First Ajax Application," how JavaScript's document object model (DOM) methods can help you process this XML information. This chapter looks at these techniques in a little more detail and hopefully gives you a taste of what Ajax applications can achieve when leveraging the power of XML.

# The responseXML **Property**

Whereas the responseText property of the XMLHTTPRequest object contains a string, responseXML can be treated as if it were an XML document.

**Watch
Out!**

> You need to make sure that your server presents valid and well-formed XML to be returned via the responseXML property. In situations where XML cannot be correctly parsed by the XMLHTTPRequest object, perhaps due to well-formedness errors or problems with unsupported character encoding, the content of the responseXML is unpredictable and also likely to be different in different browsers.

**By the
Way**

> Like the responseText property, the value stored in responseXML is read-only, so you cannot write directly to this property; to manipulate it you must copy the value to another variable:
>
> ```
> var myobject = http.responseXML;
> ```

The complete structure and data contained in the XML document can now be made available by using JavaScript's DOM methods. Later in the chapter we'll demonstrate this with another working Ajax application, but first let's revisit the JavaScript DOM methods and introduce a few new ones.

## More JavaScript DOM Methods

You met some of the JavaScript DOM methods, such as getElementById and getElementsByTagName, in previous chapters. In those cases, we were mostly concerned with reading the values of the nodes to write those values into HTML page elements.

This chapter looks at the DOM methods that can be used to actually create elements, thereby changing the structure of the page.

The Document Object Model can be thought of as a treelike structure of nodes. As well as reading the values associated with those nodes, you can create and modify the nodes themselves, thereby changing the structure and content of your document.

To add new elements to a page, you need to first create the elements and then attach them to the appropriate point in your DOM tree. Let's look at a simple example using the following HTML document:

```html
<html>
<head>
  <title>Test Document</title>
</head>
<body>
We want to place some text here:<br />
<div id="displaydiv"></div>
</body>
</html>
```

In this example, we want to add the text "Hello World!" to the `<div>` container in the document body. We'll put our JavaScript routine into a function that we'll call from the body's `onLoad()` event handler.

First, we'll use the JavaScript DOM method `createTextNode()` to, well, create a text node:

```javascript
var textnode = createTextNode('Hello World!');
```

We now need to attach `textnode` to the DOM tree of the document at the appropriate point.

You first learned about child nodes in Chapter 5, "Working with the Document Object Model"; hopefully, you recall that nodes in a document are said to have *children* if they contain other document elements. JavaScript has an `appendChild()` method, which allows us to attach our new text node to the DOM tree by making it a child node of an existing document node.

In this case, we want our text to be inside the `<div>` container having the id `displaydiv`:

```javascript
var textnode = document.createTextNode('Hello World!');
document.getElementById('displaydiv').appendChild(textnode);
```

> Compare this DOM-based method of writing content to the page with the `innerHTML` method used in the project in Chapter 13.

**By the Way**

Let's look at the complete source of the page, after wrapping up this JavaScript code into a function and adding the `onLoad()` event handler to execute it:

```html
<html>
<head>
 <title>Test Document</title>
 <script Language="JavaScript">
```

```
function hello()
{
 var textnode = document.createTextNode('Hello World!');
 document.getElementById('displaydiv').appendChild(textnode);
}
</script>
</head>
<body onLoad="hello()">
We want to place some text here:<br />
<div id="displaydiv"></div>
</body>
</html>
```

Figure 21.1 shows the browser display after loading this page.

**FIGURE 21.1**
The DOM says
"Hello World!"

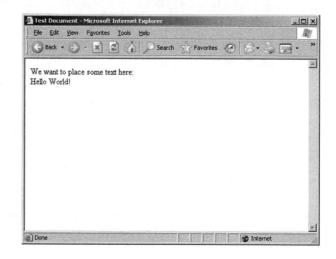

> If you display the source code of this document in your browser, you won't see the
> 'Hello World!' text inside the <div> container. The browser builds its DOM rep-
> resentation of the HTML document and then uses that model to display the page.
> The amendments made by your code are made to the DOM, not to the document
> itself.

**By the Way**

When you want to create other page elements besides text nodes, you can do so
using the createElement() method, which works pretty much like
createTextNode(). We could, in fact, have used createElement() to create the
<div> container itself, prior to adding our 'Hello World!' text node:

```
var newdiv = document.createElement("div");
```

In general, you simply pass the type of the required page element as an argument to `createElement()` to generate the required type of element.

# An Overview of DOM Methods

This book is not just about JavaScript DOM techniques, so we're not going to reproduce here a comprehensive guide to all the available methods and properties. However, Table 21.1 itemizes some of the more useful ones.

---

If you need a more comprehensive account of the JavaScript DOM methods and properties, Andrew Watt gives a useful list in his excellent book *Sams Teach Yourself XML in 10 Minutes* (Sams Publishing, ISBN 0672324717).

---

**TABLE 21.1**   Some JavaScript DOM Properties and Methods

**Node Properties**

| | |
|---|---|
| `childNodes` | Array of child nodes |
| `firstChild` | The first child node |
| `lastChild` | The last child node |
| `nodeName` | Name of the node |
| `nodeType` | Type of node |
| `nodeValue` | Value contained in the node |
| `nextSibling` | Next node sharing the same parent |
| `previousSibling` | Previous node sharing same parent |
| `parentNode` | Parent of this node |

**Node Methods**

| | |
|---|---|
| `AppendChild` | Add a new child node |
| `HasChildNodes` | True if this node has children |
| `RemoveChild` | Deletes a child node |

**Document Methods**

| | |
|---|---|
| `CreateAttribute` | Make a new attribute for an element |
| `CreateElement` | Make a new document element |
| `CreateTextNode` | Make a text item |
| `GetElementsByTagName` | Create an array of tagnames |
| `GetElementsById` | Find an element by its ID |

# Project—An RSS Headline Reader

Let's now take what we've learned about returning XML data from the server and use these techniques to tackle a new project.

XML data is made available on the Internet in many forms. One of the most popular is the RSS feed, a particular type of XML source usually containing news or other topical and regularly updated items. RSS feeds are available from many sources on the Web, including most broadcast companies and newspaper publishers, as well as specialist sites for all manner of subjects.

We'll write an Ajax application to take a URL for an RSS feed, collect the XML, and list the titles and descriptions of the news items contained in the feed.

The following is part of the XML for a typical RSS feed:

```
<rss version="0.91">
<channel>
<title>myRSSfeed.com</title>
<link>http://www.********.com/</link>
<description>My RSS feed</description>
<language>en-us</language>
<item>
<title>New Store Opens</title>
<link>http://www.**********.html</link>
<description>A new music store opened today in Canal Road.
➥The new business, Ajax Records, caters for a wide range of
➥musical tastes.</description>
</item>
<item>
<title>Bad Weather Affects Transport</title>
<link>http://www.***********.html</link>
<description>Trains and buses were disrupted badly today
➥due to sudden heavy snow.  Police advised people not to
➥travel unless absolutely necessary.</description>
</item>
<item>
<title>Date Announced for Mayoral Election</title>
<link>http://www.*********.html</link>
<description>September 4th has been announced as the date
➥for the next mayoral election.  Watch local news for more
➥details.</description>
</item>
</channel>
</rss>
```

From the first line

```
<rss version="0.91">
```

we see that we are dealing with RSS version 0.91 in this case. The versions of RSS differ quite a bit, but for the purposes of our example we only care about the <title>, <link>, and <description> elements for the individual news items, which remain essentially unchanged from version to version.

## The HTML Page for Our Application

Our page needs to contain an input field for us to enter the URL of the required RSS feed and a button to instruct the application to collect the data. We also will have a <div> container in which to display our parsed data:

```
<html>
<head>
<title>An Ajax RSS Headline Reader</title>
</head>
<body>
<h3>An Ajax RSS Reader</h3>
<form name="form1">
URL of RSS feed: <input type="text" name="feed" size="50"
➥value="http://"><input type="button" value="Get Feed">
<br /><br />
<div id="news"><h4>Feed Titles</h4></div>
</form>
</html>
```

If we save this code to a file rss.htm and load it into our browser, we see something like the display shown in Figure 21.2.

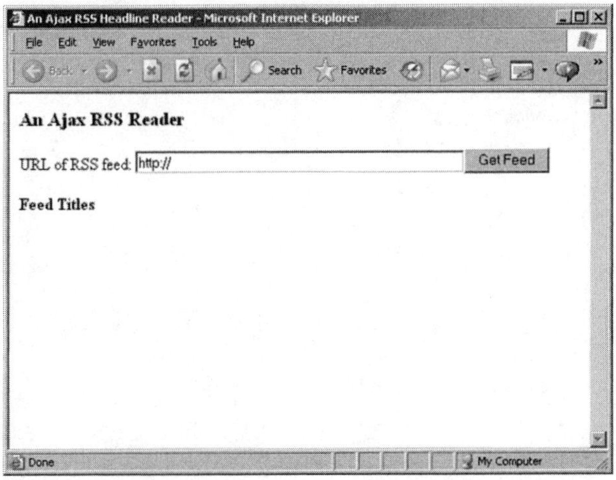

**FIGURE 21.2**
Displaying the base HTML document for our RSS headline reader.

Much of the code for our reader will be familiar by now; the means of creating an instance of the XMLHTTPRequest object, constructing and sending a server request, and checking when that request has been completed are all carried out much as in previous examples.

This time, however, instead of using responseText we will be receiving data in XML via the responseXML property. We'll use that data to modify the DOM of our HTML page to show the news items' titles and descriptions in a list within the page's <div> container. Each title and description will be contained in its own paragraph element (which we'll also construct for the purpose) and be styled via a style sheet to display as we want.

## The Code in Full

Let's jump right in and look at the code, shown in Listing 21.1.

**LISTING 21.1**　Ajax RSS Headline Reader

```
<html>
<head>
<title>An Ajax RSS Headline Reader</title>
</head>
<style>
.title {
font: 16px bold helvetica, arial, sans-serif;
padding: 0px 30px 0px 30px;
text-decoration:underline;
}
.descrip {
font: 14px normal helvetica, arial, sans-serif;
text-decoration:italic;
padding: 0px 30px 0px 30px;
background-color:#cccccc;
}
.link {
font: 9px bold helvetica, arial, sans-serif;
padding: 0px 30px 0px 30px;
}
.displaybox {
border: 1px solid black;
padding: 0px 50px 0px 50px;
}
</style>
<script language="JavaScript" type="text/javascript">
function getXMLHTTPRequest() {
try {
req = new XMLHttpRequest(); /* e.g. Firefox */
} catch(e) {
  try {
  req = new ActiveXObject("Msxml2.XMLHTTP");
  /* some versions IE */
  } catch (e) {
    try {
```

**LISTING 21.1** Continued

```
      req = new ActiveXObject("Microsoft.XMLHTTP");
      /* some versions IE */
    } catch (E) {
      req = false;
    }
  }
}
return req;
}

var http = getXMLHTTPRequest();

function getRSS() {
  var myurl = 'rssproxy.php?feed=';
  var myfeed = document.form1.feed.value;
    myRand = parseInt(Math.random()*999999999999999);
    // cache buster
  var modurl = myurl+escape(myfeed)+"&rand="+myRand;
  http.open("GET", modurl, true);
  http.onreadystatechange = useHttpResponse;
  http.send(null);
}

function useHttpResponse() {
   if (http.readyState == 4) {
     if(http.status == 200) {
        // first remove the childnodes
        // presently in the DM
        while (document.getElementById('news')
➥.hasChildNodes())
        {
document.getElementById('news').removeChild(document
➥.getElementById('news').firstChild);
        }
        var titleNodes = http.responseXML
➥.getElementsByTagName("title");
        var descriptionNodes = http.responseXML
➥.getElementsByTagName("description");
        var linkNodes = http.responseXML
➥.getElementsByTagName("link");
        for(var i =1;i<titleNodes.length;i++)
        {
          var newtext = document
➥.createTextNode(titleNodes[i]
➥.childNodes[0].nodeValue);
          var newpara = document.createElement('p');
          var para = document.getElementById('news')
➥.appendChild(newpara);
          newpara.appendChild(newtext);
          newpara.className = "title";

          var newtext2 = document
➥.createTextNode(descriptionNodes[i]
➥.childNodes[0].nodeValue);
          var newpara2 = document.createElement('p');
          var para2 = document
```

**LISTING 21.1**    Continued

```
➥.getElementById('news').appendChild(newpara2);
        newpara2.appendChild(newtext2);
        newpara2.className = "descrip";
        var newtext3 = document
➥.createTextNode(linkNodes [i]
➥.childNodes[0].nodeValue);
        var newpara3 = document.createElement('p');
        var para3 = document.getElementById('news')
➥.appendChild(newpara3);
        newpara3.appendChild(newtext3);
        newpara3.className = "link";
    }
  }
 }
}
</script>
<body>
<center>
<h3>An Ajax RSS Reader</h3>
<form name="form1">
URL of RSS feed: <input type="text" name="feed"
➥size="50" value="http://"><input type="button"
➥onClick="getRSS()" value="Get Feed"><br><br>
<div id="news" class="displaybox">
➥<h4>Feed Titles</h4></div>
</form>
</center>
</html>
```

Mostly we are concerned with describing the workings of the callback function useHttpResponse().

# The Callback Function

In addition to the usual duties of checking the XMLHTTPRequest readyState and status properties, this function undertakes for us the following tasks:

▶ Remove from the display <div> any display elements from previous RSS listings.

▶ Parse the incoming XML to extract the title, link, and description elements.

▶ Construct DOM elements to hold and display these results.

▶ Apply CSS styles to these elements to change how they are displayed in the browser.

To remove the DOM elements installed by previous news imports (where they exist), we first identify the <div> element by using its ID and then use the hasChildNodes() DOM method, looping through and deleting the first child node from the <div> element each time until none remain:

```
while (document.getElementById('news').hasChildNodes())
{
document.getElementById('news')
➥.removeChild(document.getElementById('news').firstChild);
}
```

The following explanation describes the processing of the title elements, but, as can be seen from Listing 21.1, we repeat the process identically to retrieve the description and link information, too.

To parse the XML content to extract the item titles, we build an array titleNodes from the XML data stored in responseXML:

```
var titleNodes
➥ = http.responseXML.getElementsByTagName("title");
```

We can then loop through these items, processing each in turn:

```
for(var i =1;i<titleNodes.length;i++)
        { … processing instructions … }
```

For each title, we need to first extract the title text using the nodeValue property:

```
var newtext = document.createTextNode(titleNodes[i]
➥.childNodes[0].nodeValue);
```

We can then create a paragraph element:

```
var newpara = document.createElement('p');
```

append the paragraph as a child node of the <div> element:

```
var para = document.getElementById('news')
➥.appendChild(newpara);
```

and apply the text content to the paragraph element:

```
newpara.appendChild(newtext);
```

Finally, using the className property we can define how the paragraph is displayed. The class declarations appear in a <style> element in the document head and provide a convenient means of changing the look of the RSS reader to suit our needs.

```
newpara.className = "title";
```

Each time we enter the URL of a different RSS feed into the input field and click the button, the `<div>` content is updated to show the items belonging to the new RSS feed. This being an Ajax application, there is of course no need to reload the whole page.

## The Server-Side Code

Because of the security constraints built into the XMLHTTPRequest object, we can't call an RSS feed directly; we must use a script having a URL on our own server, and have this script collect the remote XML file and deliver it to the Ajax application.

In this case, we do not require that the server-side script rssproxy.php should *modify* the XML file but simply route it back to us via the responseXML property of the XMLHTTPRequest object. We say that the script is acting as a proxy because it is retrieving the remote resource on behalf of the Ajax application.

Listing 21.2 shows the code of the PHP script.

### LISTING 21.2    Server Script for the RSS Headline Reader

```php
<?php
$mysession = curl_init($_GET['feed']);
curl_setopt($mysession, CURLOPT_HEADER, false);
curl_setopt($mysession, CURLOPT_RETURNTRANSFER, true);
$out = curl_exec($mysession);
header("Content-Type: text/xml");
echo $out;
curl_close($mysession);
?>
```

The script uses the cURL PHP library, a set of routines for making Internet file transfer easier to program. A full description of cURL would not be appropriate here; suffice to say that this short script first receives the URL of the required RSS feed by referring to the feed variable sent by the Ajax application. The two lines that call the curl_setopt() function declare, respectively, that we don't want the headers sent with the remote file, but we do want the file contents. The curl_exec() function then makes the data transfer.

After that it's simply a matter of adding an appropriate header by using the familiar PHP header() command and returning the data to our Ajax application.

**Did you Know?**

For a full description of using cURL with PHP, see the PHP website at http://uk2.php.net/curl and/or the cURL site at http://curl.haxx.se/.

Figure 21.3 shows the RSS reader in action, in this case displaying content from a CNN newsfeed.

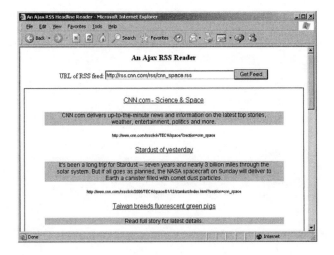

**FIGURE 21.3**
The Ajax RSS reader in action.

# Summary

The JavaScript DOM methods, when used with the XMLHTTPRequest object and XML data, provide a powerful means of transferring, organizing, and either displaying or otherwise processing data that has a sophisticated structure.

In this chapter you saw how DOM elements can be added, deleted, and manipulated to restructure an application's DOM in accordance with XML data received in the XMLHTTPRequest object's responseXML property.

# CHAPTER 22

# Web Services and the REST and SOAP Protocols

---

## What You'll Learn in This Chapter:

- ▶ Introduction to Web Services
- ▶ REST—Representational State Transfer
- ▶ Using REST in Practice
- ▶ Web Services Using SOAP
- ▶ The SOAP Protocol
- ▶ Using Ajax and SOAP
- ▶ Reviewing SOAP and REST

In this chapter you will learn the basics of web services and how to implement them using the REST (Representational State Transfer) and SOAP (Simple Object Access Protocol) protocols.

## Introduction to Web Services

So far you have seen several example applications in which we have called server-side scripts to carry out tasks. In each case we devised data structures to transfer the information and written routines to handle data transfer both to and from the server.

Suppose, though, that you wanted to make your server-side programs more generally available. Perhaps you can imagine that several different web applications might interface with such scripts for their own purposes. As well as browsers requesting pages directly, perhaps other applications (for example Ajax applications operating via XMLHTTPRequest calls) might also make data requests and expect to receive, in response, data that they can understand and manipulate.

In such cases it would be beneficial to have some form of standardization in the interfaces that your program makes available. This principle provides the basis of what have come to be known as *web services*.

As an example, suppose that our server application produces XML-formatted weather forecast data in response to a request containing geographical information.

The nature of this type of service makes it broadly applicable; such an application might have a wide variety of "clients" ranging from simple web pages that present weather forecasts in their local area to complex aviation or travel planning applications that require the data for more demanding uses.

This type of service is just one small example of what a web service might be capable of doing. Thousands of web services are active on the Internet, providing a mind-boggling array of facilities including user authentication, payment processing, content syndication, messaging, and a host of others.

In general, a web service makes available an application programming interface (API), which allows client applications to build interfaces to the service. Although any Internet protocol might be used to create web services, XML and HTTP are popular options.

A number of protocols and techniques have emerged that help you to create and utilize web services. This chapter looks at perhaps the simplest of those, called *REST* (*Representational State Transfer*), and another protocol, this time called *SOAP* (the *Simple Object Access Protocol*). Each section highlights in particular how they may be useful in Ajax applications.

# REST—Representational State Transfer

REST is centered on two main principles for generalized network design:

- ▶ Resources are represented by URLs—A resource can be thought of as a "noun" and refers to some entity we want to deal with in the API of a web service; this could be a document, a person, a meeting, a location, and so on. Each resource in a REST application has a unique URL.

- ▶ Operations are carried out via standard HTTP methods—HTTP methods such as GET, POST, PUT, and DELETE are used to carry out operations on resources. In this way we can consider such operations as "verbs" acting on resources.

# A Hypothetical REST Example

To understand how and why we might apply these ideas, let's look at a hypothetical example.

Suppose that we have a web service that allows writers to submit, edit, and read articles. Applying so-called RESTful principles to the design of this application, the following occurs:

▶ Each submitted article has a unique URL, for example:

```
http://somedomain.com/articles/173
```

We only require that the URL be unique for each article; for instance

```
http://somedomain.com/articles/list.php?id=173
```

also fulfils this requirement.

> Although REST requires that URLs be unique, it does not follow that each resource must have a corresponding physical page. In many cases the resource is generated by the web service at the time of the request—for example, by reference to a database.

**Did you Know?**

▶ To retrieve an article to read or edit, our client application would simply use an HTTP GET request to the URL of the article in question.

▶ To upload a new article, a POST request would be used, containing information about the article. The server would respond with the URL of the newly uploaded article.

▶ To upload an edited article, a PUT request would be used, containing the revised content.

▶ HTTP DELETE would be employed to delete a particular article.

In this way, the web service is using an interface familiar to anyone who has used the World Wide Web. We do not need to devise a library of API methods for sending or retrieving information; we already have them in the form of the standard HTTP methods.

> The World Wide Web itself is a REST application.

**By the Way**

## Query Information Using GET

An important issue concerning the use of the HTTP GET request in a RESTful application is that it should never change the server state. To put it another way: We only use GET requests to ask for information from the server, never to add or alter information already there.

POST, PUT, and DELETE calls can all change the server status in some way.

## Stateless Operation

All server exchanges within a RESTful application should be *stateless*. By stateless we mean that the call itself must contain all the information required by the server to carry out the required task, rather than depending on some state or context currently present on the server. We cannot, for example, require the server to refer to information sent in previous requests.

# Using REST in Practice

Let's expand on the example quoted earlier involving our articles web service.

## Reading a List of Available Articles

The list of available articles is a resource. Because the web service conforms to REST principles, we expect the service to provide a URL by which we can access this resource, for instance:

```
http://somedomain.com/articles/list.php
```

Because we are querying information, rather than attempting to change it, we simply use an HTTP GET request to the preceding URL. The server may return, for example, the following XML:

```
<articles>
    <article>
        <id>173</id>
        <title>New Concepts in Ajax</title>
        <author>P.D. Johnstone</author>
    </article>
    <article>
        <id>218</id>
        <title>More Ajax Ideas</title>
        <author>S.N. Braithwaite</author>
    </article>
    <article>
```

```
            <id>365</id>
            <title>Pushing the Ajax Envelope</title>
            <author>Z.R. Lawson</author>
        </article>
</articles>
```

## Retrieving a Particular Article

Because this is another request for information, we are again required to submit an
HTTP GET request. Our web service might perhaps allow us to make a request to

```
http://somedomain.com/articles/list.php?id=218
```

and receive in return

```
<article>
    <id>218</id>
    <title>More Ajax Ideas</title>
    <author>S.N. Braithwaite</author>
</article>
```

## Uploading a New Article

In this instance we need to issue a POST request rather than a GET request. In cases
similar to the hypothetical one outlined previously, it is likely that the server will
assign the id value of a new article, leaving us to encode parameter and value pairs
for the title and author elements:

```
var articleTitle = 'Another Angle on Ajax';
var articleAuthor = 'K.B. Schmidt';
var url = '/articles/upload.php';
var poststring = "title="+encodeURI(articleTitle)
➥+"&author="+encodeURI(articleAuthor);
http.onreadystatechange = callbackFunction();
http.open('POST', url, true);
http.setRequestHeader("Content-type",
➥"application/x-www-form-urlencoded");
http.setRequestHeader("Content-length", poststring.length);
http.send(poststring);
```

## Real World REST—the Amazon REST API

Leading online bookseller Amazon.com makes available a set of REST web services
to help developers integrate Amazon browsing and shopping facilities into their web
applications.

> Amazon.com often refers to the REST protocol as *XML-over-HTTP* or *XML/HTTP*.

By first creating a URL containing parameter/value pairs for the required search parameters (such as publisher, sort order, author, and so on) and then submitting a GET request to this URL, the Amazon web service can be persuaded to return an XML document containing product details. We may then parse that XML to create DOM objects for display in a web page or to provide data for further processing as required by our application.

> Amazon requires that you obtain a *developer's token* to develop client applications for its web services. You will need this token in constructing REST requests to Amazon's web services. You can also obtain an Amazon Associate's ID to enable you to earn money by carrying Amazon services on your website. See http://www.amazon.com for details.

Let's see this in practice by developing a REST request to return a list of books. Many types of searches are possible, but in this example, we request a list of books published by Sams.

We start to construct the GET request with the base URL:

```
$url = 'http://xml.amazon.com/onca/xml3';
```

We then need to add a number of parameter/value pairs to complete the request:

```
$assoc_id = "XXXXXXXXX";   // your Amazon Associate's ID
$dev_token = "ZZZZZZZZZZ";   // Your Developer Token
$manuf = "Sams";
$url = "http://xml.amazon.com/onca/xml3";
$url .= "?t=".$assoc_id;
$url .= "&dev-t=".$dev_token;
$url .= "&ManufacturerSearch=".$ manuf;
$url .= "&mode=books";
$url .= "&sort=+salesrank";
$url .= "&offer=All";
$url .="&type=lite";
$url .= "&page=1";
$url .= "&f=xml";
```

Submitting this URL, we receive an XML file containing details of all matching books. I won't reproduce the whole file here (there are more than 5,000 titles!), but Listing 22.1 shows an extract from the XML file, including the first book in the list.

**LISTING 22.1**  Example of XML Returned by Amazon Web Service

```
<?xml version="1.0" encoding="UTF-8" ?>
 <ProductInfo xmlns:xsi="http://www.w3.org/
➥2001/XMLSchema-instance"
➥ xsi:noNamespaceSchemaLocation
➥="http://xml.amazon.com/schemas3/dev-lite.xsd">
 <Request>
 <Args>
  <Arg value="Mozilla/4.0 (compatible; MSIE 6.0;
➥Windows NT 5.1; SV1; .NET CLR 1.1.4322)"
➥ name="UserAgent" />
  <Arg value="0G2CGCT7MRWB37PXAS4B" name="RequestID" />
  <Arg value="All" name="offer" />
  <Arg value="us" name="locale" />
  <Arg value="1" name="page" />
  <Arg value="ZZZZZZZZZZZ" name="dev-t" />
  <Arg value="XXXXXXXXXX" name="t" />
  <Arg value="xml" name="f" />
  <Arg value="books" name="mode" />
  <Arg value="Sams" name="ManufacturerSearch" />
  <Arg value="lite" name="type" />
  <Arg value="salesrank" name="sort" />
  </Args>
  </Request>
  <TotalResults>5051</TotalResults>
  <TotalPages>506</TotalPages>
 <Details url="http://www.amazon.com/exec/obidos/ASIN/
➥0672327236/themousewhisp-20?dev-t=
➥1WPTTG90FS816BXMNFG2%26camp=2025%26link_code=xm2">
  <Asin>0672327236</Asin>
  <ProductName>Sams Teach Yourself Microsoft SharePoint
➥2003 in 10 Minutes (Sams Teach Yourself
➥in 10 Minutes)</ProductName>
  <Catalog>Book</Catalog>
 <Authors>
  <Author>Colin Spence</Author>
  <Author>Michael Noel</Author>
  </Authors>
  <ReleaseDate>06 December, 2004</ReleaseDate>
  <Manufacturer>Sams</Manufacturer>
  <ImageUrlSmall>http://images.amazon.com/images/P/
➥0672327236.01.THUMBZZZ.jpg</ImageUrlSmall>
  <ImageUrlMedium>http://images.amazon.com/images/P/
➥0672327236.01.MZZZZZZZ.jpg</ImageUrlMedium>
  <ImageUrlLarge>http://images.amazon.com/images/P/
➥0672327236.01.LZZZZZZZ.jpg</ImageUrlLarge>
  <Availability>Usually ships in 24 hours</Availability>
  <ListPrice>$14.99</ListPrice>
  <OurPrice>$10.19</OurPrice>
  <UsedPrice>$9.35</UsedPrice>
  </Details>
```

Clearly we can now process this XML document in any way we want. For example, Chapter 21, "Returning Data as XML," discussed how to use JavaScript DOM methods to select information from the XML document and place it in page elements added to the DOM of our document.

## REST and Ajax

You know already that the XMLHTTPRequest object has methods that allow you to directly deal with HTTP request types and URLs.

Accessing RESTful web services is therefore simplified to a great extent. Because you know that each resource exposed by the web service API has a unique URL, and that the methods made available by the service are standard HTTP methods, it becomes a simple matter to construct the required XMLHTTPRequest calls.

The prospect of being able to access a wide variety of web services from within Ajax applications, and use the returned information within those applications, is attractive—even more so if you can use a consistent and simple interface protocol.

# Web Services Using SOAP

In the last section, we discussed web services and in particular saw how the REST (Representational State Transfer) protocol can be used to provide a consistent application programming interface (API) to such services.

REST is a good example of a protocol designed to operate with *resource-oriented* services, those that provide a simple mechanism to locate a resource and a set of basic methods that can manipulate that resource. In a resource-oriented service, those methods normally revolve around creating, retrieving, modifying, and deleting pieces of information.

In the case of REST, the methods are those specified in the HTTP specifications—GET, POST, PUT, and DELETE.

In certain cases, however, we are more interested in the *actions* a web service can carry out than in the resources it can control. We might perhaps call such services *action-oriented*. In these situations the resources themselves may have some importance, but the key issues concern the details of the activities undertaken by the service.

Perhaps the most popular and widely used protocol for designing action-oriented web services is SOAP, the Simple Object Access Protocol.

By the Way

The full name Simple Object Access Protocol has been dropped in the later versions of the SOAP specifications, as it was felt that the direction of the project had shifted and the name was no longer appropriate. The protocol continues to be referred to as SOAP.

## The Background of the SOAP Protocol

SOAP began in the late 1990s when XML was itself a fledgling web technology and was offered to the W3C in 2000. SOAP and another XML-based web service protocol, called XML-RPC, had a joint upbringing.

SOAP was designed essentially as a means of packaging remote procedure calls (requests to invoke programs on remote machines) into XML wrappers in a standardized way.

Numerous enterprises contributed to the early development of SOAP, including IBM, Microsoft, and Userland. The development of SOAP later passed to the XML Protocols Working Group of the W3C.

Did you Know?

You can get the latest information on the SOAP specification from the W3c website at http://www.w3.org/2000/xp/Group/.

# The SOAP Protocol

SOAP is an XML-based messaging protocol. A SOAP request is an XML document with the following main constituents:

- An *envelope* that defines the document as a SOAP request

- A body element containing information about the call and the expected responses

- Optional header and fault elements that carry supplementary information

Let's look at a skeleton SOAP request:

```
<?xml version="1.0"?>
<SOAP-ENV:Envelope
xmlns:SOAP-ENV="http://schemas.xmlsoap.org/soap/envelope/"
SOAP-ENV:encodingStyle=
➥"http://schemas.xmlsoap.org/soap/encoding/">
<SOAP-ENV:Header>
  ... various commands . . .
</SOAP-ENV:Header>
```

```
<SOAP-ENV:Body>
... various commands . . .
  <SOAP-ENV:Fault>
... various commands . . .
  </SOAP-ENV:Fault>
</SOAP-ENV:Body>
</SOAP-ENV:Envelope>
```

Note that the SOAP request is an XML file, which has as its root the `Envelope` element.

The first line of the `Envelope` is

```
<SOAP-ENV:Envelope xmlns:SOAP-EN =
➡"http://schemas.xmlsoap.org/soap/envelope/"
SOAP-ENV:encodingStyle=
➡"http://schemas.xmlsoap.org/soap/encoding/">
```

This line declares the `xmlns:soap` namespace, which must always have the value `xmlns:soap="http://schemas.xmlsoap.org/soap/envelope/"`.

A *namespace* is an identifier used to uniquely group a set of XML elements or attributes, providing a means to qualify their names, so that names in other schemas do not conflict with them.

The `encodingStyle` attribute contains information defining the data types used in the message.

Next appears the `Header` element, which is optional but must, if present, be the first element in the message. Attributes defined in the `Header` element define how the message is to be processed by the receiving application.

The body element of the SOAP message contains the message intended for the final recipient.

The serialized method arguments are contained within the SOAP request's body element. The call's XML element must immediately follow the opening XML tag of the SOAP body and must have the same name as the remote method being called.

The body may also contain a `Fault` element (but no more than one). This element is defined in the SOAP specification and is intended to carry information about any errors that may have occurred. If it exists, it must be a child element of the body element. The `Fault` element has various child elements including `faultcode`, `faultstring`, and `detail`, which contain specific details of the fault condition.

# Code Example of a SOAP Request

Let's see how a typical SOAP request might look:

```
<?xml version="1.0"?>
<SOAP-ENV:Envelope xmlns:SOAP-ENV=
➥"http://schemas.xmlsoap.org/soap/envelope/" SOAP
➥ENV:encodingStyle="http://schemas.xmlsoap.org/
➥soap/encoding/">
<SOAP-ENV:Body>
   <m:GetInvoiceTotal xmlns:m=
➥"http://www.somedomain.com/invoices">
      <m:Invoice>77293</m:Invoice>
   </m:GetInvoiceTotal>
</SOAP-ENV:Body>
</SOAP-ENV:Envelope>
```

In the preceding example, the `m:GetInvoiceTotal` and `m:Invoice` elements are specific to the particular application, and are not part of SOAP itself. These elements constitute the message contained in the SOAP envelope.

Let's see what the SOAP response from the web service might look like:

```
<?xml version="1.0"?>
<SOAP-ENV:Envelope xmlns:SOAP-ENV=
➥"http://schemas.xmlsoap.org/soap/envelope/" SOAP
➥ENV:encodingStyle="http://schemas.xmlsoap.org/
➥soap/encoding/">
<SOAP-ENV:Body>
   <m:ShowInvoiceTotal xmlns:m=
➥"http://www.somedomain.com/invoices">
      <m:InvoiceTotal>3295.00</m:InvoiceTotal>
   </m:ShowInvoiceTotal>
</SOAP-ENV:Body>
</SOAP-ENV:Envelope>
```

# Sending the SOAP Request Via HTTP

A SOAP message may be transmitted via HTTP GET or HTTP POST. If sent via HTTP POST, the SOAP message requires at least one HTTP header to be set; this defines the Content-Type:

```
Content-Type: text/xml
```

After a successful SOAP exchange, you would expect to receive the SOAP response preceded by an appropriate HTTP header:

```
HTTP/1.1 200 OK
Content-Type: text/xml
Content-Length: yyy
<?xml version="1.0"?>
```

```
<SOAP-ENV:Envelope xmlns:SOAP-ENV=
➥"http://schemas.xmlsoap.org/soap/envelope/" SOAP-
ENV:encodingStyle="http://schemas.xmlsoap.org/soap/encoding/">
<SOAP-ENV:Body>
   <m:ShowInvoiceTotal xmlns:m=
➥"http://www.somedomain.com/invoices">
       <m:InvoiceTotal>3295.00</m:InvoiceTotal>
   </m:ShowInvoiceTotal>
</SOAP-ENV:Body>
</SOAP-ENV:Envelope>
```

# Using Ajax and SOAP

To use SOAP with Ajax, you need to perform a number of separate steps:

1. Create the SOAP envelope.

2. Serialize the application-specific information into XML.

3. Create the SOAP body containing a serialized version of your application-specific code.

4. Send an HTTP request via the `XMLHTTPRequest` object, containing the SOAP message as a payload.

The callback function then needs to be responsible for unpacking the SOAP response and parsing the XML contained inside it.

## Code Example

How might the resulting code look? Let's see an example using the fictitious SOAP web service of the previous example:

```
var invoiceno = '77293';
http.open("POST", "http://somedomain.com/invoices",true);
http.onreadystatechange=function()  {
  if (http.readyState==4)   {
    if(http.status==200) {
      alert('The server said: '+ http.responseText)
    }
  }
 }
http.setRequestHeader("Content-Type", "text/xml")
var mySOAP = '<?xml version="1.0"?>'
  + '<SOAP-ENV:Envelope xmlns:SOAP-ENV=
➥"http://schemas.xmlsoap.org/soap/envelope/"'
  + ' SOAP-ENV:encodingStyle=
```

```
➥"http://schemas.xmlsoap.org/soap/encoding/">'
  + '<SOAP-ENV:Body>'
  + '<m:GetInvoiceTotal xmlns:m=
➥"http://www.somedomain.com/invoices">'
  + '<m:Invoice>'+invoiceno+'</m:Invoice></m:GetInvoiceTotal>'
  + '</SOAP-ENV:Body></SOAP-ENV:Envelope>';
http.send(mySOAP);
```

Here we have constructed the entire SOAP envelope in a JavaScript string variable, before passing it to the send() function of the XMLHTTPRequest object.

The value returned from the server needs to be parsed first to remove the SOAP response wrapper and then to recover the application data from the body section of the SOAP message.

# Reviewing SOAP and REST

Over the course of this chapter, we've looked at the REST and SOAP approaches to using web services.

Although other web services protocols exist, a significant REST versus SOAP argument has been waged among developers over the last couple of years.

I don't intend to join that argument in this book. Instead, let's summarize the similarities and differences between the two approaches:

▶ REST leverages the standard HTTP methods of PUT, GET, POST, and DELETE to create remote procedure calls having comparable functions. Web service implementations using the REST protocol seem particularly suited toward resource-based services, where the most-used methods generally involve creating, editing, retrieving, and deleting information. On the downside, REST requires a little more knowledge about the HTTP protocol.

▶ The SOAP protocol adds substantial complexity, with the necessity to serialize the remote call and then construct a SOAP envelope to contain it. Further work arises from the need to "unpack" the returned data from its SOAP envelope before parsing the data. These extra steps can also have an impact on performance, with SOAP often being a little slower in operation than REST for a similar task. SOAP does, however, make a more complete job of separating the remote procedure call from its method of transport, as well as add a number of extra features and facilities, such as the Fault element and type checking via namespaces.

# Summary

In this chapter we considered web services using the REST and SOAP protocols.

Either style of web service can be used via `XMLHTTPRequest` requests, though they differ somewhat in the complexity of the code involved.

# CHAPTER 23

# A JavaScript Library for Ajax

---

## *What You'll Learn in This Chapter:*

▶ An Ajax Library
▶ Reviewing `myAHAHlib.js`
▶ Implementing Our Library
▶ Using the Library

In this chapter you will learn how to encapsulate some of the techniques studied up to now into a small JavaScript library that you can call from your applications.

## An Ajax Library

Through the chapters and code examples up to now, we have developed a number of JavaScript code techniques for implementing the various parts of an Ajax application. Among these methods are

▶ A method for generating an instance of the `XMLHTTPRequest` object, which works across the range of currently popular browsers

▶ Routines for building and sending `GET` and `POST` requests via the `XMLHTTPRequest` object

▶ Techniques for avoiding unwanted caching of `GET` requests

▶ A style of callback function that checks for correct completion of the `XMLHTTPRequest` call prior to carrying out your wishes

▶ Methods of providing user feedback

▶ Techniques for dealing with text data returned in `responseText`

▶ Techniques for dealing with XML information returned in `responseXML`

In addition, you saw in Chapter 20, "AHAH—Asynchronous HTML and HTTP," how some of these methods could be abstracted into a small JavaScript "library" (in that case containing only two functions).

This chapter extends that idea to build a more fully featured library that allows Ajax facilities to be added simply to an HTML page with minimal additional code.

Of necessity, our Ajax library will not be as complex or comprehensive as the open source projects described later in the book; however, it will be complete enough to use in the construction of functional Ajax applications.

# Reviewing myAHAHlib.js

Listing 23.1 shows the code of myAHAHlib.js, reproduced from Chapter 20.

### LISTING 23.1    myAHAHlib.js

```
function callAHAH(url, pageElement, callMessage) {
    document.getElementById(pageElement).innerHTML
➥ = callMessage;
    try {
    req = new XMLHttpRequest(); /* e.g. Firefox */
    } catch(e) {
      try {
      req = new ActiveXObject("Msxml2.XMLHTTP");
      /* some versions IE */
      } catch (e) {
        try {
        req = new ActiveXObject("Microsoft.XMLHTTP");
        /* some versions IE */
        } catch (E) {
         req = false;
        }
      }
    }
    req.onreadystatechange =
➥function() {responseAHAH(pageElement);};
    req.open("GET",url,true);
    req.send(null);
  }

function responseAHAH(pageElement) {
  var output = '';
  if(req.readyState == 4) {
    if(req.status == 200) {
        output = req.responseText;
        document.getElementById(pageElement).innerHTML
➥ = output;
      }
    }
  }
```

Let's consider how we may extend the capabilities of this library:

▶ There is currently support only for HTTP GET requests. It would be useful to be able to support at least the HTTP POST request, too, especially if you intend to build applications using the REST protocol (as described in Chapter 22).

▶ The library currently only deals with text information returned via responseText and has no means to deal with responseXML.

# Implementing Our Library

Having identified what needs to be done, we'll now put together a more capable Ajax library.

## Creating XMLHTTPRequest Instances

Let's turn our attention first to the routine for creating instances of the XMLHTTPRequest object.

Currently this function is coupled tightly with the routine for constructing and sending HTTP GET requests. Let's decouple the part responsible for the creation of the XMLHTTPRequest instance and put it into a function of its own:

```
function createREQ() {
try {
    req = new XMLHttpRequest(); /* e.g. Firefox */
    } catch(err1) {
      try {
      req = new ActiveXObject("Msxml2.XMLHTTP");
      /* some versions IE */
      } catch (err2) {
        try {
        req = new ActiveXObject("Microsoft.XMLHTTP");
        /* some versions IE */
        } catch (err3) {
         req = false;
        }
      }
    }
    return req;
}
```

We can now create XMLHTTPRequest object instances by simply calling the following function:

```
var myreq = createREQ();
```

## HTTP GET and POST Requests

We'll start with the GET request because we already support that type of request:

```
function requestGET(url, query, req) {
myRand=parseInt(Math.random()*99999999);
req.open("GET",url+'?'+query+'&rand='+myRand,true);
req.send(null);
}
```

To this request we must pass as arguments the URL to which the request will be sent and the identity of the XMLHTTPRequest object instance.

We could exclude the query argument because, in a GET request, it's encoded into the URL. We keep the two arguments separate here to maintain a similar interface to the function for making POST requests.

The query argument must be suitably encoded prior to calling the function, though the cache-busting random element is added by the function.

Next, the POST function:

```
function requestPOST(url, query, req) {
req.open("POST", url,true);
req.setRequestHeader('Content-Type',
➥'application/x-www-form-urlencoded');
req.send(query);
}
```

## The Callback Function

How do we deal with the callback function? We are going to add a further function:

```
function doCallback(callback,item) {
eval(callback + '(item)');
}
```

This function uses JavaScript's eval() function to execute another function whose name is passed to it as an argument, while also passing to that function an argument of its own, via item.

Let's look at how these functions might interact when called from an event handler:

```
function doAjax(url,query,callback,reqtype,getxml) {
// create the XMLHTTPRequest object instance
var myreq = createREQ();
myreq.onreadystatechange = function() {
if(myreq.readyState == 4) {
  if(myreq.status == 200) {
    var item = myreq.responseText;
    if(getxml==1) {
       item = myreq.responseXML;
```

```
        }
    doCallback(callback, item);
      }
  }
}
if(reqtype=='post') {
requestPOST(url,query,myreq);
} else {
requestGET(url,query,myreq);
}
}
```

Our function doAjax now takes five arguments:

- ► url—The target URL for the Ajax call

- ► query—The encoded query string

- ► callback—Identity of the callback function

- ► reqtype—'post' or 'get'

- ► getxml—1 to get XML data, 0 for text

Listing 23.2 shows the complete JavaScript source code.

**LISTING 23.2**   The Ajax Library myAJAXlib.js

```
function createREQ() {
try {
    req = new XMLHttpRequest(); /* e.g. Firefox */
    } catch(err1) {
      try {
      req = new ActiveXObject("Msxml2.XMLHTTP");
➡   /* some versions IE */
      } catch (err2) {
        try {
        req = new ActiveXObject("Microsoft.XMLHTTP");
➡   /* some versions IE */
        } catch (err3) {
          req = false;
        }
      }
    }
    return req;
}

function requestGET(url, query, req) {
myRand=parseInt(Math.random()*99999999);
req.open("GET",url+'?'+query+'&rand='+myRand,true);
req.send(null);
}

function requestPOST(url, query, req) {
req.open("POST", url,true);
```

**LISTING 23.2**    Continued

```
req.setRequestHeader('Content-Type', 'application/
➥x-www-form-urlencoded');
req.send(query);
}

function doCallback(callback,item) {
eval(callback + '(item)');
}

function doAjax(url,query,callback,reqtype,getxml) {
// create the XMLHTTPRequest object instance
var myreq = createREQ();

myreq.onreadystatechange = function() {
if(myreq.readyState == 4) {
   if(myreq.status == 200) {
      var item = myreq.responseText;
      if(getxml==1) {
         item = myreq.responseXML;
      }
      doCallback(callback, item);
   }
  }
}
if(reqtype=='post') {
requestPOST(url,query,myreq);
} else {
requestGET(url,query,myreq);
}
}
```

# Using the Library

To demonstrate the use of the library, we're going to start with another simple HTML page, the code for which is shown here:

```
<html>
<head>
</head>
<body>
<form name="form1">
<input type="button" value="test">
</form>
</body>
</html>
```

This simple page displays only a button labeled "Test". All the functionality on the form will be created in JavaScript, using our new Ajax library.

The steps required to "Ajaxify" the application are

1. Include the Ajax library myAJAXlib.js in the <head> area of the page.

2. Write a callback function to deal with the returned information.

3. Add an event handler to the page to invoke the server call.

We'll start by demonstrating a GET request and using the information returned in the responseText property. This is similar to the situation we faced when dealing with AHAH in Chapter 20.

Including the Ajax library is straightforward:

```
<head>
<script Language="JavaScript" src="myAJAXlib.js"></script>
```

Next, we need to define our callback function to deal with the value stored in the responseText property. For these examples, we'll simply display the returned text in an alert:

```
<head>
<script Language="JavaScript" src="myAJAXlib.js"></script>
<script Language="JavaScript">
function cback(text) {
alert(text);
}
</script>
```

Finally, we need to add an event handler call to our button:

```
onClick="doAjax('libtest.php','param=hello',
➥'cback','get','0')"
```

Our server-side script libtest.php simply echoes back the parameter sent as the second argument:

```
<?php
echo "Parameter value was ".$param;
?>
```

Meanwhile the remaining parameters of the function call declare that the callback function is called cback, that we want to send an HTTP GET request, and that we expect the returned data to be in responseText. Listing 23.3 shows the complete code of our revised HTML page.

**LISTING 23.3    HTML Page Rewritten to Call** `myAJAXlib.js`

```
<html>
<head>
<script Language="JavaScript" src="myAJAXlib.js">
➥</script>
<script Language="JavaScript">
function cback(text) {
alert(text);
}
</script>
</head>
<body>
<form name="form1">
<input type="button" value="test"onClick=
➥"doAjax('libtest.php','param=hello',
➥'cback','get','0')">
</form>
</body>
</html>
```

Figure 23.1 shows the result of running the program.

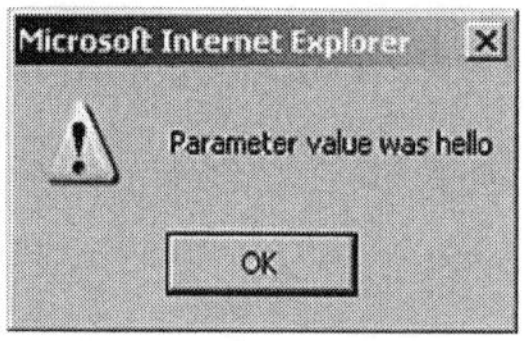

FIGURE 23.1
Returning text
following an
HTTP GET
request.

To use the same library to retrieve XML data, we'll once again use the server-side script of Chapter 13, "Our First Ajax Application," which you may recall delivers the current server time in a small XML document:

```
<?php
header('Content-Type: text/xml');
echo "<?xml version=\"1.0\" ?><clock1><timenow>"
➥.date('H:i:s')."</timenow></clock1>";
?>
```

Our callback function must be modified because we now need to return the parsed XML. We'll use some DOM methods that should by now be familiar:

```
<script>
function cback(text) {
var servertime = text.getElementsByTagName("timenow")[0]
➥.childNodes[0].nodeValue;
alert('Server time is '+servertime);
}
</script>
```

The only other thing we need to change is the call to our doAjax() function:

```
onClick="doAjax('telltimeXML.php','','cback','post','1')"
```

Here we have decided to make a POST request. Our server-side script telltimeXML.php does not require a query string, so in this case the second argument is left blank. The final parameter has been set to '1' indicating that we expect the server to respond with XML in the property responseXML.

Figure 23.2 shows the result of running the program.

**FIGURE 23.2**
Returning the server time in XML via a POST request.

**Try It Yourself** ▼

### Extending the Ajax Library

The current library might be improved in a number of ways. These will be left as an exercise for the reader, though in many cases the techniques have been covered elsewhere in the book.

User feedback, for example, has not been addressed; we previously discussed how the display of suitable text or a graphic image can alert the user that a request is currently in progress. It would be useful to revise the library to include the techniques discussed in Chapter 13 and elsewhere.

Error handling, too, has been excluded from the code and would prove a useful addition. For example, it should not be too difficult to modify the library to detect XMLHTTPRequest status properties other than 200 and output a suitable error message to the user.

Feel free to experiment with the code and see what you can achieve. ▲

# Summary

This chapter combined many of the techniques discussed to date to produce a compact and reusable JavaScript library that can be called simply from an HTML page.

The code supports both HTTP GET and HTTP POST requests and can deal with data returned from the server as text or XML.

Using such a library allows Ajax to be introduced to web pages using relatively small additions to the HTML markup. This not only keeps the code clean and easy to read but also simplifies the addition of Ajax facilities to upgrade legacy HTML.

In Chapter 24, "Ajax 'Gotchas,'" the last chapter of Part V, we'll discuss some potential problems and pitfalls awaiting the programmer in developing Ajax applications.

# CHAPTER 24

# Ajax Gotchas

## What You'll Learn in This Chapter:

- ▶ Common Ajax Errors
- ▶ The Back Button
- ▶ Bookmarking and Links
- ▶ Telling the User That Something Is Happening
- ▶ Making Ajax Degrade Elegantly
- ▶ Dealing with Search Engine Spiders
- ▶ Pointing Out Active Page Elements
- ▶ Don't Use Ajax Where It's Inappropriate
- ▶ Security
- ▶ Test Code Across Multiple Platforms
- ▶ Ajax Won't Cure a Bad Design
- ▶ Some Programming Gotchas

In this chapter you'll learn about some of the common Ajax mistakes and how to avoid them.

## Common Ajax Errors

Ajax has some common pitfalls waiting to catch the unwary developer. In this chapter, the last chapter of Part V, we'll review some of these pitfalls and discuss possible approaches to finding solutions.

The list is not exhaustive, and the solutions offered are not necessarily appropriate for every occasion. They should, however, provide some food for thought.

# The Back Button

All browsers in common use have a Back button on the navigation bar. The browser maintains a list of recently visited pages in memory and allows you to step back through these to revisit pages you have recently seen.

Users have become used to the Back button as a standard part of the surfing experience, just as they have with the other facets of the page-based web paradigm.

**Did you Know?**

> JavaScript has its own equivalent of the Back button written into the language. The statements
>
> ```
> onClick = "history.back()"
> ```
>
> and
>
> ```
> onClick = "history.go(-1)"
> ```
>
> both mimic the action of clicking the Back button once.

Ajax, as you have learned, does much to shake off the idea of web-based information being delivered in separate, page-sized chunks; with an Ajax application, you may be able to change page content over and over again without any thought of reloading the browser display with a whole new page.

What then of the Back button?

This issue has caused considerable debate among developers recently. There seem to be two main schools of thought:

▶ Create a means of recording state programmatically, and use that to re-create a previous state when the Back button is pressed.

▶ Persuade users that the Back button is no longer necessary.

Artificially re-creating former states is indeed possible but adds a great deal of complexity to Ajax code and is therefore somewhat the province of the braver programmer!

Although the latter option sounds a bit like it's trying to avoid the issue, it does perhaps have some merit. If you use Ajax to re-create desktop-like user interfaces, it's worthy of note that desktop applications generally don't have—or need—a Back button because the notion of separate "pages" never enters the user's head!

# Bookmarking and Links

This problem is not unrelated to the Back button issue.

When you bookmark a page, you are attempting to save a shortcut to some content. In the page-based metaphor, this is not unreasonable; although pages can have some degree of dynamic content, being able subsequently to find the page itself usually gets us close enough to seeing what we saw on our previous visit.

Ajax, however, can use the same page address for a whole application, with large quantities of dynamic content being returned from the server in accordance with a user's actions.

What happens when you want to bookmark a particular screen of information and/or pass that link to a friend or colleague? Merely using the URL of the current page is unlikely to produce the results you require.

Although it may be difficult to totally eradicate this problem, it may be possible to alleviate it somewhat by providing permanent links to specially chosen states of an application.

# Telling the User That Something Is Happening

This is another issue somewhat related to the change of interface style away from separate pages.

The user who is already familiar with browsing web pages may have become accustomed to program activity coinciding with the loading of a new or revised page.

Many Ajax applications therefore provide some consistent visual clue that activity is happening; perhaps a stationary graphic image might be replaced by an animated version, the cursor style might change, or a pop-up message appear. Some of these techniques have been mentioned in some of the chapters in this book.

# Making Ajax Degrade Elegantly

The chapters in this book have covered the development of Ajax applications using various modern browsers. It is still possible, though, that a user might surprise you by attempting to use your application with a browser that is too old to support the necessary technologies. Alternatively, a visitor's browser may have JavaScript and/or ActiveX disabled (for security or other reasons).

It is unfortunate if an Ajax application should break down under these conditions.

At the least, the occurrence of obvious errors (such as a failure to create an instance of the `XMLHTTPRequest` object) should be reported to the user. If the Ajax application is so complex that it cannot be made to automatically revert to a non-Ajax mode of operation, perhaps the user can at least be redirected to a non-Ajax version of the application.

*Did you Know?*

> You can detect whether JavaScript is unavailable by using the `<noscript>` … `</noscript>` tags in your HTML page. Statements between these tags are evaluated only if JavaScript is NOT available:
>
> ```
> <noscript>
> JavaScript is not available in this browser.  <br />
> ➥Please go <a href="otherplace.htm">HERE</a> for
> ➥ the HTML-only version.<br />
> </noscript>
> ```

# Dealing with Search Engine Spiders

Search engines gather information about websites through various means, an important one being the use of automated programs called *spiders*.

Spiders, as their name suggests, "crawl the web" by reading web pages and following links, building a database of content and other relevant information about particular websites. This database, better known as an *index*, is queried by search engine visitors using their keywords and phrases and returns suggestions of relevant pages for them to visit.

This can create a problem for highly dynamic sites, which rely on user interaction (rather than passive surfing) to invoke the loading of new content delivered on-demand by the server. The visiting spider may not have access to the content that would be loaded by dynamic means and therefore never gets to index it.

The problem can be exacerbated further by the use of Ajax, with its tendency to deliver even more content in still fewer pages.

It would seem wise to ensure that spiders can index a static version of all relevant content somewhere on the site. Because spiders follow links embedded in pages, the provision of a hypertext linked site map can be a useful addition in this regard.

# Pointing Out Active Page Elements

Without careful design, it may not be apparent to users which items on the page they can click on or otherwise interface with to make something happen.

It is worth trying to use a consistent style throughout an application to show which page elements cause server requests or some other dynamic activity. This is somewhat reminiscent of the way that hypertext links in HTML pages tend to be styled differently than plain text so that it's clear to a user that they perform an additional function.

At the expense of a little more coding effort, instructions and information about active elements can be incorporated in ToolTip-style pop-ups. This is, of course, especially important when a click on an active link can have a major effect on the application's state. Figure 24.1 shows an example of such a pop-up information box.

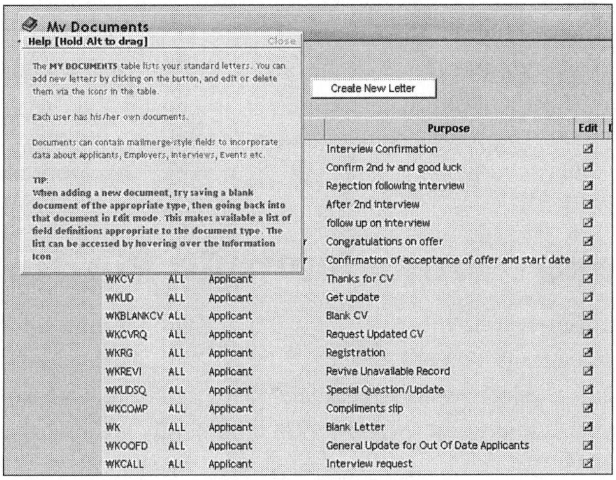

**FIGURE 24.1**
Pop-up information helps users to understand interfaces.

# Don't Use Ajax Where It's Inappropriate

Attractive as Ajax undoubtedly is for improving web interfaces, you need to accept that there are many situations where the use of Ajax detracts from the user experience instead of adding to it.

This is especially true where the page-based interface metaphor is perfectly adequate for, perhaps even of greater relevance to, the content and style of the site. Text-based sites with subjects split conveniently into chapter-styled pages can often benefit as much from intelligently designed hyperlinking as they can from the addition of Ajax functionality.

Small sites in particular may struggle to get sufficient benefit from an Ajax interface to balance the associated costs of additional code and added complexity.

# Security

Ajax does not itself seem to present any security issues that are not already present when designing web applications. It is notable, however, that Ajax-enhanced applications tend to contain more client-side code than they did previously.

Because the content of client-side code can be viewed easily by any user of the application, it is important that sensitive information not be revealed within it. In this context, sensitive information is not limited to such things as usernames and passwords (though they are, of course, sensitive), but also includes business logic. Make the server-side scripts responsible for carrying out such issues as database connection. Validate data on the server before applying it to any important processing.

# Test Code Across Multiple Platforms

It will be clear from the content of this book that the various browsers behave differently in their implementation of JavaScript. The major difference in the generation of XMLHTTPRequest object instances between Microsoft and non-Microsoft browsers is a fundamental example, but there is a host of minor differences, too.

The DOM, in particular, is handled rather differently, not only between browsers but also between different versions of the same browser. CSS implementation is another area where minor differences still proliferate.

Although it has always been important to test new applications on various browsers, this is perhaps more important than ever when faced with the added complexity of Ajax applications.

Hopefully browsers will continue to become more standards-compliant, but until then test applications on as many different platforms and with as many different browsers as possible.

# Ajax Won't Cure a Bad Design

All the dynamic interactivity in the world won't correct a web application with a design that is fundamentally flawed.

All the tenets of good web design still apply to Ajax applications:

▶ Write for multiple browsers and validate your code.

▶ Comment and document your code well so that you can debug it later.

▶ Use small graphics wherever possible so that they load quickly.

▶ Make sure that your choices of colors, backgrounds, font sizes, and styles don't make pages difficult to read.

---

The W3C offers a free online validator at http://validator.w3.org/.

*Did you*
*Know?*

---

# Some Programming Gotchas

Some of these have been alluded to in various chapters, but it's worth grouping them here. These are probably the most common programming issues that Ajax developers bump up against at some time or other!

## Browser Caching of GET Requests

Making repeated GET requests to the same URL can often lead to the response coming not from the server but from the browser cache. This problem seems especially significant when using Internet Explorer.

Although in theory this can be cured with the use of suitable HTTP headers, in practice the cache can be stubborn.

An effective way of sidestepping this problem is to add a random element to the URL to which the request is sent; the browser interprets this as a request to a different page and returns a server page rather than a cached version.

In the text we achieved this by adding a random number. Another approach favored by many is to add a number derived from the time, which will of course be different every time:

```
var url = "serverscript.php"+"?rand="+new Date().getTime();
```

## Permission Denied Errors

Receiving a Permission Denied error usually means that you have fallen foul of the security measure preventing cross-domain requests from being made by an XMLHTTPRequest object.

Calls must be made to server programs existing in the same domain as the calling script.

**Watch**
*Out!*

> Be careful that the domain is written in exactly the same way. Somedomain.com may be interpreted as referring to a different domain from www.somedomain.com, and permission will be denied.

## Escaping Content

When constructing queries for GET or POST requests, remember to escape variables that could contain spaces or other nontext characters. In the following code, the value idValue has been collected from a text input field on a form, so we escape it to ensure correct encoding:

```
http.open("GET", url + escape(idValue) + "&rand=" + myRandom, true);
```

# Summary

Ajax undoubtedly has the potential to greatly improve web interfaces. However, the paradigm change from traditional page-based interfaces to highly dynamic applications has created a few potholes for developers to step into. In this chapter we've tried to round up a few of the better-known ones.

Some of these issues have already been encountered in the other chapters in this book, whereas others will perhaps not become apparent until you start to develop real-world applications.

This chapter concludes Part V, "More Complex Ajax Technologies." If you have followed the chapters through to this point, you will by now have a good grip on the fundamentals of the XMLHTTPRequest object, JavaScript, XML, and the Document Object Model, and be capable of creating useful Ajax applications from first principles.

Fortunately, you don't have to always work from first principles. Many open source and commercial projects on the Internet offer a wide variety of Ajax frameworks, tools, and resources.

Part VI, "Ajax Tools and Resources," of the book concludes our journey through Ajax development by looking at some of these resources and their capabilities.

# PART VI

# Ajax Tools and Resources

# CHAPTER 25

# The prototype.js Toolkit

---

## What You'll Learn in This Chapter:

▶ Introducing `prototype.js`
▶ Wrapping `XMLHTTPRequest`—the Ajax Object
▶ Example Project—Stock Price Reader

In this chapter you will learn about the prototype.js JavaScript library and how it can reduce the work required for building capable Ajax applications.

## Introducing prototype.js

Part VI, "Ajax Tools and Resources," looks at some available code libraries and frameworks for Ajax development.

We begin this chapter with Sam Stephenson's *prototype.js*, a popular JavaScript library containing an array of functions useful in the development of cross-browser JavaScript routines, and including specific support for Ajax. You'll see how your JavaScript code can be simplified by using this library's powerful support for DOM manipulation, HTML forms, and the `XMLHTTPRequest` object.

> You'll find the on the CD that accompanies this book a recent version (at the time of writing) of prototype.js
>
> The latest version of the prototype.js library can be downloaded from http://www.prototypejs.org/

**On the CD**

At the time of writing, prototype.js is at version 1.6.0. If you download a different version, check the documentation to see whether there are differences between your version and the one described here.

Including the library in your web application is simple, just include in the <head> section of your HTML document the following line:

```
<script src="prototype.js" Language="JavaScript"
➥type="text/javascript"></script>
```

prototype.js contains a broad range of functions that can make writing JavaScript code quicker, and the resulting scripts cleaner and easier to maintain.

The library includes general-purpose functions providing shortcuts to regular programming tasks, a wrapper for HTML forms, an object to encapsulate the XMLHTTPRequest object, methods and objects for simplifying DOM tasks, and more.

Let's take a look at some of these tools.

## The $() Function

$() is essentially a shortcut to the getElementById() DOM method. Normally, to return the value of a particular element you would use an expression such as

```
var mydata = document.getElementById('someElementID');
```

The $() function simplifies this task by returning the value of the element whose ID is passed to it as an argument:

```
var mydata = $('someElementID');
```

Furthermore, $() (unlike getElementById()) can accept multiple element IDs as an argument and return an array of the associated element values. Consider this line of code:

```
mydataArray = $('id1','id2','id3');
```

In this example:

- ▶ mydataArray[0] contains the value of an element with ID id1.

- ▶ mydataArray[1] contains the value of an element with ID id2.

- ▶ mydataArray[2] contains the value of an element with ID id3.

# The $F() **Function**

The $F() function returns the value of a form input field when the input element or its ID is passed to it as an argument. Look at the following HTML snippet:

```
<input type="text" id="input1" name="input1">
<select id="input2" name="input2">
 <option value="0">Option A</option>
 <option value="1">Option B</option>
 <option value="2">Option C</option>
</select>
```

Here we could use

```
$F('input1')
```

to return the value in the text box and

```
$F('input2')
```

to return the value of the currently selected option of the select box. The $F() function works equally well on check box and text area input elements, making it easy to return the element values regardless of the input element type.

# The Form **Object**

prototype.js defines a Form object having several useful methods for simplifying HTML form manipulation.

You can return an array of a form's input fields by calling the getElements() method:

```
inputs = Form.getElements('thisform');
```

The serialize() method allows input names and values to be formatted into a URL-compatible list:

```
inputlist = Form.serialize('thisform');
```

Using the preceding line of code, the variable inputlist would now contain a string of serialized parameter and value pairs:

```
field1=value1&field2=value2&field3=value3…
```

Form.disable('thisform') and Form.enable('thisform') each do exactly what it says on the tin.

## The `Try.these()` **Function**

Previous chapters discussed the use of exceptions to enable you to catch runtime errors and deal with them cleanly. The `Try.these()` function provides a convenient way to encapsulate these methods to provide a cross-browser solution where JavaScript implementation details differ:

```
return Try.these(function1(),function2(),function3(), …);
```

The functions are processed in sequence, operation moving on to the next function when an error condition causes an exception to be thrown. Operation stops when any of the functions completes successfully, at which point the function returns true.

Applying this function to the creation of an `XMLHTTPRequest` instance shows the simplicity of the resulting code:

```
return Try.these(
   function() {return new ActiveXObject('Msxml2.XMLHTTP')},
   function() {return new ActiveXObject('Microsoft.XMLHTTP')},
   function() {return new XMLHttpRequest()}
   )
```

> You may want to compare this code snippet with Listing 10.1 to see just how much code complexity has been reduced and readability improved.

# **Wrapping** XMLHTTPRequest—**the** Ajax Object

prototype.js defines an `Ajax` object designed to simplify the development of your JavaScript code when building Ajax applications. This object has a number of classes that encapsulate the code you need to send server requests, monitor their progress, and deal with the returned data.

## Ajax.Request

`Ajax.Request` deals with the details of creating an instance of the `XMLHTTPRequest` object and sending a correctly formatted request. Calling it is straightforward:

```
var myAjax = new Ajax.Request( url, {method: 'post',
➥parameters: mydata, onComplete: responsefunction} );
```

In this call, url defines the location of the server resource to be called, method may be either post or get, mydata is a serialized string containing the request parameters, and responsefunction is the name of the callback function that handles the server response.

---

The second argument is constructed using a notation often called *JSON* (*JavaScript Object Notation*). The argument is built up from a series of parameter:value pairs, the whole contained within braces. The parameter values themselves may be JSON objects, arrays, or simple values.

JSON is popular as a data interchange protocol due to its ease of construction, ease of parsing, and language independence. You can find out more about it at http://www.json.org.

*Did you Know?*

---

The onComplete parameter is one of several options corresponding to the possible values of the XMLHTTPRequest readyState properties, in this case a readyState value of 4 (Complete). You might instead specify that the callback function should execute during the prior phases Loading, Loaded, or Interactive, by using the associated parameters onLoading, onLoaded, or onInteractive.

There are several other optional parameters, including

```
asynchronous:false
```

to indicate that a server call should be made synchronously. The default value for the asynchronous option is true.

## Ajax.Updater

On occasions when you require the returned data to update a page element, the Ajax.Updater class can simplify the task. All you need to do is to specify which element should be updated:

```
var myAjax = new Ajax.Updater(elementID, url, options);
```

The call is somewhat similar to that for Ajax.Request but with the addition of the target element's ID as the first argument. The following is a code example of Ajax.Updater:

```
<script>
  function updateDIV(mydiv)
  {
      var url = 'http://example.com/serverscript.php';
      var params = 'param1=value1&param2=value2';
      var myAjax = new Ajax.Updater
```

```
              (
              mydiv,
              url,
              {method: 'get', parameters: params}
              );

     }
</script>
<input type="button" value="Go" onclick="updateDIV(targetDiv)">
<div id="targetDiv"></div>
```

Once again, several additional options may be used when making the call. A noteworthy one is the addition of

```
evalscripts:true
```

to the options list. With this option added, any JavaScript code returned by the server will be evaluated.

## Ajax.PeriodicalUpdater

The `Ajax.PeriodicalUpdater` class can be used to repeatedly create an `Ajax.Updater` instance. In this way you can have a page element updated after a certain time interval has elapsed. This can be useful for such applications as a stock market ticker or an RSS reader because it ensures that the visitor is always viewing reasonably up-to-date information.

`Ajax.PeriodicalUpdater` adds two further parameters to the `Ajax.Updater` options:

- ▶ `frequency`—The delay in seconds between successive updates. Default is two seconds.

- ▶ `decay`—The multiplier by which successive delays are increased if the server should return unchanged data. Default value is 1, which leaves the delay constant.

Here's an example call to `Ajax.PeriodicalUpdater`:

```
var myAjax = new Ajax.PeriodicalUpdater(elementID, url,
➡{frequency: 3.0, decay: 2.0});
```

Here we elected to set the initial delay to 3 seconds and have this delay double in length each time unchanged data is returned by the server.

# Example Project—Stock Price Reader

Let's use the prototype.js library to build a simple reader that updates periodically to show the latest value returned from the server. In this example, we'll use a simple server-side script rand.php to simulate a changing stock price:

```php
<?php
srand ((double) microtime( )*1000000);
$price = 50 + rand(0,5000)/100;
echo "$price";
?>
```

This script first initializes PHP's random number routine by calling the srand() function and passing it an argument derived from the current time. The rand(0,5000) function is then used to generate a random number that is manipulated arithmetically to produce phony "stock prices" in the range 50.00 to 100.00.

Now let's build a simple HTML page to display the current stock price. This page forms the basis for our Ajax application:

```html
<!DOCTYPE HTML PUBLIC "-//W3C//DTD HTML 4.01 Transitional//EN"
"http://www.w3.org/TR/html4/loose.dtd">
<html>
<head>
<script src="prototype.js" Language="JavaScript"
➥type="text/javascript"></script>
<title>Stock Reader powered by Prototype.js</title>
</head>
<body>
<h2>Stock Reader</h2>
<h4>Powered by Prototype.js</h4>
<p>Current Stock Price:</p>
<div id="price"></div>
</body>
</html>
```

Note that we included the prototype.js library by means of a <script> tag in the document head. We also defined a <div> with id set to "price", which will be used to display the current stock price.

We now need to implement the Ajax.PeriodicalUpdater class, which we'll attach to the document body element's onLoad event handler. Listing 25.1 shows the complete script.

**LISTING 25.1**   Ajax Stock Price Reader Using prototype.js

```
<!DOCTYPE HTML PUBLIC "-//W3C//DTD HTML 4.01
➥ Transitional//EN"
➥"http://www.w3.org/TR/html4/loose.dtd">
<html>
<head>
<script src="prototype.js" Language="JavaScript"
➥type="text/javascript"></script>
<script>
function checkprice()
{
var myAjax = new Ajax.PeriodicalUpdater('price',
➥'rand.php', {method: 'post', frequency: 3.0,
➥ decay: 1});
}
</script>
<title>Stock Reader powered by Prototype.js</title>
</head>
<body onLoad="checkprice()">
<h2>Stock Reader</h2>
<h4>Powered by Prototype.js</h4>
<p>Current Stock Price:</p>
<div id="price"></div>
</body>
</html>
```

Look how simple the code for the application has become through using prototype.js. Implementing the application is merely a matter of defining a one-line function `checkprice()` to instantiate our repeating Ajax call and calling that function from the body element's `onLoad` event handler.

From the arguments passed to `Ajax.PeriodicalUpdater`, you'll see that a 3-second repeat interval has been specified. This period does not change with subsequent calls because the `decay` value has been set to 1.

Figure 25.1 shows the application running. What cannot be seen from the figure, of course, is the stock price updating itself every 3 seconds to show a new value.

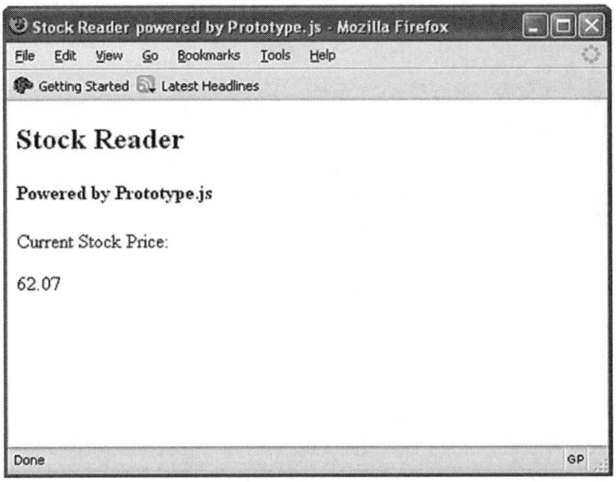

**FIGURE 25.1**
Ajax stock
reader.

This simple example does not come close to showing off the power and versatility of the prototype.js library. Rather, it is intended to get you started with your own experiments by offering an easy point of access to this great resource.

## Try It Yourself ▼

### Using prototype.js

Review some of the example JavaScript and Ajax applications from earlier in the book, and see which can be rewritten more simply or more effectively by using tools from the prototype.js toolkit. ▲

# Summary

In this first chapter in Part VI of the book, we discussed the use of the powerful and elegant prototype.js JavaScript library.

The functions made available by this library greatly simplify some of the trickier programming tasks when developing Ajax applications.

The library offers good support for the XMLHTTPRequest object, along with time-saving shortcuts for DOM handling, HTML forms, and many other techniques relevant to Ajax development.

# CHAPTER 26

# Using Rico

---

## *What You'll Learn in This Chapter:*

- ▶ Introducing Rico
- ▶ Rico's Other Interface Tools

In this chapter you will learn the basics of using Rico, a powerful Ajax and user interface development framework.

## Introducing Rico

In Chapter 25, "The prototype.js Toolkit," we looked at prototype.js, a powerful and useful JavaScript library that simplifies many of the programming tasks facing the Ajax developer.

In this chapter we'll take a look at using Rico, a sophisticated Ajax framework employing the prototype.js library.

You'll find Rico on the CD that accompanies this book, in the Frameworks folder.

On the
CD

Rico is an open source library that extends the capabilities of prototype.js to provide a rich set of interface development tools. In addition to the Ajax development techniques discussed so far, Rico offers a whole range of tools such as drag-and-drop, cinematic effects, and more.

> *Rico* is the Spanish word for *rich*, which seems appropriate for a toolkit designed for building rich user interfaces!

## Using Rico in Your Applications

To start using Rico to build applications with rich user interfaces, you need to include both Rico and prototype.js libraries in the <head>...</head> section of your web pages.

```
<script src="scripts/prototype.js"></script>
<script src="scripts/rico.js"></script>
```

## Rico's AjaxEngine

The inclusion of rico.js causes an instance called `ajaxEngine` of an `AjaxEngine` object to be created automatically ready for you to use. The `AjaxEngine` is Rico's mechanism for adding Ajax capabilities to your web pages.

The `AjaxEngine` requires a three-step process to update page elements via Ajax:

1. Register the request handler. Registering the request handler associates a unique name with a particular URL to be called via Ajax.

2. Register the response handler. Rico can deal with the return of both HTML data and JavaScript code within the XML returned from the server. In the former case, the response handler identifies a page element that is to be updated using the returned data; in the latter case, a JavaScript object that handles the server response.

3. Make the Ajax call from the page by using an appropriate event handler.

We first register our request handler by making a call to the `registerRequest()` method of `ajaxEngine`:

```
ajaxEngine.registerRequest('getData','getData.php');
```

We have now associated the name `getData` with a request to the server routine `getData.php`. That server-side routine is required to return a response in well-formed XML. The following is an example of a typical response:

```
<ajax-response>
   <response type="element" id="showdata">
     <div class="datadisplay">
        The <b>cat</b> sat on the <b>mat</b>
     </div>
   </response>
</ajax-response>
```

Such responses always have a root element <ajax-response>. The <response> element it contains in this example has two attributes, type element and id showdata. These signify, respectively, that the response contains HTML, and that this HTML is to be used to update the page element having id showdata. This element is updated via its innerHTML property.

> Rico is capable of updating multiple page elements from one request. To achieve this, the <ajax-response> element may contain multiple <response> elements.

*Did you Know?*

The other form of response that Rico can return is a JavaScript object. Here's an example:

```
<ajax-response>
  <response type="object" id="myHandler">
    <sentence>The cat sat on the mat.</sentence>
  </response>
</ajax-response>
```

Here the type has been set to object, indicating that the content is to be dealt with by a JavaScript object, the identity of which is contained in the id value (here myHandler). The content of the response is always passed to the ajaxUpdate method of this object.

How the response handler is registered depends on which type of response we are dealing with. For responses of type element, you can simply call

```
ajaxEngine.registerAjaxElement('showdata');
```

In the case of responses containing a JavaScript object, you will need

```
ajaxEngine.registerAjaxObject('myHandler', new myHandler());
```

Whereas responses of type element are simply intended for the updating of HTML page elements, responses of type object can have handlers to process responses in any way they want. This allows Rico applications to be built ranging from simple to sophisticated.

# A Simple Example

We can see Rico in action by using the simple script of Listing 26.1. This application updates two HTML elements with a single call to Rico's ajaxEngine object. The script for the application is in Listing 26.1.

**LISTING 26.1** A Simple Rico Application

```
<!DOCTYPE HTML PUBLIC "-//W3C//DTD HTML 4.01
➥ Transitional//EN"
➥"http://www.w3.org/TR/html4/loose.dtd">
<html>
<head>
<title>Testing OpenRico</title>
<script src="prototype.js"></script>
<script src="rico.js"></script>
<script type="text/javascript">
function callRICO()
{
ajaxEngine.registerRequest('myRequest', 'ricotest.php');
ajaxEngine.registerAjaxElement('display');
ajaxEngine.registerAjaxElement('heading');
}
</script>
</head>
<body onload=" callRICO();">
<div id="heading"><h3>Demonstrating Rico</h3></div>
<input type="button" value="Get Server Data"
➥ onclick="ajaxEngine.sendRequest('myRequest');"/>
<div id="display"><p>This text should be replaced with
➥server data ...</p></div>
</body>
</html>
```

You will see from the code that the single function callRICO() is used to register both the single request handler myRequest and two response handlers. The response handlers are used to update two <div> containers; one of these contains the page's heading, the other a short text message. On making the Rico request, the contents of both are updated, leaving the page with a new title and now displaying some server information instead of the previous text message. Figure 26.1 shows before and after screenshots.

The server routine is a simple PHP script that outputs the required XML data. The script uses PHP's $_SERVER['SERVER_SIGNATURE'] global variable. Note that the script constructs and returns two separate <response> elements, each responsible for updating a particular element in the HTML page.

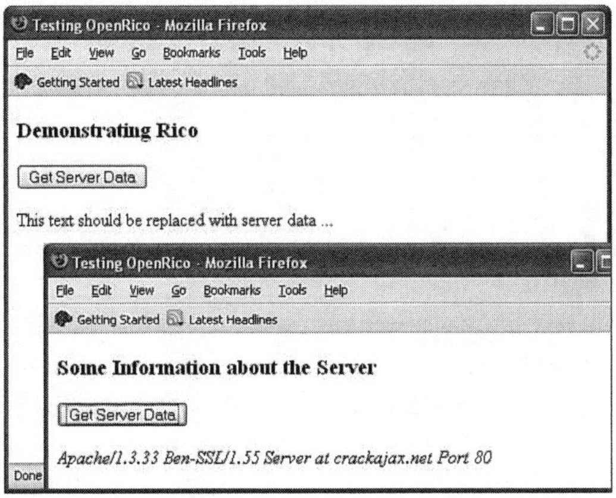

**FIGURE 26.1**
Updating multiple page elements with Rico.

Listing 26.2 shows the server script.

**LISTING 26.2**    The Server Script for Generating `<ajax-response>`

```php
<?php
header("Content-Type:text/xml");
header("Cache-Control:no-cache");
header("Pragma:no-cache");
echo "<ajax-response><response type=\"element\"
➥id=\"display\"><p>"
➥.$_SERVER['SERVER_SIGNATURE']
➥."</p></response>
➥<response type=\"element\" id=\"heading\">
➥<h3>Some Information about the Server</h3>
➥</response></ajax-response>";
?>
```

Chapter 11, "Talking with the Server," discussed problems that can occur due to the browser cache. In that chapter we used a workaround involving adding a parameter of random value to the URL of the server resource that we wanted to call.

This script example uses another technique, including the header commands

```
header("Cache-Control:no-cache");
header("Pragma:no-cache");
```

instructing the browser not to cache this page, but to collect a new copy from the server each time.

*Did you*
*Know?*

> PHP's $_SERVER global array variable was introduced in PHP 4.1.0. If you have an older version of PHP installed, you'll need the global variable $HTTP_SERVER_VARS instead.

# Rico's Other Interface Tools

Rico's capabilities aren't limited to aiding the development of Ajax applications. Let's now look at some other capabilities you can add to your user interfaces using the Rico toolkit. Although these techniques do not themselves use Ajax, it takes little imagination to realize what they might achieve when combined with Rico's Ajax tools.

## Drag-and-Drop

Both desktop applications and the operating systems on which they run make widespread use of drag-and-drop to simplify the user interface. The JavaScript techniques required to implement drag-and-drop can be tricky to master, not least because of the many cross-browser issues that arise.

Drag-and-drop using Rico, however, is simple.

Including the rico.js file in your application automatically causes the creation of an object called dndMgr, Rico's Drag and Drop Manager. Using the dndMgr object is much like using AjaxEngine; this time, though, we need to register not Ajax requests and responses, but *draggable* items and *drop zones* (page elements that can receive dragged items).

These tasks are carried out via the registerDraggable and registerDropZone methods:

```
dndMgr.registerDraggable( new Rico.Draggable('test',
➥'dragElementID') );
dndMgr.registerDropZone( new Rico.Dropzone
➥('dropElementID') );
```

These two simple commands declare, respectively, a page element with ID dragElementID as being draggable, and another element with ID dropElementID as a drop zone. The argument 'test' of the registerDraggable() method defines a type for the draggable item, which can be tested and used by subsequent code, if required.

# Example of a Drag-and-Drop Interface

Listing 26.3 shows how simple it is to implement drag-and-drop using Rico. The displayed HTML page is shown in Figure 26.2.

**LISTING 26.3**   Simple Drag-and-Drop Using Rico

```
<!DOCTYPE HTML PUBLIC "-//W3C//DTD HTML 4.01
➥ Transitional//EN"
➥"http://www.w3.org/TR/html4/loose.dtd">
 <html>
<head>
  <script src="prototype.js"></script>
  <script src="rico.js"></script>
  <style>
  body {
  font: 10px normal arial, helvetica, verdana;
  background-color:#dddddd;
  }

  div.simpleDropPanel {
   width    : 260px;
   height   : 180px;
   background-color: #ffffff;
   padding  : 5px;
   border   : 1px solid #333333;
  }

  div.box {
   width         : 200px;
   cursor        : hand;
   background-color: #ffffff;
   -moz-opacity     : 0.6;
   filter        : alpha(Opacity=60);
   border: 1px solid #333333;
  }
  </style>
</head>
<body>
<table width="550">
<tr>
  <td><h3>Drag and Drop</h3>
  <p>Drag and drop data items into the target fields
➥using the left mouse button in the usual way.
➥Note how available target fields change colour
➥during the drag operation.</p>
  <p>Reload the page to start again.</p>
  <div class="box" id="draggable1">This is a piece
➥of draggable data</div>
  <div class="box" id="draggable2">
➥This is another</div>
  <div class="box" id="draggable3">
➥And this is a third</div>
```

**LISTING 26.3**    Continued

```
<br/>
<table>
<tr>
  <td>
    <div id="droponme" class="simpleDropPanel">
        <b>Drop Zone 1</b><br />A simple text area
    </div>
  </td>
  <td>
    <b>Drop Zone 2</b><br />
    A form text entry field.
    <form><textarea name="dropzone" id="droponme2"
➥ rows="6" cols="30"></textarea></form>
  </td>
 </tr>
 </table>
 </td>
</tr>
</table>
<script>
  dndMgr.registerDraggable( new
➥Rico.Draggable('foo','draggable1') );
  dndMgr.registerDraggable( new
➥Rico.Draggable('foo','draggable2') );
  dndMgr.registerDraggable( new Rico.
➥Draggable('foo','draggable3') );
  dndMgr.registerDropZone( new Rico.Dropzone
➥('droponme') );
  dndMgr.registerDropZone( new Rico.Dropzone
➥('droponme2') );
</script>
</body>
</html>
```

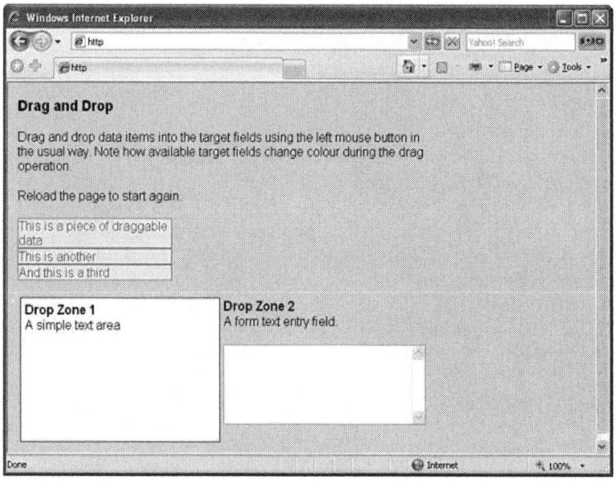

**FIGURE 26.2**
The simple
drag-and-drop
application.

The two JavaScript libraries rico.js and prototype.js are included in the <head> of the document along with style definitions for various page elements.

Note that two page elements in particular, a <div> container and a <textarea> input field, have been given IDs of dropzone1 and dropzone2. Further down the listing, these two elements are defined as drop zones for our drag-and-drop operations by the lines

```
dndMgr.registerDropZone( new Rico.Dropzone('droponme') );
dndMgr.registerDropZone( new Rico.Dropzone('droponme2') );
```

You'll see too that three small <div> containers have been defined in the page and given IDs of draggable1, draggable2, and draggable3. As you have no doubt guessed, they are to become draggable page elements and are defined as such by the following code lines:

```
dndMgr.registerDraggable( new Rico.Draggable('foo',
➥'draggable1') );
dndMgr.registerDraggable( new Rico.Draggable('foo',
➥'draggable2') );
dndMgr.registerDraggable( new Rico.Draggable('foo',
➥'draggable3') );
```

That's all there is to it! Rico takes care of all the details, even changing the look of the available drop zones while something is being dragged, as shown in Figure 26.3.

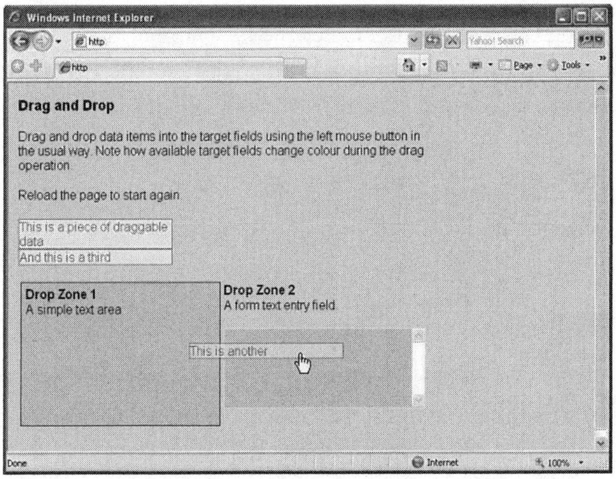

**FIGURE 26.3**
Drop zones highlighted during drag operation.

When released above an available drop zone, draggable items position themselves inline with the HTML code of the drop zone element, as shown in Figure 26.4.

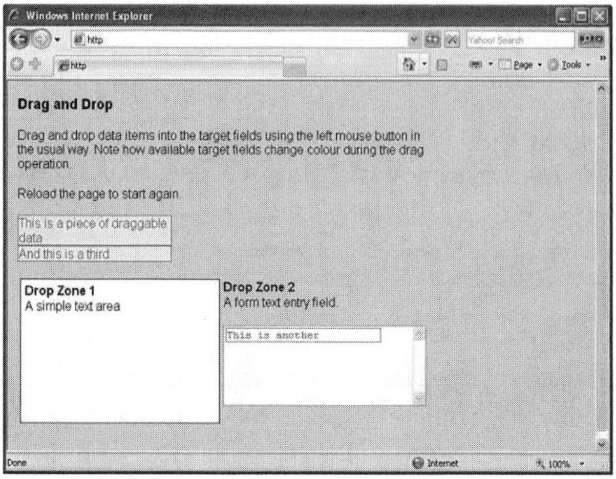

**FIGURE 26.4**
After completing
the drag-and-
drop.

## Cinematic Effects

In addition to Ajax and drag-and-drop tools, Rico also makes available a host of
user interface gadgets known collectively as *cinematic effects*.

**By the Way**

> Rico's cinematic effects are extensions to the `Effect` class found in prototype.js.

These effects include animation of page elements (changing their sizes and/or
shapes), fading effects (altering the opacity of page elements), applying rounded
corners to objects, and manipulating object colors.

Used alongside the interface techniques previously discussed, these effects can help
you to build sophisticated, eye-catching, and user-friendly interfaces much more
reminiscent of desktop applications than of web pages.

## Summary

Following our examination of the prototype.js library in the Chapter 25, this chapter moved on to experiment with Rico. Rico is an open source framework based on
prototype.js that offers a simple way to integrate Ajax, along with drag-and-drop
and other visual effects, into user interface designs.

In Chapter 27, we'll have a brief look at another toolkit based on prototype.js,
namely Script.aculo.us.

# CHAPTER 27

# Using Script.aculo.us

---

## What You'll Learn in This Chapter:

▶ Downloading the Library

▶ Including the Files

▶ Using Effects

▶ Building the Script

We have already seen in previous chapters how powerful the prototype.js library is, and we have used the Rico library, built on prototype.js, to create some visual effects with very little code.

In this chapter you will learn the basics of using Script.aculo.us, a powerful Ajax and user interface development framework, also based on prototype.js.

To see how simple it is to use, you will now create an example script that includes the Script.aculo.us library and use event handlers to demonstrate several of the available effects.

This example was created using version 1.5.1 of the Script.aculo.us library. It should work with later versions, but the library might have changed since this was written. If you have trouble, you might need to use this specific version.

**Watch Out!**

## Downloading the Library

To use the library, you will need to obtain it and copy the files you need to the same folder where you will store your script.

You will find a copy of Script.aculo.us on the CD accompanying this book. Alternatively, you can download the latest version of the library from the Script.aculo.us website at http://script.aculo.us/downloads.

The download is available as a Zip file. Inside the Zip file you will find a folder called `scriptaculous-js-x.x.x`. You will need the following files from the folders under this folder:

- `prototype.js` (the Prototype library) from the `lib` folder
- `effects.js` (the effects functions) from the `src` folder

Copy both of these files to a folder on your computer, and be sure to create your demonstration script in the same folder.

The Script.aculo.us download includes many other files, and you can include the entire library if you intend to use all of its features. For this example, you only need the two files described here.

## Including the Files

To add the library to your HTML document, simply use `<script>` tags to include the two JavaScript files you copied from the download:

```
<script type="text/javascript" src="prototype.js"> </script>
<script type="text/javascript" src="effects.js"> </script>
```

If you include these statements as the first things in the `<head>` section of your document, the library functions will be available to other scripts or event handlers anywhere in the page.

## Using Effects

After you have included the library, you simply need to include a bit of JavaScript to trigger the effects. We will use a section of the page wrapped in a `<div>` tag with the id value `test` to demonstrate the effects. Each effect is triggered by a simple event handler on a button. For example, this code defines the Fade Out button:

```
<input type="button" value="Fade Out"
    onClick="new Effect.Fade($('test'))">
```

This uses the $ function built into Prototype to obtain the object for the element with the id value test, and then passes it to the Effect.Fade function built into Script.aculo.us.

> This example will demonstrate six effects: Fade, Appear, SlideUp, SlideDown, Highlight, and Shake. There are more than 16 effects in the library, plus methods for supporting Drag and Drop and other features. See http://script.aculo.us for details.

# Building the Script

After you have included the libraries, you can combine them with event handlers and some example text to create a complete demonstration of Script.aculo.us effects. The complete HTML document for this example is shown in Listing 27.1.

**LISTING 27.1    The Complete Library Effects Example**

```html
<html>
<head>
<title>Testing script.aculo.us effects</title>
<script type="text/javascript" src="prototype.js"> </script>
<script type="text/javascript" src="effects.js"> </script>
</head>
<body">
<h1>Testing script.aculo.us Effects</h1>
<form name="form1">
<input type="button" value="Fade Out"
    onClick="new Effect.Fade($('test'))">
<input type="button" value="Fade In"
    onClick="new Effect.Appear($('test'))">
<input type="button" value="Slide Up"
    onClick="new Effect.SlideUp($('test'))">
<input type="button" value="Slide Down"
    onClick="new Effect.SlideDown($('test'))">
<input type="button" value="Highlight"
    onClick="new Effect.Highlight($('test'))">
<input type="button" value="Shake"
    onClick="new Effect.Shake($('test'))">
</form>
<div id="test"
    style="background-color:#CCC; margin:20px; padding:10px;">
<h2>Testing Effects</h2>
<hr>
<p>This section of the document is within a &lt;div&gt; element
with the <b>id</b> value <b>test</b>. The event handlers on the
buttons above send this object to the
<a href="http://script.aculo.us/">script.aculo.us</a> library
to perform effects. Click the buttons to see the effects.
</p>
</div>
</body>
</html>
```

This document starts with two `<script>` tags to include the library's files. The effects are triggered by the event handlers defined for each of the six buttons. The `<div>` section at the end defines the `test` element that will be used to demonstrate the effects.

To try this example, make sure the `prototype.js` and `effects.js` files from Script.aculo.us are stored in the same folder as your script, and then load it into a browser. The display should look like Figure 27.1, and you can use the six buttons at the top of the page to trigger effects.

**FIGURE 27.1**
The library effects example as displayed by Firefox.

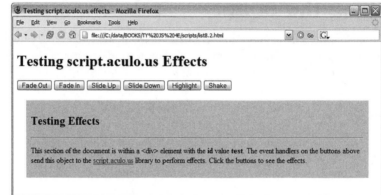

## Try It Yourself

### Exploring Script.aculo.us

Explore the facilities available in the Script.aculo.us framework and compare the approach taken to that of the Rico library discussed in Chapter 26.

Feel free to experiment with the other functionality that the library offers and see what you can achieve.

# Summary

Script.aculo.us is another powerful and easy-to-use toolkit based on the prototype.js library. With just a few lines of code, you can add impressive effects to your page elements.

This chapter has barely scratched the surface of what Script.aculo.us can achieve. Read the package documentation and experiment with the library to see how you can build powerful and impressive interactive pages with minimal additional programming.

# CHAPTER 28

# Using XOAD

---

## What You'll Learn in This Chapter:

▶ Introducing XOAD

▶ XOAD HTML

▶ Advanced Programming with XOAD

In this chapter you will learn about XOAD, a server-side framework with Ajax support written by Stanimir Angeloff.

# Introducing XOAD

So far in this part of the book we have looked at the prototype.js, script.aculo.us and Rico libraries and how they can help you to develop Ajax applications. Unlike these client-side libraries, which are written in JavaScript, XOAD is a *server-side* Ajax toolkit written in PHP.

This chapter discusses some of the concepts behind XOAD and the basics of its use.

> *XOAD* is an acronym for *XMLHTTP Object-oriented Application Development.*

All our work so far has concentrated on the use of JavaScript to handle both the server request and the returned data in Ajax applications. XOAD is a server-based solution written in PHP that takes a slightly different approach.

XOAD applications make server-based PHP functions available to the client-side JavaScript interpreter by passing serialized versions of them as JavaScript objects.

**By the Way**

Under the hood, XOAD employs JSON (JavaScript Object Notation) for communications. JSON was introduced in Chapter 25, "The prototype.js Toolkit."

## Downloading and Installing XOAD

**On the CD**

A recent version of XOAD is included on the companion CD. To make sure you have the most up-to-date version, see the following download instructions.

XOAD is made up of many PHP and supporting scripts and can be downloaded as an archive file from http://sourceforge.net/projects/xoad. To install XOAD successfully, you need FTP access to a web server that supports PHP and (to use the more advanced features of XOAD) the MySQL database. Detailed instructions for installing XOAD can be found in the downloaded material, and there is a public forum at http://forums.xoad.org/.

## A Simple XOAD Page

Let's take a look at an example of the simplest XOAD page. Suppose that you have a PHP class that you want to use in your XOAD application. This class is stored in the PHP file myClass.class.php:

```php
<?php
class myClass {
  function stLength($mystring) {
      return strlen($mystring);
    }
  function xoadGetMeta() {
      XOAD_Client::mapMethods($this, array('stLength'));
      XOAD_Client::publicMethods($this, array('stLength'));
    }
}
?>
```

This simple class has only one function, stLength(), which merely returns the length of a string variable. We also added some *metadata* to the class in the form of the function xoadGetMeta(). This information tells XOAD which methods from the class are available to be exported to the main application. In this case there is just one, stLength().

**Watch Out!**

It is not absolutely necessary to include metadata in the class, but it is recommended. Without metadata, all methods will be public, and method names will be converted to lowercase.

Now you need to start constructing the main application script xoad.php.

The Ajax applications developed in previous chapters were HTML files with file extensions .htm or .html. Because our XOAD application contains PHP code, it must have a suitable file extension. Most web server and PHP implementations will accept a file extension of .php, and some will allow other extensions such as .php4 or .phtml.

**Did you Know?**

Listing 28.1 shows the XOAD application. This is a fairly pointless program that simply returns the length of a string, "My XOAD Application". Nevertheless, it demonstrates the concept of methods from server-side PHP classes being made available on the client side as JavaScript objects.

**LISTING 28.1**  A Simple XOAD Application

```php
<?php
require_once('myClass.class.php');
require_once('xoad.php');
XOAD_Server::allowClasses('myClass');
if (XOAD_Server::runServer()) {
  exit;
  }
?>
<?= XOAD_Utilities::header('.') ?>
<script type="text/javascript">
var myobj = <?= XOAD_Client::register(new myClass()) ?>;
var mystring = 'My XOAD Application';
myobj.onStLengthError = function(error) {
  alert(error.message);
  return true;
  }
myobj.stLength(mystring, function(result) {
  document.write('String: ' + mystring
 + '<br />Length: ' + result);
  });
</script>
```

On loading the preceding document into a browser, the page simply says:

```
String: My XOAD Application
Length: 19
```

I won't go into much detail about how the PHP code works; we've discussed the PHP language elsewhere. It's important, though, to understand the concepts that underpin the code, so let's step through Listing 28.1 and try to understand what's happening:

```php
<?php
require_once('myClass.class.php');
require_once('xoad.php');
XOAD_Server::allowClasses('myClass');
```

```
if (XOAD_Server::runServer()) {
  exit;
  }
?>
<?= XOAD_Utilities::header('.') ?>
```

The first part of the script includes both xoad.php and the required class file myClass.class.php, and informs XOAD which classes it may access (in this case only one).

The XOAD function runServer() checks whether the XOAD request is a client callback, and if so handles it appropriately. The header() function is used to register the client header files.

Now let's look at the remainder of the script:

```
<script type="text/javascript">
var myobj = <?= XOAD_Client::register(new myClass()) ?>;
var mystring = 'My XOAD Application';
myobj.onStLengthError = function(error) {
  alert(error.message);
  return true;
  }
myobj.stLength(mystring, function(result) {
  document.write('String: ' + mystring
➥+ '<br />Length: ' + result);
  });
</script>
```

See how the remainder of the script is a <script>...</script> element? The line

```
var myobj = <?= XOAD_Client::register(new myClass()) ?>;
```

exports the public methods declared in myClass.class.php to a JavaScript object. We now have a JavaScript object with a method stLength() that allows us to use the method of the same name from the PHP class myClass.

# XOAD HTML

XOAD HTML is an extension that allows for the easy updating of HTML page elements using XOAD. The following examples show the use of the XOAD_HTML::getElementBy ID() and XOAD_HTML::getElementsByTagName() methods, which do exactly the same thing as their equivalent JavaScript DOM methods.

## XOAD_HTML::getElementById()

You will recognize the layout of the code in Listing 28.2 as being similar in structure to the basic XOAD program discussed earlier.

Rather than include an external class file, in this example we have defined a class, Updater, within the application itself. The class contains a single function, change().

The first line in that function uses XOAD_HTML::getElementById() to identify the page element with and ID of display. Subsequent program lines proceed to change the text and background color of the page element.

The function change() is made available as a method of the JavaScript object myobj and can then be called like any other JavaScript method:

```
<a href="#server" onclick="myobj.change();
➥return false;">Change It!</a>
```

Figure 28.1 shows the program's operation.

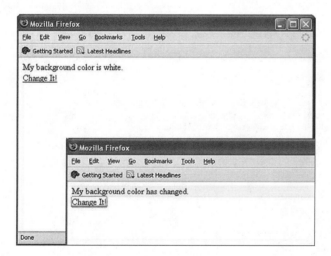

**FIGURE 28.1**
Using
XOAD_HTML:
:getElement
ById().

**LISTING 28.2**   Application to Use XOAD_HTML::getElementById

```php
<?php
class Updater
{
   function change()
   {
     $mytext =& XOAD_HTML::getElementById('display');
     $mytext->style['backgroundColor'] = 'yellow';
     $mytext->innerHTML = 'My background
```

**LISTING 28.2    Continued**

```
➥ color has changed.';
    }
}
define('XOAD_AUTOHANDLE', true);
require_once('xoad.php');
?>
<?= XOAD_Utilities::header('.') ?>
<div id="display">My background color is white.</div>
<script type="text/javascript">
var myobj = <?= XOAD_Client::register(new Updater()) ?>;
</script>
<a href="#server" onclick="myobj.change();
➥return false;">Change It!</a>
```

# XOAD_HTML::getElementsByTagName()

The XOAD_HTML::getElementsByTagName() method, like its JavaScript equivalent, returns an array of elements with a certain element type. Listing 28.3 identifies all page elements of type <div> and changes some of their style attributes.

**LISTING 28.3    Changing All Page Elements of a Given Type**

```
<?php
class Updater
{
    function change()
    {
        $mydivs =& XOAD_HTML::getElementsByTagName('div');
        $mydivs->style['height'] = '60';
        $mydivs->style['width'] = '350';
        $mydivs->style['backgroundColor'] = 'lightgreen';
        $mydivs->innerHTML =
➥'Size and color changed by XOAD';
    }
}
define('XOAD_AUTOHANDLE', true);
require_once('xoad.php');
?>
<?= XOAD_Utilities::header('.') ?>
<script type="text/javascript">
var myobj = <?= XOAD_Client::register(new Updater()) ?>;
</script>
<style>
div {
border:1px solid black;
height:80;
width:150
}
</style>
<div>Div 1</div>
```

**LISTING 28.3**  Continued

```
<br />
<div>Div 2</div>
<br />
<div>Div 3</div>
<a href="#server" onclick="myobj.change();
return false;">Update All Divs</a>
```

The three <div> elements in the page are identified by XOAD_HTML::getElementsBy
TagName() and have their styles and sizes changed.

Figure 28.2 shows the program in operation.

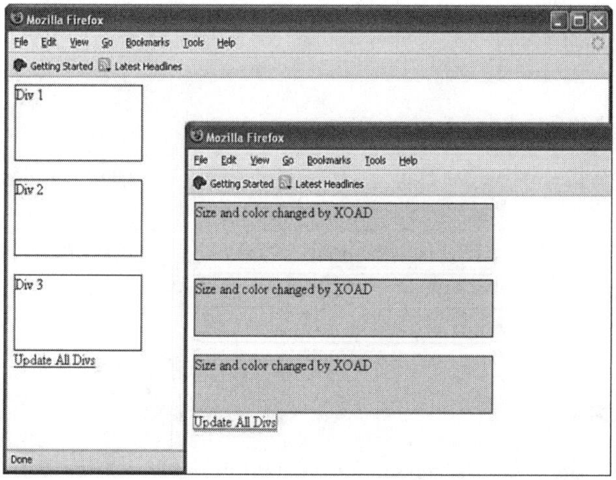

**FIGURE 28.2**
Selecting multiple page elements with XOAD_HTML.

---

XOAD_HTML has many other capabilities. Details of all the functions available within XOAD_HTML are in the XOAD download.

*Did you Know?*

# Advanced Programming with XOAD

XOAD has a range of advanced capabilities over and above those discussed in this chapter. In case you want to investigate the limits of what is possible using XOAD, here is an overview of the currently supported techniques.

## XOAD Events

The XOAD framework also has support for *events*. An XOAD event instigated on one client's computer can be stored on the server and subsequently detected by other clients, making it possible to build complex applications in which users can interact. Such applications might, for instance, include chat, groupware, or similar collaborative tools.

## Cache Handling with XOAD

XOAD allows for the caching on the server using the XOAD_Cache class. Caching results gives significant performance improvements, especially when server-side routines are time-intensive (such as sorting a large data set or performing queries on a sizeable database table).

## XOAD Controls

You can define custom client controls in XOAD using the XOAD_Controls class.

At the time of writing, the current version of XOAD is 0.6.0.0. If the version you download is different, consult the documentation included in the download.

# Summary

This chapter examined a server-side implementation of an Ajax toolkit, in the form of XOAD.

XOAD allows the methods contained within PHP classes stored on the server to be made available to client programs using JavaScript. This forms an interesting contrast in approach compared to the client-side techniques discussed in Chapters 25 and 26.

This concludes Part VI of the book and, in fact, the book itself. You should now have a good understanding of JavaScript programming, PHP programming and Ajax application architecture.

# APPENDIX

# JavaScript, PHP, and Ajax Websites

Although you've learned a lot about JavaScript, PHP, and Ajax, there's still a lot to know. If you'd like to move on to advanced features of JavaScript or learn more, the resources listed in this appendix will be helpful.

## JavaScript Websites

The following websites will help you learn more about JavaScript:

▶ The JavaScript Workshop is a weblog about JavaScript written by Michael Moncur, the author of this book. There you'll find updates on the JavaScript language and the DOM, as well as detailed tutorials on beginning and advanced tasks.

http://www.jsworkshop.com/

▶ The DOM Scripting Task Force, part of the Web Standards Project, works toward better use of standards in scripting, and has an informative weblog with the latest on JavaScript and DOM standards.

http://domscripting.webstandards.org/

▶ The Mozilla Project's JavaScript section has information on the latest updates to the JavaScript language, as well as documentation, links to resources, and information about JavaScript implementations.

http://www.mozilla.org/js/

# PHP Websites

The following sites are invaluable for PHP Developers:

▶ The PHP home site offers downloads, documentation, tutorials, FAQs, and much more, including user-submitted code.

http:// www.php.net/

▶ PHPBuilder is a meeting point for anybody interested in PHP, and includes a Code Library, Community pages, PHP news, and much more.

http://www.phpbuilder.com/

▶ Planet PHP maintains a list of many important PHP-related blogs. Here you can find news, views, and opinions from influential people in the world of PHP.

http://www.planet-php.net/

# Web Development Sites

The following sites have news and information about web technologies, including JavaScript, XML, and the DOM, as well as basic HTML:

▶ The W3C (World Wide Web Consortium) is the definitive source for information about the HTML and CSS standards.

http://www.w3.org/

▶ WebReference.com has information and articles about web technologies ranging from Java to plug-ins.

http://www.webreference.com/

▶ *Digital Web Magazine* features regular online articles on everything from JavaScript and web design to running a web business.

http://www.digital-web.com/

# Ajax Websites

Some useful websites dedicated to Ajax programming:

- ▶ Ajax Matters contains a wide range of in-depth articles about all aspects of Ajax.

  http://www.ajaxmatters.com/

- ▶ Ajaxian is a well respected and massive resource with news, podcasts, articles, and more about every aspect of Ajax programming.

  http://ajaxian.com/

- ▶ Crack Ajax contains tutorials, code snippets, demos, and completely worked projects, as well as a forum for Ajax programmers.

  http://www.crackajax.net.

# Glossary

The following are some terms relating to web development that are used throughout this book. Although most of them are explained in the text of the book, this section can serve as a useful quick reference while reading the book, or while reading other sources of JavaScript, PHP, or Ajax information.

**ActiveX** A technology developed by Microsoft to allow components to be created, primarily for Windows computers. ActiveX components, or controls, can be embedded in web pages.

**AHAH (Asynchronous HTML and HTTP)** A simplified subset of Ajax, useful for updating text on a web page without page refresh.

**Ajax (Asynchronous JavaScript and XML)** a combination of technologies that allows JavaScript to send requests to a server, receive responses, and update sections of a page without loading a new page.

**algorithm** The process, method or routine used to solve a problem.

**anchor** In HTML, a named location within a document, specified using the <a> tag. Anchors can also act as links.

**applet** A Java program that is designed to be embedded in a web page.

**argument** A parameter that is passed to a function when it is called. Arguments are specified within parentheses in the function call.

**array** A set of variables that can be referred to with the same name and a number, called an index.

**attribute** A property value that can be defined within an HTML tag. Attributes specify style, alignment, and other aspects of the element defined by the tag.

**assignment** The setting of a variable to a particular value.

**Boolean** A type of variable that can store only two values: true and false.

**browser sensing** A scripting technique that detects the specific browser in use by clients to provide compatibility for multiple browsers.

**cache** The internal memory used by a browser to store visited pages, making them faster to load when next requested.

**Cascading Style Sheets (CSS)** The W3C's standard for applying styles to HTML documents. CSS can control fonts, colors, margins, borders, and positioning.

**class** A construction within an object-oriented programming language that allows the creation of objects.

**comment** Programmer's notes written within sections of code to clarify how code operates and make it easier to maintain later. Comments are ignored when code is executed.

**Common Gateway Interface (CGI)** A standardized method for running server-side programs, irrespective of the language they are written in.

**concatenate** The act of combining two strings into a single, longer string.

**conditional** A statement that performs an action if a particular condition is true, typically using the if statement.

**constructor** A class method used to create and initialize a new object.

**debug** The act of finding errors, or bugs, in a program or script.

**declaration** A statement of a variable's name and type.

**decrement** To decrease the value of a variable by one. In JavaScript and PHP, this can be done with the decrement operator, `--`.

**deprecated** A term the W3C applies to HTML tags or other items that are no longer recommended for use, and may not be supported in the future. For

example, the `<font>` tag is deprecated in HTML 4.0 because style sheets can provide the same capability.

**Domain Name Service (DNS)** The system used to associate domain names with IP addresses across the Internet.

**Document Type Declaration (DTD)** A declaration made at the beginning of a HTML document that states what version of HTML the document adheres to.

**Document Object Model (DOM)** The set of objects that JavaScript can use to refer to the browser window and portions of the HTML document. The W3C (World Wide Web Consortium) DOM is a standardized version supported by the latest browsers, and allows access to every object within a web page.

**Dynamic HTML (DHTML)** The combination of HTML, JavaScript, CSS, and the DOM, which allows dynamic web pages to be created. DHTML is not a W3C standard or a version of HTML.

**element** A single member of an array, referred to with an index. In the DOM, an element is a single node defined by an HTML tag.

**error handling** The use of coding techniques to make a script deal elegantly with any error situations that may arise.

**event** A condition, often the result of a user's action, that can be detected by a script.

**event handler** A JavaScript statement or function that will be executed when an event occurs.

**expression**   A combination of variables, constants, and operators that can be evaluated to a single value.

**feature sensing**   A scripting technique that detects whether a feature, such as a DOM method, is supported before using it to avoid browser incompatibilities.

**Firefox**   Mozilla's popular standards-compliant web browser.

**float**   A floating point decimal number.

**form**   An HTML construct to allow website users to send information to the server

**formatting**   Use of indents, new lines and whitespace to make code easier to read and understand.

**function**   A group of statements that can be referred to using a function name and arguments.

**global variable**   A variable that is available to all code in a web page. It is declared (first used) outside any function.

**Greasemonkey**   An extension for the Firefox browser that allows user scripts to modify the appearance and behavior of web pages.

**Hypertext Markup Language (HTML)**   The language used in web documents. JavaScript statements are not HTML, but can be included within an HTML document, and will be executed in the visitor's browser. Blocks of PHP code can also be embedded within HTML, and will be executed at the server.

**Hypertext Transfer Protocol (HTTP)**   The standard by which web servers and browsers communicate

**increment**   To increase the value of a variable by one. In JavaScript and PHP, this is done with the increment operator, ++.

**integer**   A whole number (positive or negative).

**Internet Explorer (IE)**   Microsoft's web browser, available for various platforms including Windows and Mac.

**interpreter**   A program that interprets code statements and acts on them. The JavaScript interpreter is embedded in the visitor's web browser. The PHP interpreter is installed on the web server.

**Java**   An object-oriented language developed by Sun Microsystems. Java applets can be embedded within a web page. JavaScript has similar syntax, but is not the same as Java.

**JavaScript**   A scripting language for web documents, loosely based on Java's syntax, developed by Netscape. JavaScript is now supported by the most popular browsers.

**layer**   An area of a web page that can be positioned and can overlap other sections in defined ways. Layers are also known as positionable elements.

**local variable**   A variable that is available to only one function. It is declared (first used) within the function.

**loop**   A set of program statements that are executed a number of times, or until a certain condition is met.

**method**   A specialized type of function that can be stored in an object, and acts on the object's properties.

**Navigator**   A browser developed by Netscape, and the first to support JavaScript.

**node**   In the DOM, an individual container or element within a web document. Each HTML tag defines a node.

**null**   An identifier used in a computer language to indicate the absence of a value; for instance to indicate that a function returned no data.

**object**   A type of variable that can store multiple values, called properties, and functions, called methods.

**operator**   A character used to divide variables or constants used in an expression.

**parameter**   A variable sent to a function when it is called, also known as an argument.

**PHP**   A very popular and open source server-side scripting language.

**progressive enhancement**   The approach of building a basic page that works on all browsers, and then adding features such as scripting that will work on newer browsers without compromising the basic functionality of the page.

**property**   A variable that is stored as part of an object. Each object can have any number of properties.

**readyState**   Property of the `XMLHTTPRequest` object containing information about the progress of an Ajax request.

**Really Simple Syndication (RSS)**   A family of formats used for publishing frequently updated information via XML.

**Representational State Transfer (REST)**   A popular web service protocol.

**responseText**   Property of the `XMLHTTPRequest` object containing string-formatted data returned by the server.

**responseXML**   Property of the `XMLHTTPRequest` object containing XML data returned by the server.

**rule**   In CSS, an individual element of a style block that specifies the style for an HTML tag, class, or identifier.

**scope**   The part of a program that a variable was declared in and is available to.

**selector**   In a CSS rule, the first portion of the rule that specifies the HTML tag, class, or identifier that the rule will affect.

**Simple Object Access Protocol (SOAP)**   A popular protocol for offering and consuming web services.

**stateless protocol**   A communications

protocol that does not retain information between successive requests. HTTP is such a protocol.

**statement**    A single line of a script or program.

**string**    A group of text characters that can be stored in a variable.

**stylesheet**    A document containing CSS styling information.

**syntax**    Grammar defining a programming language.

**table**    HTML element designed for showing tabular data on a page.

**tag**    In HTML, an individual element within a web document. HTML tags are contained within angle brackets, as in <body> and <p>.

**text node**    In the DOM, a node that stores a text value rather than an HTML element. Nodes that contain text, such as paragraphs, have a text node as a child node.

**unobtrusive scripting**    A set of techniques that make JavaScript accessible and avoid trouble with browsers by separating content, presentation, and behavior.

**variable**    A container, referred to with a name, that can store a number, a string, or an object.

**VBScript**    A scripting language devel-

oped by Microsoft, with syntax based on Visual Basic. VBScript is supported only by Microsoft Internet Explorer.

**Web 2.0**    A popular term used to describe websites using Ajax and similar techniques to enhance the user's experience.

**World Wide Web Consortium (W3C)**    An international organization that develops and maintains the standards for HTML, CSS, and other key web technologies.

**XHTML (Extensible Hypertext Markup Language)**    A new version of HTML developed by the W3C. XHTML is similar to HTML, but conforms to the XML specification.

**XML (Extensible Markup Language)**    A generic language developed by the W3C (World Wide Web Consortium) that allows the creation of standardized HTML-like languages, using a DTD (Document Type Definition) to specify tags and attributes.

**XMLHTTPRequest object**    The built-in JavaScript object used to make Ajax calls.

# Index

## SYMBOLS

&& (And operator), 120

\* (multiplication operator), 198

@ characters, PHP methods, 253

\ (backslashes)

  escaping strings, 202

  \n character sequence, newline characters, 192

{} (braces)

  code indentation rules, 216

  loop syntax, 126

  use in conditional statements, 216

[] (brackets), use in conditional statements, 216

$ (dollar sign)

  $ SERVER global array variable, 320

  $() function, 306

  $F() function, 307

  variables, 195

= (equal sign)

  = (assignment operator), 119

  == (equality operator), 119, 203

! (Not operator), 120

< (less than sign)

  <ajax-response> elements, Rico, 317-319s

  <div> ... <div> elements, 176

  <div> containers, 179

  <response> elements, Rico, 317-319

  <script> ... <script> elements, 177

— (minus sign), 84

  — (decrement operator), 199

  - (subtraction operator), 198

% (modulus operator), 199

. (period), 71

|| (Or operator), 119-120

data() function, 178

date and time, displaying, **54-60**

date command, **189**

date formats

converting, 143, 213

listing of, 213

storage overview, 209-210

Unix timestamp, 210

date function, **210-211, 224**

Date object, **56, 140-141**

Date.parse() method, **143**

Date.UTC() method, **143**

decimal numbers, rounding, **136**

declaring

arrays, 95, 207

variables, 82, 196

decrement operator (—), **199**

decrementing variables, **84**

default argument values, functions, **226-227**

defining

functions, 104

multiple parameters, 105

simple example, 224-225

objects, 110

DELETE requests, **273-274**

developer's tokens, **276**

displaying

dates and times, 54-60

error messages, 60

Displaying the System Date and Time (Listing 1.1), **190-191**

dissecting strings

sublen function, 206

subpos function, 206

substr function, 205-206

<div> ... <div> elements, **176**

<div> containers, **179**

division operator (/), **199**

DNS (Domain Name Service) servers, **14**

do loops, **221**

do...while loops, **128**

doAjax function, **289-293**

DOCTYPE elements, **23**

document object, **74**

methods, 76

properties, 75

document.write statement, **56**

Dojo library, **144**

dollar sign ($)

$ SERVER global array variable, 320

$() function, 306

$F() function, 307

variables, 195

DOM (Document Object Model)

appendChild() method, 259

child nodes, adding to, 259

createElement() method, 260

createTextNode() method, 259

document methods table, 261

elements, deleting, 267

getElementByID method, 258

getElementsByTagName method, 258

history of, 73

level standards, 74

methods, 73

node methods table, 261

node properties table, 261

objects, 72

document, 74-76

hierarchy, 73

properties, 73

double data types, **197**

double quotes (" "), strings, **197, 202**

downloading Script.aculo.us library, **325**

# E

echo command, **189**

A Badly Formatted Script That Displays the Date and Time (Listing 1.3), 192

browser, outputting to, 191-192

Using echo to Send Output to the Browser (Listing 1.2), 191-192

else clause, multiple condition branches, **218-219**

else keyword, **121-124**

elseif keyword, multiple condition branches, **218-219**

email

gmail web mail service (Google), 45

Internet development, 10

return values, mail function example, 226

email_validation_class (third-party), **234-235**

## variables

**BOOKS ONLINE**

**ENABLED**

# THIS BOOK IS SAFARI ENABLED

## INCLUDES FREE 45-DAY ACCESS TO THE ONLINE EDITION

The Safari® Enabled icon on the cover of your favorite technology book means the book is available through Safari Bookshelf. When you buy this book, you get free access to the online edition for 45 days.

Safari Bookshelf is an electronic reference library that lets you easily search thousands of technical books, find code samples, download chapters, and access technical information whenever and wherever you need it.

**TO GAIN 45-DAY SAFARI ENABLED ACCESS TO THIS BOOK:**

- Go to **http://www.samspublishing.com/safarienabled**
- Complete the brief registration form
- Enter the coupon code found in the front of this book on the "Copyright" page

If you have difficulty registering on Safari Bookshelf or accessing the online edition, please e-mail customer-service@safaribooksonline.com.

# Sams Teach Yourself

## When you only have time for the answers™

Whatever your need and whatever your time frame, there's a Sams **TeachYourself** book for you. With a Sams **TeachYourself** book as your guide, you can quickly get up to speed on just about any new product or technology—in the absolute shortest period of time possible. Guaranteed.

Learning how to do new things with your computer shouldn't be tedious or time-consuming. Sams **TeachYourself** makes learning anything quick, easy, and even a little bit fun.

### Adobe Flash CS3 Professional in 24 Hours

Phillip Kerman
**ISBN-10:** 0-672-32937-9
**ISBN-13:** 978-0-672-32937-1

**PHP, MySQL and Apache All in One**

Julie C. Meloni
**ISBN-10:** 0-672-32725-2
**ISBN-13:** 978-0-672-32725-4

**Adobe Dreamweaver CS3 in 24 Hours**

Betsy Bruce
**ISBN-10:** 0-672-32936-0
**ISBN-13:** 978-0-672-32936-4

**HTML & CSS in 24 Hours**

Dick Oliver
Michael Morrison
**ISBN-10:** 0-672-32841-0
**ISBN-13:** 978-0-672-32841-1

**JavaScript in 24 Hours**

Michael Moncur
**ISBN-10:** 0-672-32879-8
**ISBN-13:** 978-0-672-32879-4

Sams Teach Yourself books are available at most retail and online bookstores. For more information or to order direct, visit our online bookstore at **informit.com/sams**.

Online editions of all Sams Teach Yourself titles are available by subscription from Safari Books Online at **safari.informit.com**.

# Safari Library
## Subscribe Now!
http://safari.informit.com/library

**Safari's entire technology collection is now available with no restrictions. Imagine the value of being able to search and access thousands of books, videos, and articles from leading technology authors whenever you wish.**

## EXPLORE TOPICS MORE FULLY

Gain a more robust understanding of related issues by using Safari as your research tool. With Safari Library you can leverage the knowledge of the world's technology gurus. For one flat, monthly fee, you'll have unrestricted access to a reference collection offered nowhere else in the world—all at your fingertips.

With a Safari Library subscription, you'll get the following premium services:

- **Immediate access to the newest, cutting-edge books**—Approximately eighty new titles are added per month in conjunction with, or in advance of, their print publication.

- **Chapter downloads**—Download five chapters per month so you can work offline when you need to.

- **Rough Cuts**—A service that provides online access to prepublication information on advanced technologies. Content is updated as the author writes the book. You can also download Rough Cuts for offline reference

- **Videos**—Premier design and development videos from training and e-learning expert lynda.com and other publishers you trust.

- **Cut and paste code**—Cut and paste code directly from Safari. Save time. Eliminate errors.

- **Save up to 35% on print books**—Safari Subscribers receive a discount of up to 35% on publishers' print books.

**Safari** Books Online

Addison Wesley · Cisco Press · Microsoft Press · Peachpit Press · Redbooks · AdobePress · FT Press FINANCIAL TIMES · New Riders · PRENTICE HALL · Wharton School Publishing · SAMS · ALPHA · lynda.com · O'REILLY · Que · IBM Press